EVALUATING LITERACY INSTRUCTION

"An essential text for all literacy educators, particularly those with a direct impact on school and district evaluation, this book focuses on common practices in evaluating literacy educators, how evaluation policies impact teaching and learning, and action steps we can take toward a more positive and meaningful approach to teacher evaluation. With chapters written by leaders in the field, Gabriel and Allington offer a text that develops understandings of a timely and essential topic."

Danielle Dennis, Associate Professor of Literacy Studies,
University of South Florida, USA

This must-read book for all literacy educators illuminates the intersection of research on literacy instruction and teacher evaluation. Since 2009, 46 states have changed or revised policies related to evaluating teachers and school leaders. In order for these new policies to be used to support and develop effective literacy instruction, resources are needed that connect the best of what is known about teaching literacy with current evaluation policies and support practices. A major contribution to meeting this need, the volume brings together a range of perspectives on tools, systems, and policies for the evaluation of teaching, organized into two sections:

- Crafting Systems and Policies for Evaluating Literacy Instruction
- Examples of Alternative Systems/Approaches for Evaluating Literacy Instruction

Across the text, expert scholars in the field emphasize the need for literacy professionals to do more than merely apply generic observation instruments for teacher evaluation, but also to consider how these tools reflect professional values, how elements of effective literacy instruction can be unearthed or included within them, and how teacher evaluation systems and policies can be used to increase students' opportunities to develop literacy.

Rachael E. Gabriel is Assistant Professor of Reading Education, Neag School of Education, University of Connecticut, USA.

Richard L. Allington is Professor of Education, Literacy Studies Program, University of Tennessee, USA.

EVALUATING LITERACY INSTRUCTION

Principles and Promising Practices

Edited by
Rachael E. Gabriel and Richard L. Allington

 Routledge
Taylor & Francis Group

NEW YORK AND LONDON

First published 2016
by Routledge
711 Third Avenue, New York, NY 10017

and by Routledge
2 Park Square, Milton Park, Abingdon, Oxon, OX14 4RN

Routledge is an imprint of the Taylor & Francis Group, an informa business

© 2016 Taylor & Francis

Library of Congress Cataloging-in-Publication Data
Evaluating literacy instruction : principles and promising practices /
    [edited] by Rachael E. Gabriel and Richard Allington.
       pages cm
    Includes bibliographical references and index.
   1. Reading.   2. Literacy.   I. Gabriel, Rachael E.   II. Allington, Richard L.
    LB1050.E93 2015
    428.4—dc23
    2015008677

ISBN: 978-1-138-84307-3 (hbk)
ISBN: 978-1-138-84359-2 (pbk)
ISBN: 978-1-315-73094-3 (ebk)

Typeset in Bembo
by Apex CoVantage, LLC

Printed and bound in the United States of America by Publishers Graphics, LLC on sustainably sourced paper.

CONTENTS

PREFACE

The chapters in this book tackle one by one problems of identification and the shortcomings of tools for supporting teacher development, by highlighting research-based principles and promising practices for putting such principles in action. Each chapter begins with a description of the challenge or problem related to evaluating literacy instruction, provides evidence from research about possible solutions, and concludes with a set of action steps that readers can use to put these research-based ideas into action.

The book is organized in two sections, each introduced by a practicing principal from a US public school.

Section I: Crafting Systems and Policies for Evaluating Literacy Instruction

In Chapter 2, my colleague, Sarah Woulfin, and I (Gabriel) describe the current state of knowledge about the impact of various observation tools on teaching and learning in the settings where they are employed. We explore open questions about how to select and structure observation rubrics or checklists, and share evidence from a recent study that has implications for ways administrators might frame and/or modify their tools to keep their focus on what is most important for literacy learning in the classrooms they evaluate.

Chapters 3–5 provide even more specific suggestions for developing or modifying observation instruments to better reflect the best of what we know to support literacy learning.

Beyond classroom observations, new generation teacher evaluation systems all include an increased emphasis on rating teachers by comparing student outcomes on standardized tests. In his chapter related to assessment in the context of teacher evaluation, Afflerbach (Chapter 3) not only outlines the central tensions in using such assessments to measure and support achievement, he suggests possibilities for ways to integrate the assessments that matter most for literacy instruction. The action steps in this chapter will ensure that important aspects of literacy teaching and learning are not ignored by the inherent limitations of traditional assessment schemes. Instead, Afflerbach outlines what a "construct-valid" evaluation of literacy instruction might include.

Continuing with the theme of assessment, Turkan (Chapter 4) offers a rare and uniquely accessible peek behind the measurement curtain by presenting her analysis of the challenges of measuring quality instruction for English language learners (ELLs). As an ETS scientist, Turkan has access to and experience with the cutting edge of measurement tools and approaches for complex classroom contexts. She particularly highlights the need for explicit attention to ELLs in the design of classroom observation instruments, explains the problems with using generic tools to address the specific needs of ELLs, and provides actionable suggestions for those designing or using existing tools with students from linguistically diverse backgrounds.

Turkan demonstrates that "unless any of the three instruments incorporates teaching ELLs as part of their construct definition, their use for making any high stakes claims about effective teaching of reading and literacy to ELLs cannot be valid." In the chapter that follows, Lavigne and Oberg de la Garza (Chapter 5) take on two widely used observation instruments, demonstrating where they fall short in terms of reflecting culturally relevant pedagogies for diverse student populations. They also provide specific additions that evaluators can lay on top of existing tools in order to ensure they are identifying and supporting culturally relevant pedagogies. Taken together, these chapters can be used to ensure that the focus on evaluation and measurement does not eclipse the need for expansive notions of excellence in teaching that can support teachers in meeting the needs of linguistically and culturally diverse students.

When the complex act of teaching is reduced and narrowed so that it can be measured reliably, students bear the brunt of these reductive versions of what counts as effective teaching. The first four chapters in Section I provide readers with concrete tools and suggestions to guard against the reductive limits of existing tools in order to preserve a focus on what matters most for literacy instruction.

This section concludes with another rare behind-the-scenes look. This time it's a first-hand glimpse at exactly how a tool for observation is developed, tested, and deployed in classrooms. Coker and colleagues (Chapter 6) illuminate the challenges, tensions, and assumptions that go into the construction of all tools for classroom observations, as well as specific considerations for observing the teaching of writing—an aspect of literacy instruction that is rarely explicitly referenced in existing tools for observation. This chapter will not only give readers an understanding of how and why observation instruments are constructed in particular ways but also specific suggestions for how to select and use them based on this understanding.

Section II: Examples of Alternative Systems/Approaches for Evaluating Literacy Instruction

Section II moves beyond the challenges and solutions associated with current tools and provides examples of approaches to evaluating literacy instruction that have a demonstrated track record within research settings, with clear implications for practice in everyday school settings. The section begins with Peterson's chapter (Chapter 7), which details the school-change observation system used in several large-scale, multiyear studies of school-wide literacy improvement programs. Next, Sailors and Hoffman (Chapter 8) discuss tools for evaluating the text environment as it relates to opportunities to develop the teaching and learning of literacy in elementary school settings. Connecting back to Chapters 3 and 4 in Section I, López, Proctor, and Scanlan (Chapter 9) discuss tools for linking specific kinds of formative data collection to teacher evaluations that specifically support the needs of ELLs. Like Afflerbach's earlier chapter, their discussion goes beyond tools for observation to discuss options and considerations for the assessments used to measure and support progress across the year.

Section II concludes with a chapter by Connor and colleagues (Chapter 10) which returns to the idea that commercially available tools for teacher evaluation largely fail to provide adequate guidelines on what evaluators might look for when evaluating the effectiveness of reading instruction. Connor et al. review the research on observation tools that do predict students' literacy outcomes and provide a system for educational leaders that discriminates between more and less effective first grade literacy instruction.

The concluding chapter (McAbee, Chapter 11), written by an elementary school principal who is currently engaged in the everyday work of teacher evaluation and supporting more effective literacy instruction across his elementary school, provides one example of how the content and ideas in this text can be used to let evaluation be a part of positive transformations in literacy teaching and learning. More than simply summarizing the ideas presented by authors throughout the text, McAbee offers a framework for thinking about the role of teacher evaluation in supervising and supporting effective literacy instruction, as well as specific action steps for school administrators based on of his first-hand experience of supervising and evaluating literacy instruction over the last decade.

Across the entire text, each author echoes the need to do more than merely apply generic observation instruments for teacher evaluation, emphasizing that literacy professionals must also consider how these tools reflect their values, how elements of effective literacy instruction can be unearthed or included within them, and how teacher evaluation systems and policies can be used to increase students' opportunities to develop literacy. We hope that you will find action steps and new questions to consider in each of these chapters. Happy reading!

1

EVALUATING LITERACY INSTRUCTION

An Introduction

Rachael E. Gabriel and Richard L. Allington

The purpose of this book is to place a spotlight on the intersection of research on effective literacy instruction and teacher evaluation. Since 2009, 46 states and the District of Columbia have changed or revised policies related to the evaluation of teachers and school leaders. In order for new teacher evaluation policies to be used to support and develop effective literacy instruction, teachers and school leaders will need resources that connect the best of what we know about teaching literacy with current evaluation policies and support practices. As teacher evaluation policies shift and change, this book will serve as a resource for selecting and improving evaluation schemes that bring them into alignment with the best of what we know about literacy teaching.

Any teacher evaluation system requires an explanation of what constitutes effective teaching. Historic and contemporary studies of teacher effectiveness have often centered on reading instruction in particular for several important reasons. As Lipson and Wixson (2012) point out, "some view reading and writing as the basis for most other learning. Others care about it because they view it as a general indicator of the health of public schools. Finally, some care about it because the methods of instruction may be emblematic of philosophical or personal orientations toward larger issues" (p. 11). Taken together, these points may explain why reading assessments and achievement are so often the focus of public policies, and why studies of teacher effectiveness so often hinge on the effective teaching of reading.

Research on effective reading instruction is central to the work of defining effectiveness in teaching because of its emblematic status as an indicator of overall educational quality. It is also practically central because of the increased role of student outcomes on measures of reading achievement (and other measures that depend on literacy skills) in teacher evaluations in the Race To The Top era. As we will describe later in this introduction, during the years since Race To The Top, teacher evaluation schemes have hinged on identifying and supporting the effective teaching of reading more than ever before.

In this introduction we begin by providing a brief outlined summary of what we view as the research base on effective reading instruction. We then discuss how reading teacher effectiveness has been researched and defined in the last century, and end by discussing its definition in our contemporary policy context, and discussing the role this text might play in linking the research base on effective reading instruction with teacher evaluation policy.

What We Know about Teaching Reading

Classroom-level influences on reading development in U.S. public schools have consistently been a topic of study since the early 1900s (e.g., Fulton, 1914; Goodykuntz et al.,1925; Betts, 1949). Though conceptualizations and methodologies have evolved over time, the central notion that teachers themselves matter has remained constant. Likewise, several aspects of reading instruction have consistently been noted as key elements of effectively developing children as readers. We will describe these but also note that none of these characteristics seem common in classroom reading lessons offered in American classrooms today. The five factors that have evidence of their influence on reading development are outlined below.

Access to Texts That Can Be Read with Accuracy

We have good evidence that enhancing children's access to a wide range of texts is related to improved reading achievement (Lindsay, 2013). Classroom libraries are often the vehicle for ensuring easy access to a range of texts, but many classrooms have inadequate classroom libraries and fail to make access easy. Our view is that all classrooms, K-12, should have classroom libraries with 500 to 1,000 titles that reflect a range of genres and topics and reflect levels of text difficulty that ensure that books that can be read accurately by every student in the class.

Besides access to physical texts, opportunities to engage with text are also related to improved reading achievement (e.g., Allington et al., 2010). Even in classrooms with a large number of available texts, and literacy blocks with 60–90 minutes of allocated time, the actual time students spend engaged in reading or writing is often minimal (Hiebert, 2002; Hiebert & Mesmer, 2013). Of the time students spend with text in front of them, much is spent reading a whole-class text at or near grade level regardless of the individual levels of students, thus this text experience is unlikely to approach optimal levels of opportunity to develop literacy (Hiebert & Martin, 2009).

Since Anderson, Wilson, and Fielding (1988) noted the strength of the relationship between the volume of voluntary out-of-school reading and student reading development, we have had evidence (e.g., Langer, 2001) that reading practice is important in reading development, even in middle and high school settings. Of course, reading volume is not only a matter of allocating time for reading, but requires both ease of access to books and an orientation toward student-selection of text.

Choice of Text

We know that when children are allowed to self-select books both engagement in reading and reading achievement are powerfully affected (Guthrie & Humenick, 2004). To us this suggests that it is time to end the one-text-fits-all model of reading instruction. That is where the lesson is offered from a single text selected by the teacher (or by corporate executives many miles away). This would not necessarily end small group reading lessons but would largely eliminate whole class reading lessons.

Literate Conversations

In today's classrooms, if there is a focus on comprehension, that focus is on lower-order literal recall as teachers ask questions that generally require a single-word answer or sometimes a phrase or sentence segment as the response. However, we have good evidence that when classroom reading lessons focus on higher-order understanding and engage students in literate conversations students benefit enormously (Ivey & Johnston, 2013; Nystrand, 2006; Taylor, Pearson, Peterson, & Rodriguez, 2003).

Focused, Explicit Instruction

Explicit decoding instruction is best accomplished in kindergarten and first grade classrooms (National Reading Panel, 2000) with roughly 10 minutes per day allocated for providing explicit decoding instruction. The National Reading Panel also noted that there is little evidence that decoding lessons after first grade are effective even with those students who seem not to acquire decoding proficiencies in K-1 classrooms. Though researchers have long disagreed about the place and relative importance of basic skills instruction, research over the last decade has consistently highlighted the need to address both—basic skills, in the context of meaning-focused instruction—rather than one or the other. Indeed embedded decoding lessons seem to work at least as well or better than the typical commercial decoding material lessons (Mathes et al., 2005). Though it is easier to plan, measure, and execute basic skills instruction than meaning-focused instruction, teachers cannot allow one to supplant the other if meaning-making is to be maintained as the goal of literacy instruction.

The large-scale, exemplary teacher studies (Pressley et al., 2001; Allington & Johnston, 2002) demonstrated that a balanced approach to literacy instruction that included some skill instruction with meaning-focused instruction was not only possible across settings and policy environments, it was far more powerful than instruction that privileged one or the other approach to literacy development.

Writing to Real Audiences

Students who struggle with reading skills and engagement may find their way into literacy through writing because it gives them a medium with which to accomplish something that matters to them. Like explicit comprehension instruction, writing instruction is all too often supplanted by elements of literacy that are more easily assessed (e.g., fluency, decoding), or crowded out by worksheets and brief writing assignments that are so structured and contrived they are no better than a fill-in-the-blank task. When students have control over what they are writing, to whom they are writing, and what form that writing takes they are purposefully engaged with texts of various types and purposes, and with encoding words, syntax, and imagery they will then be able to decode as readers (Graham & Hebert, 2011; Hebert, Simpson, & Graham, 2013). Both for the reciprocal skill development and potential for engagement with text, the place of real writing (where students come up with all the words) to a real audience (to whom the piece is actually delivered) cannot be overestimated.

Teachers Matter

Orchestrating opportunities to develop literacy like the five outlined above requires knowledge and commitment to literacy development that are not always supported by school and district policy environments. Still, despite the role of curricula, programs, policies, and changing student demographics, research over the past 40 years has consistently highlighted the importance of teachers in facilitating literacy development.

In the 1970s, teacher evaluation research had a process–product orientation that favored observing teacher "behaviors," measuring student learning on discrete and/or standardized measures, and attempting to correlate certain behaviors with certain student outcomes. The most influential study of this era was the California Beginning Teacher Evaluation Study (BTES), a multiphase project that investigated the behaviors of second and fifth grade teachers over five years. The largest contribution of the BTES studies was the conceptualization of "Academic Learning Time" (ALT; Berliner, 1981), which was described as the amount of time students are engaged in tasks of the appropriate level of difficulty. ALT was strongly and positively correlated with academic achievement in both reading and math, though the strength of the correlation varies across subjects, grades, and students' beginning levels of performance (Fisher & Berliner, 1985; Fisher et al., 1980). Though ALT is possible when students work independently, it is more likely to occur when teachers are actively directing activities. These findings suggested that (1) time on task is an important factor in predicting student achievement, and (2) that teacher-directed and/or teacher-supervised activities were more likely to result in *engaged* and *appropriate* time on task (ALT) than seatwork or teacher-centered instruction that is not interactive.

The notion of ALT, and the strength of its correlation to higher achievement, supported a widespread focus on ensuring "time on task," essentially viewing allocated time as evidence of opportunity to learn. In some states the idea that allocating time for reading instruction would increase the likelihood of higher achievement led to state laws requiring specific amounts of time for reading instruction like, for example, the 90-minute reading block.

ALT also prompted an emphasis on interactive instruction, with later phases of the BTES study noting that substantial teacher-student interaction was likely to be associated with increased engagement during interactions as well as in the group work or independent work that followed.

This process-product orientation to teacher effectiveness research influenced teacher preparation and evaluation by constructing a version of effectiveness that was centered on the orchestration of maximum ALT. This included observable factors like room arrangement, planning, and pacing, as well as elements of classroom management such as effective rules and procedures with a focus on efficiency to maximize time on task. Though states and districts often established allocations of time specifically for reading, and focused on the logistics of maximizing time on task, the orchestration of engaging and appropriate tasks requires more than logistics. This fits a general interest in efficiency in public education, supported by the increasing involvement of the business community in state and federal education policy (Cross, 2004).

Throughout the 1990s there was a shift in focus from process-product research to an interest in variables that are not behavioral or easily observable: specifically, teacher knowledge. The National Commission on Teaching and America's Future (NCTAF) explicitly linked the notion of teacher quality to proxies for teacher knowledge such as test scores earned and degrees or certifications held. The first of three core premises boasts: "What teachers know and can do is the most important influence on what students learn" (NCTAF, 1997, p. 8). Though researchers have struggled to find stable and meaningful connections between observable practices and proxies for teacher knowledge like degrees and test scores, the central message of the BTES was that teaching required more than just attention to efficient classroom management. Teachers need specialized knowledge and skills to generate, orchestrate, and monitor engaging and appropriate activities. According to NCTAF, this requires deep knowledge of subject matter as well as a robust understanding of how students learn. Therefore it was measured by indicators of knowledge acquisition such as degrees and scored portfolios that demonstrated proficiency on standards for what teachers should know and be able to do.

Just as the process-product approach emphasized efficiency of observable behavior for a teaching force that mostly held two- or four-year degrees in teaching, the next phase in research on teacher effectiveness emphasized teacher knowledge and was associated with a professionalization of teaching via standards and policies aimed to raise the bar for initial and continuing certification.

One high-profile example of research from this period was initiated as a study of class size, but generated findings that suggested teacher effects account for a large portion of student achievement, and that teachers' qualifications matter. In the Tennessee Student Teacher Achievement Ratio (STAR) Project, researchers compared the achievement of students in classes with varying student-adult ratios over four years (1990–1994). Nearly 12,000 students were randomly assigned to a small class (13–17 students), regular class (22–26 students), or a regular class with an instructional aide in addition to a teacher. In general, smaller classes had higher achievement, especially in high-poverty schools (Achilles, 1999). The addition of an instructional aide did not improve achievement, and some larger classes outscored small classes, thus indicating that the individual teacher, along with class size, was a factor influencing student achievement (Boyd-Zaharias & Pate-Bain, 1998). The differences in student achievement by teacher were significant and lasted over several years, especially if students had higher performing teachers two or more years in a row (Finn, Gerber, Achillles, & Boyd-Zaharias, 2001; Nye, Konstantopoulos, & Hedges, 2004; Nye, Hedges, & Konstantopoulos, 1999). Moreover, minority and lower-performing students seemed to benefit most from a year or more with a high-performing teacher.

The variation in effect between teachers and instructional aides bolstered arguments that knowledge specific to teaching, and advanced degrees in education, were necessary to have an effect on student achievement. However, the variation within teachers, the differences in associated student achievement for some over others, also indicated that more than just a teaching degree was at work in the classrooms of highly effective teachers.

Building on the idea that teachers themselves matter, not just because they manage time or hold degrees, but because they know what to do with time to maximize student learning, researchers became interested in the differences in the nature of instruction exemplary teachers provided. The mid-to-late 1990s marked a return to classroom observation, but rather than observing all teachers to generate correlations between behaviors and outcomes, these researchers specifically identified "exemplary," "effective," or "beating-the-odds" teachers. The first of this generation of research (e.g., Knapp, 1995) was a two-year study of 140 classrooms in high-poverty schools where students demonstrated high achievement despite low socioeconomic status. The main finding of this and other studies, including those focused on high school (Langer, 2001), first grade classrooms (Pressley et al., 2001), and fourth grade classrooms (Allington & Johnston, 2002), was that a balanced version of reading instruction was more effective than skills-emphasis reading lessons. This is because the effective teachers actually taught useful skills, including decoding, but in the context of actual reading activity rather than as skills in isolation.

Taylor and Pearson and their colleagues (Taylor, Pearson, Clark, & Walpole, 2000; Taylor, Pearson, Peterson, & Rodriguez, 2003, 2005) at the federally funded Center for Improving Early Reading Achievement (CIERA) found similar links. In the series of CIERA studies the students were primarily children from low-income families. The higher-achieving classrooms featured substantially more reading and writing activities and classroom teachers who asked higher-order questions during and after the reading.

In some ways, these exemplary teacher studies represented the unification of process-product and teacher-characteristic approaches by acknowledging that exemplary teachers routinely spent more allocated time on academic tasks (Allington & Johnston, 2002), but adding that the focus of these tasks matters significantly. It is not enough for classrooms to be busy and efficient if the work is not focused on the construction of meaning. Herein lies the rub: effective literacy instruction may not be readily observable on lesson plans, classroom walk-throughs, or examinations of classroom bulletin boards or libraries. Even teachers working with the same scripted curricula next door to one another may do so in subtly but powerfully different ways that impact the engagement and achievement of their students (Gabriel & Lester, 2013). It takes some knowledge of literacy processes and a clear-eyed focus on uncovering and encouraging the five factors above to identify effective literacy instruction. Yet, most instruments used to guide observations and feedback within teacher evaluations are not literacy or language arts specific and so rarely direct an observer's attention to these critical aspects of effective literacy lessons.

Most commercially available instruments for observation are agnostic when it comes to grade level, content area, or curricular context (ranging from highly scripted to teacher-directed). This ensures teachers across grades and content areas are held to a similar standard but, as the chapters in Section I of this volume describe, they do so at the expense of explicitly directing evaluators to attend to those factors that matter most for literacy development. In the section that follows we briefly explain the context and shape of what we will refer to as "new generation teacher evaluation policies"—those policies that were inspired by Race To The Top competition criteria, and reinforced by criteria for states applying for a No Child Left Behind (NCLB) waiver. New generation policies are discussed in terms of their implied theories of action and their resulting constitution as tools that measure, but do not necessarily support, effective literacy instruction.

Measuring Literacy Instruction for Teacher Evaluation

The theory of action behind new generation teacher evaluation systems is outlined below in Figure 1.1.

This figure demonstrates that there are two, sometimes conflicting, goals for teacher evaluation as inspired by Race To The Top and NCLB waiver criteria:

1. Differentiate effectiveness so that ineffective teachers can be released from the teaching corps
2. Improve effectiveness so that average and high performers continuously increase effectiveness

Differentiating effectiveness requires knowing how teachers are different from each other in terms of practices, processes and student outcomes. New generation policies have benefitted from relatively recent advances in statistical modeling like value-added modeling (VAM; McCaffery et al., 2004), structural equation modeling, multilevel modeling, and student-learning objectives (Lacireno-Pacquet, Morgan, & Mello, 2014) to infer teacher effects on student achievement with more nuance than was possible in the 1990s (Campbell, Kyriakides, Muijs, & Robinson, 2004). Since 2009, VAM, in particular, has been heralded by the media as a gold standard—in spite of a range of cautions from statisticians (e.g., Baker & Welner, 2012; Ewing, 2011) researchers (Whitehurst, Chingos, & Lindquist, 2015; Baker et al., 2010) and several lawsuits (Baker, Oluwole, & Green, 2013; Amrein-Beardsley & Collins, 2012). Still, the perceived ability to estimate a teacher's effect on student achievement provided a way to validate observation

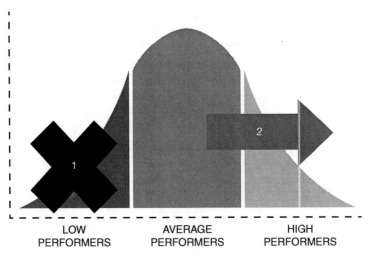

LOW   AVERAGE   HIGH
PERFORMERS   PERFORMERS   PERFORMERS

FIGURE 1.1 New generation teacher evaluation systems' theory of action

instruments against something that appears to be an objective outcome measure of instruction.

To date, most research on the reliability and validity of observation instruments has sought to correlate scores on these instruments with student achievement and/or some teacher effect measure (Porter, Polikoff, Goldring, Murphy, Elliott, & May, 2010). Yet, as Mintrop and Trujillo (2007) demonstrated in their observations of high-performing schools in California:

> (If one) expected to encounter visible signs of an overall higher quality of students' educational experience at the high-performing schools, they would be disappointed. Rather, they would have to settle on a narrower definition of quality that is more proximate to the effective acquisition of standards-aligned and test-relevant knowledge. (p. 319)

If the goal of teacher evaluation is to coach teachers into having a more positive effect on student achievement, we must understand the construction and optimization of such tools in order to ensure we are focusing on the most useful aspects of instruction. That is the focus of Section I of this text. If, on the other hand (or in addition), we are interested in high-quality instruction that involves *but is not limited to* high scores on standardized tests, we must understand where the instructional utility and face validity of these instruments start and end so that modifications and additions may be supplied (Gabriel & Allington, 2012). This is the focus of Section II.

Still, even observation instruments that most reliably differentiate effectiveness as measured by differential student outcomes do not automatically generate data that could guide improvement. They focus on indicators that align with higher test scores, but these indicators may not be the most salient, powerful, or foundational aspects of instruction for generating useful feedback. This is where the difficulty of linking specific practices, environments, conditions, materials, and interactions with student outcomes presents challenges for researchers and evaluators alike. We know that time spent reading matters, but how do we measure whether all students are reading during that time? How can we observe the match between reader and text both in terms of interest and difficulty? What counts as reading? Is reading aloud, reading along, or listening to peers read aloud as valuable as independent reading? Is reading in unison just as good as reading aloud independently? Is it as good as self-selected independent silent reading?

Our primary purpose in developing this book was exposure of the many new ideas that are important in effective literacy teaching to the broader public. Simple though it may be to articulate what matters for literacy development, observing and measuring in valid, reliable, and fruitful ways can be painfully difficult, especially when available tools for evaluation do not explicitly connect with literacy instruction or focus on opportunities to develop literacy. We hope this will be a first step in the adoption of new evaluation systems that are richer, more powerful predictors of literacy development.

References

Achilles, C.M. (1999). *Let's put kids first, finally: Getting class size right.* Thousand Oaks, CA: Corwin Press.

Allington, R., McGill-Franzen, A., Camilli, G., Williams, L., Graff, J., Zeig, J., Zmach, C., & Nowak, R. (2010). Addressing summer reading setback among economically disadvantaged elementary students. *Reading Psychology, 31*(5), 411–427.

Allington, R.L., & Johnston, P.H. (Eds.). (2002). *Reading to learn: Lessons from exemplary 4th grade classrooms.* New York: Guilford.

Amrein-Beardsley, A., & Collins, C. (2012). The SAS Education Value-Added AssessmentSystem (SAS® EVAAS®) in the Houston Independent School District (HISD): Intended and Unintended Consequences. *Education Policy Analysis Archives, 20*(12). Retrieved from: http://epaa.asu.edu/ojs/article/view/1096

Anderson, R., Wilson, P., & Fielding, L. (1988). Growth in reading and how children spend their time outside of school. *Reading Research Quarterly, 23,* 285–303.

Baker, B., & Welner, K.G. (2012). Evidence and rigor: Scrutinizing the rhetorical embrace of evidence-based decision making. *Educational Researcher, 41*(3), 98–101.

Baker, E., Barton, P., Darling-Hammond, L., Haertel, E., Ladd, H., Linn, R., Ravitch, R., Rothstein, R., Shavelson, R., & Shepard, L. (2010). *Problems with the use of student test scores to evaluate teachers.* Washington, DC: Economic Policy Institute.

Berliner, D.C. (1981). Academic learning time and reading achievement. In J. Guthrie (Ed.), *Comprehension and teaching: Research reviews* (pp. 203–225). Newark, DE: International Reading Association.

Betts, E.A. (1949). Adjusting instruction to individual needs. In N.B. Henry (Ed.), *The forty-eighth yearbook of the National Society for the Study of Education: Part II, reading in the elementary school* (pp. 266–283). Chicago: University of Chicago Press.

Boyd-Zaharias, J., & Pate-Bain, H. (1998). *Teacher aides and student learning: Lessons from Project STAR.* Arlington, VA: Educational Research Service.

Campbell, J., Kyriakides, L., Muijs, D., & Robinson, W. (2004). *Assessing teacher effectiveness: Developing a differentiated model.* London: Routledge.

Cross, C.T. (2004). *Political education: National policy comes of age.* New York: Teachers College Press.

Ewing, D. (2011). "Leading mathematician debunks 'value-added.'" *Washington Post,* April 5, 2011. Retrieved from: http://www.washingtonpost.com/blogs/answer-sheet/post/leading-mathematician-debunks-value-added/2011/05/08/AFb999UG_blog.html.

Finn, J.D., Gerber, S.B., Achilles, C.M., & Boyd-Zaharias, J. (2001). The enduring effects of small classes. *Teachers College Record, 103*(2), 145–183.

Fisher, C.W., & Berliner, D.C. (1985). *Perspectives on instructional time.* New York: Longmans.

Fisher, C.W., Berliner, D.C., Filby, N.N., Marliave, R., Cahen, L.S., & Dishaw, M.M. (1980). Teaching behaviors, academic learning time, and student achievement: An overview. In C. Denham & A. Lieberman (Eds.), *Time to learn* (pp. 7–32). Washington, DC: National Institute for Education, U.S. Department of Education.

Fulton, M. (1914). An experiment in teaching spelling. In R.D. Robinson (Ed.), *Readings in reading instruction: Its history, theory, and development* (pp. 123–126). Boston: Pearson.

Gabriel, R., & Allington, R.L. (2012). Constructing and measuring teacher effectiveness in global education reform. In C.S. Collins & A.W. Wiseman (Eds.), *Education strategy in the developing world: Understanding the World Bank's education policy*. (Vol. 16). Bingley, UK: Emerald Group Publishing.

Gabriel, R. & Lester, J. (2013, December). *Constructing comprehension: a discourse analysis of middle grades reading instruction*. Paper presented at the Literacy Research Association Annual Conference, Dallas, TX.

Goodykuntz, B. (1925). The relation of reading to content subjects and other school activities. In R.D. Robinson (Ed.), *Readings in reading instruction: Its history, theory, and development* (pp. 160–162). Boston: Pearson.

Graham, S., & Hebert, M. (2011). Writing to read: A meta-analysis of the impact of writing and writing instruction on reading. *Harvard Educational Review, 81*(4), 710–744.

Guthrie, J.T., & Humenick, N.M. (2004). Motivating students to read: Evidence for classroom practices that increase motivation and achievement. In P. McCardle & V. Chhabra (Eds.), *The voice of evidence in reading research.* (pp. 329–354). Baltimore: Paul Brookes Publishing.

Hebert, M., Simpson, A., & Graham, S. (2013). Comparing effects of different writing activities on reading comprehension: A meta-analysis. *Reading and Writing, 26*(1), 111–138.

Hiebert, E.H. (2002). Standards, assessments, and text difficulty. In A. Farstrup & S.J. Samuels (Eds.), *What research has to say about reading instruction* (pp. 337–369). Newark, DE: International Reading Association.

Hiebert, E.H., & Martin, L.A. (2009). Opportunity to read: A critical but neglected construct in reading instruction. In E.H. Hiebert (Ed.), *Reading more, reading better* (pp. 3–29). New York: Guilford.

Hiebert, E.H., & Mesmer, H.A.E. (2013). Upping the ante of text complexity in the Common Core State Standards: Examining its potential impact on young readers. *Educational Researcher, 42*(1), 44–51.

Ivey, G., & Johnston, P.H. (2013). Engagement with young adult literature: Outcomes and processes. *Reading Research Quarterly, 48*(3), 255–275.

Knapp, M.S. (1995). *Teaching for meaning in high-poverty classrooms*. New York: Teachers College Press.

Lacireno-Pacquet, N., Morgan, C., & Mello, D. (2014). *How states use student learning objectives in teacher evaluation systems: A review of state websites*. Washington DC: U.S. Department of Education. Retrieved from: http://ies.ed.gov/ncee/edlabs/regions/northeast/pdf/REL_2014013.pdf

Langer, J.A. (2001). Beating the odds: Teaching middle and high school students to read and write well. *American Educational Research Journal, 38*(4), 837–880.

Lindsay, J.J. (2013). Impacts of interventions that increase children's access to print material. In R.L. Allington & A. McGill-Franzen (Eds.), *Summer reading: Closing the rich/poor reading achievement gap* (pp. 20–38). New York: Teachers College Press.

Lipson, M., & Wixson, K. (2012). Assessment of reading and writing difficulties: An interactive approach (5th ed.). New York: Pearson.

Mathes, P.G., Denton, C.A., Fletcher, J.M., Anthony, J.L., Francis, D.J., & Schatschneider, C. (2005). The effects of theoretically different instruction and student characteristics on the skills of struggling readers. *Reading Research Quarterly, 40*(2), 148–182.

McCaffrey, D.F., Lockwood, J.R., Koretz, D., Louis, T.A., & Hamilton, L. (2004). Models for value-added modeling of teacher effects. *Journal of Educational and Behavioral Statistics, 29*(1), 67–101.

Mintrop, H., & Trujillo, T. (2007). The practical relevance of accountability systems for school improvement: A descriptive analysis of California schools. *Educational Evaluation and Policy Analysis, 29*(1), 319–352.

National Commission on Teaching and America's Future. (1997). *Doing what matters most: Investing in quality teaching.* New York: National Commission on Teaching and America's Future.

National Reading Panel. (2000). *Teaching children to read: An evidence-based assessment of the scientific research literature on reading and its implications for reading instruction.* Washington, DC. Retrieved from: http://www.nichd.nih.gov/publications/pubs/nrp/Pages/smallbook.aspx

Nye, B., Hedges, L.V., & Konstantopoulos, S. (1999). The long-term effects of small classes: A five-year follow-up of the Tennessee class size experiment. *Educational Evaluation and Policy Analysis, 21*, 127–142.

Nye, B., Konstantopoulos, S., & Hedges, L.V. (2004). How large are teacher effects? *Educational Evaluation and Policy Analysis, 26*(3), 237–257.

Nystrand, M. (2006). Research on the role of classroom discourse as it affects reading comprehension. *Research in the Teaching of English, 40*, 392–412.

Porter, A.C., Polikoff, M.S., Goldring, E.B., Murphy, J., Elliott, S., & May, H. (2010). Investigating the validity and reliability of the Vanderbilt Assessment of Leadership in Education. *Elementary School Journal, 111*(2), 282–313.

Pressley, M., Allington, R.L., Wharton-MacDonald, R., Collins-Block, C., & Morrow, L. (2001). *Learning to read: Lessons from exemplary first-grade classrooms.* New York: Guilford.

Taylor, B.M., Pearson, P.D., Clark, K., & Walpole, S. (2000). Effective schools and accomplished teachers: Lessons about primary grade reading instruction in low income schools. *Elementary School Journal, 101*, 121–165.

Taylor, B.M., Pearson, P.D., Peterson, D.S., & Rodriguez, M.C. (2003). Reading growth in high-poverty classrooms: The influences of teacher practices that encourage cognitive engagement in literacy learning. *Elementary School Journal, 104*(1), 4–28.

Taylor, B.M., Pearson, P.D., Peterson, D.S., & Rodriguez, M.C. (2005). The CIERA School Change Framework: An evidence-based approach to professional development and school reading improvement. *Reading Research Quarterly, 40*(1), 40–69.

Whitehurst, G.J., Chingos, M.M., & Lindquist, K.M. (2015). Getting classroom observations right. *Education Next, 15*(1). Retrieved from: http://educationnext.org/getting-classroom-observations-right/

SECTION I

Crafting Systems and Policies for Evaluating Literacy Instruction

We asked Mr. Garry, principal of South Side School in Bristol, CT about his experience with the state's new teacher evaluation policy. He told us:

> To put it simply, the state's new educator evaluation system took us by storm. Like most districts, our evaluation system had not changed in years and relied heavily on the expertise of the building leader. Broad categories, some reflecting the work of Marzano, provided a lens for feedback following observations of practice. In addition, the professional goals that all staff had to complete often lacked coherence with building and or district goals—due to both departmental and/or grade level autonomy. The adoption of the state's plan was an overwhelming experience—from the immense amount of information during roll-out with minimal training to develop a level of expertise required to effectively share this information with staff, to the misunderstandings and, at times, misinformation that seemed a regular occurrence. Sometimes information trickled down to help clear things up.
>
> Complicating matters for all was the adoption of a data system for recording and coding all observations. Each district had the option to choose a data system (either paid or free) and the state provided week-long trainings to calibrate administrators in the understanding and use of the new systems. Needless to say, the trainings did little to enhance understanding of the technology or the application of the new teacher evaluation policy to assess teacher practice. It was not a good year.
>
> The frustrations from our first year highlighted the need for clarity and coherence in terms of school goals, teacher professional goals, and observations of practice.

Where commercially available tools and state-specific systems present challenges for clarity and coherence, these chapters illuminate the construction and theoretically sound use of observation instruments and measures of student achievement.

2

EVALUATING THE STRUCTURE AND CONTENT OF OBSERVATION INSTRUMENTS

Rachael E. Gabriel and Sarah Woulfin

The state of New York has approved 10 different rubrics for rating teacher practice. Each rubric has a different history, set of assumptions about measurement, audience, structure, and framework for considering what counts as good teaching. Across the country, new-generation teacher evaluation systems—those developed in the years since Race To The Top—all have evaluative observations as part of a teacher's overall rating. However, few research studies have examined the impact of classroom observation instruments on instruction, and none compare the effects of different kinds of instruments. Nevertheless, states often approve one or more observation instruments as a way to ensure uniformity in criteria. In some places, this means a state model—often based on an existing, commercially available instrument, with room for exceptions to this model that meet similar criteria. In many cases, the choice of instrument is based on logistics, cost, and the timing of availability (Gabriel & Paulus, 2014; Gabriel, 2011), rather than the relative merit of the format or focus.

This atheoretical, unscientific approach to selecting observation instruments is troubling given their potential to change what counts as good teaching, and what kind of feedback teachers receive from evaluators. Within this volume, several of the chapters offer suggestions about the content foci that are required to support ambitious literacy instruction, especially for linguistically diverse students (see Chapters 3 and 4). In this chapter we review existing guidelines for the format and style of observation instruments, and we discuss the limited research on the impact of observations on classroom instruction. In addition, we present results of a study that compared existing tools for evaluating literacy instruction using data from the Gates Foundation's Measures of Effective Teaching Project in order to demonstrate the need for increased attention to literacy-specific indicators in any evaluation of literacy instruction.

Guidelines for Rating Observation Instruments: Conventional (Not Evidence-Based) Wisdom on the Format of Observation Instruments

In the absence of research that addresses fundamental questions about the nature and impact of instruments for classroom observations, nonprofit organizations, such as The New Teacher Project and the Gates Foundation's Measures of Effective Teaching Project, have filled the void with reports and white papers. At best, these documents summarize conventional wisdom on the subject, and—at worst—serve as advertisements for their proprietary instruments and training. We review several reports from The New Teacher Project and the Measures of Effective Teaching Project, as well as one researcher-generated report. We summarize the recommendations of each, and we critique them in an attempt to separate common sense from commercialism in selecting instruments for classroom observation.

The New Teacher Project

In 2009, The New Teacher Project (TNTP), a national non-profit organization with a policy and advocacy arm, sounded the alarm bell on teacher evaluation with their report *The Widget Effect* (Weisberg, Sexton, Mulhern, & Keeling, 2009), which revealed that less than 1% of teachers receive satisfactory ratings, despite wide-ranging student achievement. They concluded that current teacher evaluation schemes failed to differentiate effectiveness and therefore to guide human capital management (hiring, firing, promotion, and tenure) or teacher development. This report was widely cited in reports and presentations related to the construction and release of new generation teacher evaluation policies beginning in 2009. In 2011, TNTP published a presentation under the advertisement: "Teacher evaluations need serious fixing. Here's a guide to get started." The presentation makes no attempt to ground the suggestions in a field of research (e.g., corporate evaluations, institutional psychology, etc.), but advances common sense ideas about what evaluation tools should do based on their analysis about what current tools fail to do. Their criteria can be summarized as a set of questions:

1. Do the criteria and tools cover the classroom performance areas most connected to student outcomes? Do the criteria and tools set high performance expectations for teachers, or do they settle for minimally acceptable performance?
2. Are the performance expectations for teachers clear and precise? Are the criteria and tools student-centered, requiring evaluators to look for direct evidence of student engagement and learning? Are the criteria and tools concise enough for teachers and evaluators to understand thoroughly and use easily?

In their 2013 report, TNTP argues that "new teacher evaluation systems . . . will not succeed in improving instruction because they have not been updated to reflect the Common Core State Standards (CCSS)" (p. 1) and have "too many cumbersome criteria" (p. 8). They claim that this overloads observers, thus inflating ratings and limiting the value of feedback generated by observation. They therefore suggest two "must-have" changes to observation rubrics:

1. Pay more attention to lesson content; and
2. Pare observation rubrics down to make them more focused and clear.

Regarding the first must-have, they note that most observation instruments do not explicitly reflect the Common Core State Standards (CCSS), and thus cannot be used to support better instruction, "especially the importance the standards place on teaching the right content in addition to teaching that content well" (p. 1). Current instruments do focus primarily on instructional delivery and student engagement rather than content, but this may have more to do with the need for instruments that can be applied across grades and content areas than any de-valuing of content. On the other hand, recent studies of the link between instructional alignment to content standards and student achievement have shown disappointingly weak correlations (Polikoff & Porter, 2014), which troubles the assumption that standards-alignment is a clear indicator of quality.

TNTP also declares that rubrics, as instruments for evaluation and development, should focus on work that teachers are responsible for generating and enacting. Though easy to agree with on the surface, this contradicts their emphasis on teaching the "right stuff" in the right ways. In many cases, teachers are not solely responsible for choosing their curriculum or planning their own lessons. In other cases they may not even be allowed to, such as in settings with strict curriculum maps, packaged programs, or scripted curricula. The TNTP report argues that feedback related to content "is a crucial part of professional development, and it is especially important now, when teachers are adjusting to the Common Core" (p. 1). Though support for implementing the CCSS may be helpful in places where the CCSS has been adopted, and content areas where it has the most impact, the CCSS was not universally adopted (4 of the 50 states never adopted it, while others have or are in the process of disassociating), nor is it universally held in high regard. Therefore, TNTP's assertion that focusing on CCSS-related instruction ensures teachers are "teaching the right content" (p. 1) is not only misleading, it's inaccurate.

TNTP's second must-have involves paring down observation rubrics by limiting rubrics or checklists to 5–10 essential items. They suggest doing this by combining items that co-vary and describe this as "put(ting) observation rubrics on a diet." Ironically, this suggestion is about as misguided as the guidelines for a miracle diet in that there is no research to suggest that 5–10 items are optimal or even sufficient. Five to ten may be worse than 30–90, and the co-variance of indicators may not be a marker of excess, but rather a mechanism for generating patterns of behaviors, strengths, and practices. Or, multiple indicators that co-vary may support more reliable instruments, as rubrics with more indicators can have better overall reliability and validity than those with fewer. These are all open and important questions that are ignored when oversimplified ideas about of cognitive load threatens the utility of evaluations.

As the National Education Policy Center has highlighted in their critique of the 2013 TNTP report (Whitcomb, 2014), neither of the two "must-have" suggestions are research-based, nor do any deal with the fundamental assumptions of commercially available instruments for observation. Whitcomb concludes her review of the report with the following: "the report does not build a research-informed case for its conclusions; as such, the validity of the report's conclusions is questionable" (p. 4).

The TNTP report hinges on the idea that the success of both the CCSS and new-generation teacher evaluation policies are intertwined. They write that "high-quality observations and specific feedback are critical to improving practice and will be necessary for successful implementation of the Common Core" (p. 1). This concern about the combined success of simultaneous reform efforts explains (or is explained by) their affiliation with a non-profit that creates and disseminates instruments for CCSS implementation, as noted in a callout box on page 4:

> By partnering with Student Achievement Partners, a non-profit dedicated to providing supports for schools and teachers to implement the Common Core, TNTP seeks to influence the next generation of classroom observation rubrics by creating new observation criteria focused on whether Common Core content is being taught and by streamlining observation rubrics to make them easier for observers to use.

Both organizations have invested deeply in the CCSS and new generation evaluation reform efforts—efforts which often co-occur or are funded simultaneously in districts and states across the U.S. TNTP's 2013 report serves the same purpose as *The Widget Effect* report: It sounds an alarm to incite panic that sparks action—in the form of financial investment—to address a perceived gap in current practice. In this case, they exclaim that current observation instruments "threaten the success of the Common Core standards . . . and more importantly, their potential to put millions more students on the path to college and a career" (p. 1). As we will discuss below, there is only limited evidence that observation instruments matter for shaping teaching practice, instruction, or outcomes. Still, fear-mongering that concerns the very prominent CCSS is effective fear-mongering indeed.

Though we agree with the TNTP report that "We will do better when we score what counts rather than everything we can count," we argue that there is not nearly enough empirical evidence to decide what should count. It remains unclear what aspects of instruction should be tallied during observations or labeled as "effective." In this absence of evidence, practitioners may draw on the CCSS, another untested reform instrument, but should not necessarily be encouraged to do so. In fact, in light of recent findings about the lack of relationship between standards-aligned instruction and student achievement (Polikoff & Porter, 2014) or instructional practices and high achievement on state tests (Mintrop & Trujilo, 2007), we may do better by ignoring standards alignment in favor of some more proximal measure of teacher-student interaction.

Measures of Effective Teaching Project

In contrast to the call for a focus on content and fewer indicators, the Gates Foundation's Measures of Effective Teaching Project (MET Project, 2013) released a report that takes a more balanced approach. Focusing more on implementation than the content of instruments for observation, they note:

> When people talk of observations they refer only to the instruments and procedures used by evaluators. But what makes observations trustworthy are a set of system components that work together to support evaluators in using those instruments and procedures correctly. (p. 5)

Indeed the trustworthiness of evaluators and quality of routines around generating and sharing feedback may be more important for teacher and administrator development than the instruments themselves.

Based on their $45 million two-year study of teaching in over 11,000 classrooms in urban districts located across five states, which compared various measures of effectiveness for teacher evaluation (e.g., observation scores, student surveys, parent surveys, student achievement data, value-added ratings) the MET project (2010, 2012) released a short report on guidance for observation systems. Focusing on the trustworthines rather than efficiency of observation systems, they write that trustworthy observations are:

- Consistent. Results vary little by observer or lesson.
- Unbiased. Results don't reflect personal or pedagogical preferences.
- Authentic. Expectations are clear and reflect best practice for effective teaching.
- Reasonable. Performance standards are challenging but attainable.
- Beneficial. Teachers get actionable feedback and support for success. (p. 4)

Unlike TNTP's call for uniformly addressing the CCSS, in a related report, the MET Project authors concede that:

> Developing an observation instrument locally has its advantages. . . . Engaging together in this process could help promote desired professional growth

in your staff [and] . . . help ensure that the instrument reflects district or state standards for teaching practice, which in turn can garner buy-in and support for the use of the instrument in the evaluation process. (MET project, 2013)

They further note that "the development process may also serve as a catalyst for aligning district and state standards to the Common Core State Standards" though they acknowledge the inherent challenges to reliability and validity in multiple locally developed instruments. Still, the focus of this report is on developing instruments that can be *used* effectively, rather than instruments that contain the "right stuff."

Like the TNTP report, this set of recommendations is largely untested, but is based mostly on common-sense ideas about instruments for evaluation across professions and contexts. No one would argue against this list of features (who wants an inconsistent, unreasonable, detrimental instrument?) but there is little guidance about how to identify, develop, or modify instruments that meet these criteria.

More recently, Whitehurst, Chingos, and Lindquist (2014) wrote, "most of the action and nearly all the opportunity for improving teacher evaluations lie in the area of classroom observations rather than in test-score gains" (n.p.). Unlike the TNTP and MET reports, these recommendations are based on studies of four districts' policies, but, like previous reports, the recommendations are based on good guesses rather than evidence. Furthermore, they provide little specificity when it comes to enacting these recommendations. They write:

1. Teacher evaluations should include two to three annual classroom observations, with at least one of those observations being conducted by a trained observer from outside the teacher's school.
2. Classroom observations that make meaningful distinctions among teachers should carry at least as much weight as test-score gains in determining a teacher's overall evaluation score when both are available.
3. Most important, districts should adjust teachers' classroom-observation scores for the background characteristics of their students, a factor that can have a substantial and unfair influence on a teacher's evaluation rating. (n.p.)

Based on their findings that observation scores tend to be more stable, they suggest, "If the administrator's impression of individual teachers is relatively sticky from year to year, then it will be less reflective of true teacher performance as observed at a particular point of time" and recommend the addition of an outside observer. Again, this is not a tested recommendation, but a reasonable suggestion based on conventional knowledge. The idea that districts should adjust observation scores based on background is similarly inspired by evidence that students' prior achievement predicts teacher observation ratings, but not on evidence that such a modification increases the reliability or validity of the observation.

Taken together the TNTP, MET Project, and Whitehurst, Chingos, and Lindquist reports highlight good guesses about selecting and improving teacher observation systems, but more evidence is needed to make truly informed decisions about the nature and use of various instrument options.

For example, are instruments with more indicators necessarily different from instruments with fewer? Are instruments that are subject-specific more useful for feedback than generic instruments? These are some of the questions we sought to answer in our study of instruments for evaluation using the MET Project database. Before describing our study, we briefly review the handful of studies that demonstrate the potential impact of observation instruments. These studies would have been important background information for the reports described above, had the authors considered their results, because they raise an even more fundamental question about observation: Can observations be used to support teacher performance and student achievement?

Research on the Impact of Various Observation Instruments

Though few studies have investigated the impact of observation instruments on teacher satisfaction, development, or student achievement, several large-scale correlational studies have suggested that the practice of observation supports better student outcomes. One such study found that schools in the second year of implementing classroom observations for the first time had stronger reading achievement, on average, than schools that had only implemented for one year (Steinberg & Sartain, 2013). In this study, educators had recently moved from a vague checklist system to the Framework For Teaching as part of a project to improve excellence in teaching with clearer criteria, more observations and more feedback from administrators (Sartain, Stoelinga, & Brown, 2011).

In this study, the transition to the FFT corresponded with an increase in overall student achievement. However, these researchers acknowledged that the transition to a new teacher observation system impacted schools with different characteristics in different ways. For example, more advantaged schools benefitted more from the new system of observations than lower-performing, less-advantaged schools. This suggests that schools with more capacity and financial support for reform can benefit from increasing observation, while schools with less capacity and support may not.

Similarly, in Cincinnati, researchers found that mid-career teachers improved after being involved in a program of increased observations and feedback sessions (Taylor & Tyler, 2011). But, like the MET Project, they caution that "the effect is likely sensitive to the quality and reputation of the feedback." Unlike Steinberg and Sartain's 2013 study in Chicago, Taylor and Tyler found an effect for math but not reading scores. It appears there is some evidence that observation systems matter for student achievement, but little clarity around how or how much they matter.

Given the limitations of conventional wisdom on the subject, and the small, nearly equivocal available research, we set out to investigate the optimal structure and content of observation instrument using the database of classroom videos and scores generated by the MET Project. Though many of these questions are still outstanding, we present our preliminary findings here and discuss what they mean for selecting or modifying instruments for classroom evaluations in more scientifically grounded ways.

A Comparison of Instruments for Teacher Observation

Content Analysis

Our analysis of MET Project data began with an exploratory document analysis of the three observation protocols used to rate English Language Arts (ELA) instruction as part of the MET Project. This analysis involved creating a "crosswalk" between the three instruments and a description of the differences in focus, format, scope, and level of inference. Table 2.1 displays information about the observation protocols used, as well as their source, scope, and focus.

Figure 2.1 displays the relative distribution of indicators across areas of instruction:

Though some version of the FFT is used as part of many state evaluation systems, FFT devotes relatively few indicators to instruction, and weights indicators related to management just as strongly in the overall score. The version of the FFT analyzed here was modified for use in the MET Project and thus included only domains 2 & 3 (*Classroom Environment* and *Instruction*), while omitting two domains often included in state systems for use outside of classroom observations (*Planning & Preparation* and *Professional Responsibility*). Compared to subject-specific instruments, few FFT indicators are designed to generate data

TABLE 2.1 MET Project observation protocols

Observation Protocol	Focus	Indicators
1. Framework For Teaching	General teaching	General indicators of effective instructional and environmental factors
2. CLASS	General teaching	General indicators of effective socio-emotional and instructional practices
3. PLATO-Prime	ELA instruction	Indicators of high-leverage ELA practices

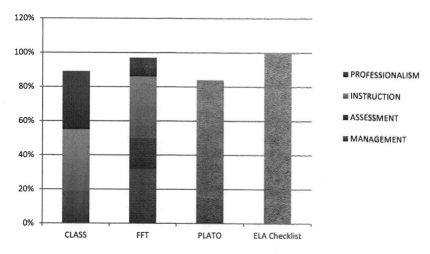

FIGURE 2.1 Distribution of indicators for observation protocols

that could be used for feedback on instruction specifically. As an ELA-specific instrument, PLATO is the most directly related to instruction, but still includes indicators of classroom and time management—thus indicating slightly different assumptions about the relative importance of various observable aspects of classroom instruction. CLASS has a dual focus on instructional and socio-emotional support, and frames what may be considered time or behavior management from a socio-emotional support perspective (e.g., safety, respect, responsiveness).

Implications from these findings include the need to consider that the use of any single instrument involves reproducing its theoretical assumptions and biases. Thus teachers and evaluators must engage in careful interrogation of the philosophical alignment between instruments for observations and reading programs. For example, some researchers have recently demonstrated a cultural and/or linguistic bias in ratings from the CLASS (e.g., Lopez, 2011, 2012). Awareness of the ways in which individual instruments privilege specific approaches may be helpful in thoughtfully applying state- or district-mandated instruments across settings and philosophies (Lavigne & Oberg de la Garza, Chapter 5, this volume).

Correlational Analysis

As in the field of medicine (e.g., Hales & Pronovost, 2006), we propose that checklists of high-impact practices might be used to identify, triangulate, and guide support for effective instruction. For instance, the checklist could ask about the five important factors for effective reading instruction outlined in the introduction to this text. Essentially: do students have to have opportunities to read, write, and talk about text? Though a checklist of principles seems in some ways to be less scientific or thorough, researchers and practitioners have consistently highlighted the burden of unwieldy, lengthy observation instruments (e.g., Sartain, Stoelinga, & Brown 2011) even as they praise the addition of a common language for thinking and talking about high-quality instruction (Tennessee Department of Education, 2010).

As a next step, we developed a checklist of essential ELA practices in order to investigate the possibility of reliable and accurate assessments of teacher effectiveness using a simple and transparent macro-level instrument. (See Table 2.2).

After scoring 216 fourth grade videos, we used a Spearman rank correlation to compare ratings on the ELA Checklist with PLATO, CLASS, and the FFT. The sample of videos was randomly selected from the population of fourth grade teachers in the MET study that had at least three videos of at least 20 minutes in length. These teachers were spread across 48 schools and five districts.

We found statistically significant correlations between ratings on the ELA Checklist and indicators on all three MET Project instruments at the lesson and teacher level. Specifically, presence of choice of text on the ELA Checklist is negatively correlated with *Classroom Discourse* on the PLATO. This is likely because offering choice of text often means students are working independently or in small groups on a text, which makes it impossible to rate *Classroom Discourse* given the limitations of sound on the video. Thus, if there was more than one text available, there was no full-class discussion to code.

Choice of text was not correlated with any indicators on the CLASS, but was negatively correlated with three indicators on the FFT: *Communicating with*

TABLE 2.2 Theoretical and empirical basis for ELA-Checklist indicators of essential practices

ELA-Checklist indicator	*Representative research base*
1. Choice of texts	Guthrie & Humenick, 2004; Malloy & Gambrell, 2010
2. Opportunities to read	Anderson, Wilson, & Fielding, 1988; Stanovich, 1986
3. Opportunities to write	Graham & Hebert, 2010; Dyson, 2000; Graham & Perrin, 2007
4. Opportunities to talk	Gutierrez, 1995 Fall, Webb, & Chudowsky, 2000
5. Explicit strategy instruction	Grossman et al., 2013; Schumaker et al., 2002; Bruce & Robinson, 2000
6. Variable grouping	Allington & Johnston, 2002; Schwartz, Smith, & Lose, 2012
7. Meaning vs. skill focus	MET Project, 2010; Langer, 2001; Knapp et al., 1995

Students, *Using Questioning and Discussion Techniques* and *Engaging Students in Learning*. Though we used choice of text as an indication of engaging, differentiated instruction, in observation it may be coded negatively because students reading different texts at the same time may limit the amount of time they are talking, engaging with each other, or learning specific content. This should not be taken as an indication that the practice of using multiple texts is a poor instructional choice. Rather it indicates that the indicators used in PLATO and FFT may privilege other instructional decisions over differentiated text options because of how they have specified their indicators of quality.

In addition, the amount of time spent on literacy activities was correlated with a range of indicators across instruments. Time spent writing is negatively correlated with *Classroom Discourse* on the PLATO, presumably because allocating time for writing replaces opportunities to talk. Student talk was positively correlated with the *Classroom Discourse*. Similarly, time spent on student talk is positively correlated with CLASS sub-scores for *Regard for Student Perspective, Instructional Learning Formats*, and *Instructional Discourse*, while time spent reading was negatively correlated with *Instructional Learning Formats* and *Content Understanding*.

Ironically, the more time teachers in our sample spent reading aloud, the less likely they were to have high scores for *Modeling* or *Strategy Instruction* on PLATO. This suggests that time allocated to read-alouds, which present opportunities for both modeling and strategy use, is rarely used in this way. In fact, teachers in this sample are more likely to model or provide strategy when students do more of the reading in lesson. Read-alouds are, however, strongly positively correlated with *Time Management* and *Behavior Management* in PLATO, which suggests that they are being enacted in ways that indicate they are a strategy for management rather than instruction.

Similarly, when comparing our ELA Checklist scores with FFT ratings, time spent reading is negatively correlated with *Using Questions and Discussion Techniques* and *Engaging Students with Learning*, though time spent on student talk is positively correlated with both. This indicates that teachers are not asking questions or leading discussions when students are reading, but also suggests that students are not being asked to read in engaging formats or with high-quality questions or discussions attached. Anecdotally, we noted that reading done in class in MET Project videos is more often accompanied by known- and closed-answer questions or even by test preparation–style multiple choice questions, neither of which would earn high ratings on indicators related to questioning, discussion, or engagement. It appears that teachers very rarely orchestrate rigorous, engaging discussion within this dataset, particularly with student-student conversation around text. This may be due to the restriction of sampling methods used across instruments which limited observations to the first 30 minutes of lesson videos (often, but not always, the first 30 minutes of a class period).

To capitalize on the indicators of the checklist that seem most correlated with indicators of other instruments, we revised the ELA Checklist into a third version using two constructs developed for a study of implementation of curricular shifts (Woulfin, in press). We then applied the revised checklist to a sample that included the highest- and lowest-scoring fourth grade teachers with videos in the MET Project database based on value-added rating.

We applied the "Accountability Focused" code to ELA instruction that was focused on skill-centered activities, including word identification and literal comprehension, with purposes and formats explicitly linked to test preparation and isolated skill demonstration. In contrast, we created and applied the "Meaning Focused" code to practices incorporating authentic engagement with text and which worked on constructing meaning from multiple sources for intrinsic or authentic purposes (Coburn, 2001; Pearson, 2007; Weaver, 1994; Woulfin, in press). We also developed inductive codes based on themes that arose from the data (Creswell, 2009; Miles & Huberman, 1994). For instance, we created a code for *Instructional Materials* to capture the types of materials used by different teachers. We created coding reports and tabulated the proportion of lessons featuring various instructional elements. This helped us describe broad trends and patterns in classroom practice. To reduce the probability of bias, researchers involved in coding were not aware of the value-added ratings of the teachers in the videos before or during the coding and analysis process. After videos were analyzed and categorized, the categories were compared to the binary category (high or low) based on value-added ratings as calculated by the MET Project.

We found that the "Meaning Focused" indicator on any category (reading, writing, or talking) predicts whether a teacher is in the highest or lowest value-added group 70% of the time. This suggests that the simple checklist can account for some but not all of the variance between teachers with the highest and lowest value-added ratings. Some teachers in both categories engage in practices that fall in both categories. This may be because value-added ratings simply do not measure what matters most for developing literacy, or because our checklist does not effectively capture what matters most either. In either case, our study has generated three important findings:

1. Features of effective literacy instruction are not explicitly reflected by commercially available instruments.
2. This means it is possible to earn high scores on observation rubrics and value-added ratings without engaging with features of effective literacy instruction.
3. More research on the nature and impact of instruments for observation is needed before anyone hands out advice on how to optimize or simplify the process of observation.

We have some evidence that observation *can* matter for teacher development, but to whatever extent it does matter, we have to know that observation instruments are focused on the most predictive and fruitful indicators for discussion and measurement.

Rather than focusing on instruments that are the best predictors of achievement, we argue that the most important direction for research and practice at this point is towards finding or modifying instruments that create the most fruitful feedback for teachers. We should take advantage of the potential to influence practice by investing in instruments that explicitly reflect elements of effective literacy instruction; these instruments could be used as starting points for discussion, reflection, and feedback that address those values. If not, and we continue down the pathway of seeking the gold standard of measurement—without agreement on what's most important to measure—then we may mislabel effective teaching as well as miss opportunities to develop it.

Take Action

When selecting, creating, or modifying an observation instrument, we suggest considering the following questions as discussion starters among colleagues exploring or evaluating a new observation instrument:

1. What elements of literacy instruction does the observation instrument address or value?
    a. If there are none, what indicators could be added or interpreted differently?
2. What forms of instruction does the instrument privilege? How does the instrument define highly effective teachers or teaching?
3. How does the instrument incorporate the principles of concurrent reform initiatives (e.g., Common Core, district's approach to literacy instruction)?
    a. Does it explicitly support or contradict other ongoing efforts? Is there alignment that could be highlighted and exploited to build coherence?
4. What is the existing track record of the instrument you are considering?
    a. Where has it been used and for what purpose?
    b. What were the results when it was deployed?
    c. Who developed it, and how closely do your purposes and values match theirs?
5. Are indicators stated in clear and simple ways so that they can be used as engaging conversation starters?
6. Do some indicators seem arbitrary, random, or smaller than others? Might they be combined or replaced?
7. Does anything you view as important to effective instruction seem to be missing or minimized by this instrument?

References

Allington, R., & Johnston, P. (2002). *Reading to learn: Lessons from exemplary 4th grade classrooms.* New York: Guilford Press.

Anderson, R., Wilson, P., & Fielding, L. (1988). Growth in reading and how children spend their time outside of school. *Reading Research Quarterly, 23,* 285–303.

Bruce, M., & Robinson, E. (2000). Effectiveness of a metacognitive reading program for poor readers. *Issues in Educational Research, 10*(1), 1–20.

Coburn, C.E. (2001). *Making sense of reading: Logics of reading in the institutional environment and the classroom.* Unpublished Ph.D. Dissertation. Stanford University, Stanford, California. Retrieved from: http://www.ncrel.org/sdrs/areas/liread.pdf.

Creswell, J. (2009). *Research design: Qualitative, quantitative and mixed methods approaches.* Thousand Oaks, CA: Sage.

Danielson, C. (2013). *The framework for teaching evaluation instrument,* 2013 edition. Princeton, NJ: The Danielson Group.

Dyson, A.H. (2000). Writing and the sea of voices: Oral language in, around, and about writing. In R. Indrisano & J. Squire (Eds.), *Perspectives on writing: Research, theory, and practice* (pp. 45–65). Newark, DE: International Reading Association.

Fall, R., Webb, N.M., & Chudowsky, N. (2000). Group discussion and large-scale language arts assessment: Effects on students' comprehension. *American Educational Research Journal, 37*(4), 911–941.

Gabriel, R. (2011). *Tennessee teacher evaluation policies under Race To The Top: A Discursive Investigation.* Ph.D. dissertation. University of Tennessee. Retrieved from: http://trace.tennessee.edu/utk_graddiss/971.

Gabriel, R., & Paulus, T. (2014). Committees and controversy: Consultants in the construction of education policy. *Educational Policy.* Retrieved from: http://epx.sagepub.com/content/early/2014/08/22/0895904814531650

Graham, S., & Hebert, M. (2010). *Writing to read: Evidence for how writing can improve reading.* New York: Carnegie Corporation.

Graham, S., & Perin, D. (2007). *Writing next: Effective strategies to improve writing of adolescents in middle and high schools.* New York: Carnegie Corporation.

Grossman, P., Loeb, S., Cohen, J., & Wyckoff, J. (2013). Measure for measure: The relationship between measures of instructional practice in middle school English language arts and teachers' value-added. *American Journal of Education, 113*(3), 445–470.

Guthrie, J., & Humenick, N. (2004). Motivating students to read: Evidence for classroom practices that increase motivation and achievement. In P.D. McCardle & V. Chhabra (Eds.), *The voices of evidence in reading research* (pp. 329–354). Baltimore: Brookes.

Gutierrez, K. (1995). Unpacking academic discourse. *Discourse Processes, 19,* 21–27.

Hales, B. & Pronovost, P. (2006). The checklist—a tool for error management and performance improvement. *Journal of Critical Care, 21*(3), 231–235

Knapp, M.S., & Associates. (1995). *Teaching for meaning in high-poverty classrooms.* New York: Teachers College Press.

Langer, J.A. (2001). Beating the odds: Teaching middle and high school students to read and write well. *American Educational Research Journal, 38*(4), 837–880.

Lopez, F. (2011). The nongeneralizability of classroom dynamics as predictors of achievement for Hispanic students in upper elementary grades. *Hispanic Journal of Behavioral Sciences, 33*(3), 350–576.

Lopez, F. (2012). Moderators of language acquisition models and reading achievement for English language learners: The role of emotional warmth and instructional support. *Teachers College Record, 114*(8), 1–30.

Malloy, J.A., & Gambrell, L.B. (2010). New insights on motivation in the literacy classroom. In J.A. Malloy, B.A. Marinak, & L.B. Gambrell (Eds.), *Essential readings on motivation* (pp. 163–172). Newark, DE: International Reading Association.

MET Project. (2010). *Learning about teaching: Initial findings from the measures of effective teaching project.* Retrieved from: www.metproject.org/ . . . /Preliminary_Finding-Policy_Brief.pdf.

MET Project. (2012). *Gathering feedback for teaching combining high-quality observations with student surveys and achievement gains.* Retrieved from: http://metproject.org/downloads/MET_Gathering_Feedback_Practioner_Brief.pdf.

MET Project. (2013). *Building trust in observations: A blueprint for improving systems to support great teaching.* Retrieved from: http://www.metproject.org/downloads/MET_Observation_Blueprint.pdf.

Miles, M., & Huberman, M. (1994). *Qualitative data analysis: An expanded sourcebook.* Thousand Oaks, CA: Sage.

Mintrop, H., & Trujilo, T. (2007). The practical relevance of accountability systems for school improvement: A descriptive analysis of California schools. *Educational Evaluation and Policy Analysis, 29*, 319. Retrieved from: http://epa.sagepub.com/content/29/4/319.

The New Teacher Project. (2011). *Rating a teacher evaluation tool: Five ways to ensure classroom observations are focused and rigorous.* Retrieved from: http://tntp.org/assets/documents/TNTP_RatingATeacherObservationTool_Feb2011.pdf.

The New Teacher Project. (2013). *Fixing classroom observations: How Common Core will change the way we look at teaching.* Retrieved from: http://tntp.org/assets/documents/TNTP_FixingClassroomObservations_2013.pdf.

Pearson, P.D. (2007). An endangered species act for literacy education. *Journal of Literacy Research, 39*(2), 145–162.

Polikoff, M., & Porter, A. (2014). Instructional alignment as a measure of teaching quality. *Educational Evaluation and Policy Analysis. 36*(4), 399–416.

Sartain, L., Stoelinga, S.R., & Brown, E.R. (2011). *Rethinking teacher evaluation in Chicago: Lessons learned from classroom observations, principal-teacher conferences, and district implementation.* Chicago: Consortium on Chicago School Research.

Schumaker, J., Deshler, D., Bulgren, J., Davis, B., Lenz, B., Grossen, B. (2002). Access of adolescents with disabilities to general education curriculum: Myth or reality? *Focus on Exceptional Children, 35*(3), 1–16.

Schwartz, R., Schmidt, M., and Lose, M. (2012). Effects of teacher-student ratio in response to intervention approaches. *The Elementary School Journal, 112*(4), 547–567.

Stanovich, K. E. (1986). Matthew effects in reading: Some consequences of individual differences in the acquisition of literacy. *Reading Research Quarterly, 21*(4), 360–407.

Steinberg, M., & Sartain, L. (2013). *Does teacher evaluation improve school performance? Experimental evidence from Chicago's excellence in teaching project.* Chicago: Consortium on Chicago School Research.

Taylor, E.S., & Tyler, J.H. (2011, March). *The effect of evaluation on performance: Evidence from longitudinal student achievement data of mid-career teachers* (Working paper 16877). Cambridge, MA: National Bureau of Economic Research.

Tennessee Department of Education. (2010). Meeting minutes of the Teacher Evaluation Advisory Committee, 5/27. Retrieved from: http://www.tn.gov/firsttothetop/programs-committee.html

Weaver, C. (1994). *Reading process and practice: From socio-psycholinguistics to whole language* (2nd ed.). Portsmouth, NH: Heinemann.

Weisberg, D., Sexton, S., Mulhern, J., & Keeling, D. (2009). *The widget effect: Our national failure to acknowledge and act on differences in teacher effectiveness.* New York: The New Teacher Project.

Whitcomb, J. (2014). Review of Fixing Classroom Observations. Boulder, CO: National Education Policy Center. Retrieved from: http://nepc.colorado.edu/files/ttr-teval-tntp.pdf

Whitehurst, G., Chingos, M., & Lindquist, K. (2014). Evaluating teachers with classroom observations: Lessons learned in four districts. Retrieved from: http://www.brookings.edu/research/reports/2014/05/13-teacher-evaluation-whitehurst-chingos

Woulfin, S. (in press). Catalysts of change: An examination of coaches' framing of reading policy. *Journal of School Leadership.*

3

HOW THE TESTS USED IN EVALUATING READING MISREPRESENT STUDENT DEVELOPMENT AND TEACHER EFFECTIVENESS

Peter Afflerbach

The evaluation of teachers, related to student reading development, includes tests that have exclusive focus on students' reading strategies, skills, and content area knowledge. The weighting of test scores varies among states and school districts, but tests are the most frequently used measure of student reading growth and teacher accomplishment. Reading strategies and skills are of central importance to students' academic development, and they deserve instructional and assessment attention. However, testing only skill, strategy, and content area knowledge while ignoring powerful factors such as motivation, engagement and self-efficacy results in an incomplete portrayal of student growth: Both accomplished cognition and healthy affect are at the center of student readers' achievement. The incomplete account of student reading development contributes to inaccurate evaluation and misrepresentation of teachers' accomplishments. Moreover, psychometric theory posits that tests should not be used for unintended purposes—and using reading tests to evaluate teachers does just that.

This chapter is comprised of two sections. In the first, I introduce a student whose reading development is misrepresented by test scores, and his teacher whose accomplishments are similarly misrepresented. Then, I describe the current state of affairs in which high-stakes reading test scores are used in teacher evaluations. I focus on how laws created in the statehouse influence students and teachers in the schoolhouse, and I demonstrate that broad educational goals are undermined by tests with narrow focus. Then, I describe aspects of student development that are missed by high stakes reading tests, and explain how an evaluation system that so ignores valuable student development persists. Next, I propose two areas that are central to students' reading development but missed by tests: motivation and self-efficacy. I suggest that teacher evaluation programs that ignore or miss teachers' important work in these areas are in need of remediation.

In the second section, I overview measurement concerns with the practice of using reading test scores to evaluate teachers. I examine the inferences that are needed to conduct such evaluations, and argue that they are not supportable. I then focus on the practice of using value-added models (VAMs) to try to discern teachers' contributions to student development, and to evaluate teaching. I conclude with suggestions for future teacher evaluation practices, as they relate to students' reading development.

Raphael: A Case for Rethinking What "Counts" in Reading Development and Teacher Evaluation

Raphael is a fourth grader with a history of failing in school. He has literally spent half his school life in the struggling reading group. His experiences with reading in every grade contribute to an affective profile that includes the following: low self-esteem, negative motivation for reading and reading tasks, a lack of engagement with schooling, a belief that things are not under his control during reading class, and attributions for his poor reading outcomes that include being stupid and having bad luck. Raphael's daily school routine includes avoidance of reading and passivity in the classroom. His third grade high stakes test results place him in the 16th percentile of students taking the test.

Raphael's teacher understands his plight, and strives to create a classroom environment that addresses both his cognitive and affective needs. Raphael's teacher believes that cognitive strategies and skills are of utmost importance for reading development; she also believes that positive motivations and high self-efficacy are intertwined with students' growth as readers. As noted by Stanovich (1986),

> Readers of differing skill soon diverge in the amount of practice they receive at reading and writing activities. They also have different histories of success, failure, and reward in the context of academic tasks. The long-term effects of such differing histories could act to create other cognitive and behavioral differences between readers of varying skill. Consider some possible examples. Many of the motivational differences between good and poor readers that are receiving increased attention (see Johnston & Winograd, 1985; Oka & Paris, 1986) may well be consequences of the history of success and failure associated with groups of differing skill. (p. 373)

In accordance with her professional experience and the findings of reading research, she adjusts cognitive strategy and skill instruction to meet Raphael at his current levels of achievement. This allows her to work with Raphael in the appropriate zone of proximal development, and to avoid situations in which particular strategy and skill instruction, and text content, are beyond Raphael's reach. Related to this intentional leveling of instructional materials to meet the student, the teacher locates books, magazines, and online reading resources that Raphael can read successfully, with some teacher support and independently. To realize this success, Raphael regularly reads texts that are one to two grade levels below many of his classroom peers.

The teacher's yearlong plan is to shore up Raphael's wavering motivation, and to build self-efficacy through the series of successful readings. She conceptualizes a second zone of proximal development—the development of positive affect related to reading—to further foster Raphael's reading. The decision to work with below-grade-level texts is appropriate and strategic—it is where Raphael can be engaged. Within the classroom environment that is marked by support and success, Raphael no longer fears reading class. He believes that he has the ability to influence the outcomes of his reading, and he has a renewed appreciation of his effort to become better at reading. The teacher's approach provides Raphael with the experience of success at reading every day, and he feels that he is in some control as he reads. Over time, his experiences help him begin to construct the understanding that reading can be meaningful, worthwhile, and sometimes entertaining.

At the end of the school year (or one month prior, when the high stakes test is given), Raphael demonstrates cognitive growth and scores in the 29th percentile. Although his reading performance has improved in relation to his previous score, it is still well below grade level expectation. Hidden in the scores (because it is not measured or reported) is the fact that Raphael is experiencing a change in his self-perception as a reader, and that this change is contributing to a turn towards positive motivations and engagement with reading, and higher self-efficacy. The story told by the test score is one of minimal improvement and a student's failure to read on level, as well as the teacher's inability to raise the student's test score to a level deemed suitable. The story the test data cannot tell is that Raphael's teacher effected positive change with caring instruction, and that Raphael is a work in progress, still quite shaky as a reader, but with good motivation and developing self-efficacy. These affective aspects of development are foundational for Raphael's ongoing improvement in reading. They are not frills, and cognitive achievements will be hampered without them. In the next sections I describe how the bifurcation of students' cognitive and affective needs happens, especially in relation to education policy making and high stakes tests.

Tests and Teacher Evaluations: Statehouse and Schoolhouse

Teacher evaluation policy is determined in state houses. Legislators and policy makers set the parameters and foci of teacher evaluations, and mandate the measures to be used in the evaluations. Many of these measures are developed from a distance by large testing companies. I assume that teacher evaluations, along with related student learning outcomes, are guided by a vision of the processes and products of an education system—the kind of people we want to help our students grow to be, and the education that fosters that growth. How do teacher evaluations "fit" with the above scenario, in which Raphael experiences positive reading experiences that contribute to his development? In developing this chapter, I examined numerous state Department of Education websites to identify such vision or mission statements. I found the following from the State of California

Our Mission

California will provide a world-class education for all students, from early childhood to adulthood. The Department of Education serves our state by innovating and collaborating with educators, schools, parents, and community partners. Together, as a team, we prepare students to live, work, and thrive in a highly connected world. (California Department of Education, 2014)

Retrieved from: http://www.cde.ca.gov

The above statement suggests the value of innovation and collaboration on the part of members of the education community, and implies schooling will contribute to helping students to live, work, and thrive. Here, my personal biases include the idea that living, working, and thriving are possible when students learn in an environment that addresses their cognitive and affective development.

Next, I examined how students' growth is gauged in relation to the above mission statement, and presumably in relation to the outcomes of California schooling. I found the following:

California Assessment of Student Performance and Progress (CAASPP)

California's new statewide student assessment system [was] established January 1, 2014. Signed into law in October 2013, Assembly Bill 484 establishes the CAASPP assessment system. For the 2013–14 school year, the CAASPP assessment system encompasses the following required assessments:

- Smarter Balanced system of assessments for mathematics and English–language arts
- California Standards Tests (CST) for Science in grades five, eight, and ten
- California Modified Assessment (CMA) for Science in grades five, eight, and ten
- California Alternate Performance Assessment (CAPA) for Science in grades five, eight, and ten and for mathematics and English–language arts in grades two through eleven. (California Department of Education, 2014)

An examination of the sample items from the above tests indicates that the California statewide assessment programs measure student-learning outcomes that include cognitive strategies and skills and content domain learning. The understanding that I construct from reading the State of California Department of Education Mission Statement and examining the means of assessing student outcomes is that there is a partial accounting of the outcomes of schooling. Cognitive development is measured by tests, and affective development is, apparently, not measured. If student outcomes are a focus of the teacher evaluation process, then it is probable that the outcome measures, most prominently high stakes test scores, will only partially represent student outcomes, and misrepresent teacher achievements. Raphael's growth, and his teacher's accomplishments, might be lost. I note that the State of California Department of Education's focus on broad goals and outcomes of schooling (communicated in the mission statement), paired with narrow testing (statewide mandated tests), is common.

What Is Missed by High Stakes Reading Tests

We have known about the limits and biases of high stakes testing for some time. A brief review of that knowledge is in order. In 1987, the annual report of the National Assessment of Educational Progress (Alexander et al., 1987) noted the following:

> Many of those personal qualities that we hold dear—resilience and courage in the face of stress, a sense of craft in our work, a commitment to justice and caring in our social relationships, a dedication to advancing the public good in communal life—are exceedingly difficult to assess. And so, unfortunately, we are apt to measure what we can, and eventually come to value what is measured over what is left unmeasured. The shift is subtle and occurs gradually. (pp. 51–52)

Decades later, the full effects of this subtle and gradual shift are on display—most states ignore students' affective and social development when it comes to assessing their growth and evaluating their teachers. Adding to Alexander et al.'s (1987) list, Gerald Bracey noted the following learning outcomes that high stakes tests fail to measure:

> Creativity, critical thinking, resilience, motivation, persistence, curiosity, endurance, reliability, enthusiasm, empathy, self-awareness, self-discipline, leadership, civic-mindedness, courage, compassion, resourcefulness, sense of beauty, sense of wonder. (Ohanion, 2005)

If the above are valued outcomes of schooling, then shouldn't their attainment, as evidenced by students and influenced by teachers, be part of all teacher evaluation schemes? Shouldn't teaching achievements around these learning outcomes be made part of teacher evaluations? And shouldn't the massive investment of resources made by states and schools in testing yield more information on how reading develops, and contributes to, such growth?

Why the System Persists

Testing culture, in which massive resources are allotted to testing programs, days and weeks are given to measuring rather than teaching and learning, academic schedules are adjusted to accommodate testing, and test scores are revered, reinforces a cognitive monopoly: strategy, skill, and content area knowledge gain are assessed by high stakes tests and the results are used to judge students and their teachers. Students becoming strategic and skillful readers and student learning in content domains are an important and expected outcome of schooling. It seems strange to remind that there are other important outcomes of schooling, but such is the power of the testing culture. Testing cares not a whit about affect or student development outside of the cognitive. Today, high stakes tests act as both a determinant of what is valued in schools, and the measure of that value.

There are several reasons for tests' foci on cognitive strategy, skill, and content area knowledge gain, and a concomitant lack of attention to students' affective development. These include recent reading education initiatives, the means by which reading programs are developed, and contentment with the status quo. Consider that consequential documents and legislation, including The National Reading Panel Report (National Institute of Child Health and Human Development, 2000) and the No Child Left Behind laws, propose that student reading problems are due to a lack of reading skill and strategy. This conclusion was reached through a process that deemed certain reading research to be definitive, and other research to be inconclusive. In the case of the National Reading Panel, definitive research findings came from studies with experimental designs that tightly controlled external factors or intervening variables. Unfortunately, these factors and intervening variables include reader affect, and they were "controlled" out of consideration. Thus, affect was not only ignored as an important aspect of reading development, it was designed out of studies that were designated as meeting a standard of scientific rigor.

Similar reinforcement of the cognitive perspective comes from the practice of basing the development of reading instruction programs on scientific evidence. Of course, it is vital for programs to be based on proven instructional approaches that address certified reading needs. However, the scientific evidence that undergirds reading programs happens to be the results of standardized reading tests. Reading programs are determined to be effective when their use leads to statistically significant differences between treatment and control groups. The dependent variables in studies that examine reading program effectiveness are test scores—based on students' learning of strategy and skill. To reinforce this strategy-skill test dependency, adequate yearly progress (AYP), the most consequential bit of information used in decision-making each school year, is based on tests. More recently, the Common Core State Standards are framed in terms of expected cognitive outcomes, and the affiliated assessment consortia are producing tests that once again have an exclusive cognitive focus. The continued dominance of cognitive strategy and skill, as measured by high stakes tests, appears certain.

Other factors influence the primacy of test scores, their focus on cognition, and their use in teacher evaluations. Economists describe how particular social practices maintain, even in the face of possibly better alternatives, using the term *path dependency*:

> The continued use of a product or practice based on historical preference or use. This holds true even if newer, more efficient products or practices are available. . . . Path dependency occurs because it is often easier or more cost effective to simply continue along an already set path than to create an entirely new one. (Investopedia, n.d.)

Beyond Alexander et al.'s (1987) notion of tests leading to valuing what is easily measured and ignoring that which is not, habits of mind may lead us to, or away from, the consideration of alternatives. While "what is tested is what is taught" predicts the nature of reading instruction, over time it may also be what is conceptualized as reading development. Finally, there is considerable economic benefit for some as the status quo in testing is maintained. Here, I assume that the people and organizations that make billions of dollars each year selling and scoring and reporting on high stakes tests act to keep the system going.

Building a Case for the Centrality of Affect in Reader Development and Teacher Evaluation

High stakes tests' exclusive focus on cognitive outcomes of schooling has been explained, in part, by the fact that there are considerable research *corpora* that describe the centrality of phonemic awareness, phonics, vocabulary, fluency, and comprehension to reading development. In fact, the report of the National Reading Panel cites the lack of such research evidence as a reason that it didn't consider other aspects of reading development as essential. The No Child Left Behind and Reading First laws reflect this skewing of instruction and testing towards aspects of reading development that have a critical mass of research behind them.

In the last two decades, research in areas not included in the National Reading Panel report has achieved critical mass status. The findings of this research have implications for teaching and learning, and the assessment of students and teachers. Two such areas are motivation and engagement and self-efficacy (Afflerbach, Cho, Kim, Crassas, & Doyle, 2013). Each area has compelling research bases to support arguments of their centrality to students' reading development, but each is ignored by high stakes tests. Thus, the development of students' motivation and engagement and self-efficacy have a difficult path to find their way into teacher evaluations.

Readers' motivation and engagement processes influence how they use their existing skills and knowledge, how well they acquire new skills and knowledge, and how well they transfer these new skills and knowledge to novel situations. Readers' intrinsic motivation predicts their acquisition of reading, competence in reading, and engagement in reading (Guthrie, Wigfield, & You, 2012). Guthrie and Klauda (in press) posit that positive motivations to read lead to engagement that is marked by student readers' "active participation as typified by effort, time, and persistence." Thus, the use and development of cognitive strategy and skill is appreciably influenced by motivational factors.

Motivated and engaged readers choose to read for a variety of purposes and comprehend the texts in the context of the situation, and elect a wide range of literacy activities for aesthetic enjoyment, knowledge gain, and interactions with others. Motivated readers are invested in their reading and self-regulate their processes, including higher-order reading strategies. Research demonstrates the powerful influence of motivation on student reading achievement. Construct-valid teacher evaluation programs should include student motivation as an indicator of teacher effectiveness. However, teachers' efforts and accomplishments in this critical area of student reading development are ignored by tests.

A second powerful affective factor in reading development is self-efficacy. Bandura (2006) states:

> Among the mechanisms of human agency, none is more central or pervasive than belief of personal efficacy. *Unless people believe they can produce desired effects by their actions, they have little incentive to act, or to persevere in the face of difficulties.* Whatever other factors serve as guides and motivators, they are rooted in the core belief that one has the power to effect changes by one's actions. (p. 170; italics added)

Self-efficacy helps students focus on and bring effort to school tasks, and it is highly correlated with academic achievement. Student readers with high self-efficacy exhibit enhanced reading comprehension, and they make fewer attributions for performance to external causes, such as luck, task difficulty, and teacher/student relationship (Shell, Colvin, & Bruning, 1995). Students with high self-efficacy use more reading strategies. Further, self-efficacy is related to motivation: When readers are efficacious, their motivation to read and to persevere at challenging reading tasks increases (Mucherah & Yoder, 2008). Student readers' high self-efficacy is associated with increased aspirations, increased and sustained efforts when challenged by a text, task, or both, considering reading problems as challenges to be overcome (and that can be overcome), and making internal attributions for poor performance, focusing on the amount of effort given. In contrast, students with low self-efficacy may "aim low" in terms of their reading performances, exhibit limited effort when encountering challenges, make debilitating attributions for their reading outcomes (e.g., luck), and avoid challenges.

As with motivation, the research base for self-efficacy is developed to the point where the necessity of self-efficacy for reading success is clear. Both motivation and self-efficacy are involved in reading development: Each is marked by established and growing research bases, evidence of influence on reading development, and evidence of dynamic relationships with other factors. Both are ignored by tests, and lacking in most teacher evaluation equations.

High stakes reading tests focus on cognitive strategies and skills that are essential for reading success. The validity of these tests represents a mapping of test tasks and items onto the cognitive domain of reading. Missing in all high stakes tests is attention to other important aspects of students' development, including affect. Given what published research and accomplished teachers describe as the essential nature of positive affect in reading, high stakes tests can be considered, at best, a partial sampling in relation to the constructs we know to be essential for reading development. Thus, these consequential tests are limited in what they can tell us about students' reading development—even though their purpose is to assess this development.

The Chain of Inferences Needed to Validate Reading Test Use in Teacher Evaluation

Pellegrino, Chudowsky, and Glaser (2001) describe the necessity of clear and concise mapping of an assessment onto the construct and related student growth it is intended to measure. In the previous sections, I demonstrated how high stakes reading tests have partial construct validity: These tests clearly sample cognitive behaviors that are integral to students' reading development. However, when an assessment offers only partial construct validity, the information it provides must be used with extreme care. A reading test that focuses on cognitive strategies and skills, and reports that students vary in their literal and inferential comprehension achievement and vocabulary, provide important but incomplete information. We should be skeptical of using such test scores to describe and certify the totality of a student's growth (or lack of growth) in reading. High stakes tests simply do not provide a comprehensive account of students' reading development.

Following from Pellegrino, Chudowsky, and Glaser's (2001) model of assessment, it is risky to privilege results of reading tests because they provide only partial, gross-grain accounts of students' reading development. Yet, this is exactly what the practice of determining students' AYP in reading requires. An even more questionable practice is using scores from tests that sample students' reading behaviors to evaluate teacher effectiveness in relation to reading development.

Simply stated, a reading comprehension test is not a teacher evaluation test. When a test is used for a purpose other than that for which it is specifically designed, those who would use test scores must make a series of inferences. These inferences must be defensible for test score use to be legitimate. Consider the inferences that must be made when using a student's high stakes reading test result as part of a teacher evaluation scheme:

- That a test created to measure student reading achievement is suitable for measuring teacher achievement.
- That the test sufficiently samples and represents what we know to be important for students' reading achievement (focusing on both cognitive and affective development), and is therefore a legitimate representation of a teacher's accomplishments.
- That a teacher's accomplishment and contribution to student achievement can be parsed from the complex collection of things a student knows and does at the beginning of the school year, and those at the end of the school year, all within the confines of a single test score.
- That the weighting of a test score, in the (hopefully) larger mix of students' reading development indicators used in teacher evaluation, is based on more than guesswork.
- That contextual factors are not operating to influence the process of using reading comprehension tests to evaluate teacher achievement (e.g., teaching to the test).

The accurate evaluation of teachers requires a comprehensive and strategic approach to gathering evidence and assigning each piece of evidence appropriate weight. The above series of inferences illustrates that a teacher evaluation that is weighted heavily to a high stakes test score is unreliable.

Reading Tests, Teacher Evaluations, and Value-Added Models (VAMs)

Recently, teacher evaluations have employed high stakes test scores in value-added model (VAM) procedures. VAMs are used to try to parse students' overall achievement into pieces attributable to a teacher, and other factors. Specific to this chapter, VAMs offer an estimate of a teacher's contributions to students' reading achievement. According to the American Statistical Association:

> Many states and school districts have adopted Value-Added Models (VAMs) as part of educational accountability systems. The goal of these models, which are also referred to as Value-Added Assessment (VAA) Models, is to estimate effects of individual teachers or schools on student achievement while accounting for differences in student background. VAMs are increasingly promoted or mandated as a component in high-stakes decisions such as determining compensation, evaluating and ranking teachers, hiring or

dismissing teachers, awarding tenure, and closing schools. (American Statistical Association, 2014, p. 1)

Value-added models are used in an attempt to make more specific a teacher's contribution to students' reading growth. For example, high stakes test scores among elementary school students who come from households with high socioeconomic status, who have parents who are college-educated and understand the United States' educational system, may not be as impressive as elevated test scores among students who are raised in poverty. Groups of students who maintain high test scores across their school careers may not be as impressive as groups of students who exhibit large gains in their test scores. Value-added models project students' expected test performances and match them with actual test performances, and attempt to assign a degree of correlation between the teacher and the reading test score. In theory, this can be beneficial in helping to identify those teachers whose work elevates the performance of students above an expected level. However, the process of assigning "value-added" status is fraught with potential problems. The American Statistical Association makes the following observations and recommendations regarding the use of VAMs (American Statistical Association, 2014):

- Estimates from VAMs should always be accompanied by measures of precision and a discussion of the assumptions and possible limitations of the model. These limitations are particularly relevant if VAMs are used for high-stakes purposes.
- VAMs are generally based on standardized test scores, and do not directly measure potential teacher contributions toward other student outcomes.
- VAMs typically measure correlation, not causation: Effects—positive or negative—attributed to a teacher may actually be caused by other factors that are not captured in the model. (pp. 1-2)

That a preeminent professional organization representing statisticians assigns the above caveats to using value-added models in teacher evaluation speaks volumes. Finally, the American Statistical Association also notes the following related to value-added models:

Value-Added Models (VAMs) should be viewed within the context of quality improvement, which distinguishes aspects of quality that can be attributed to the system from those that can be attributed to individual teachers, teacher preparation programs, or schools. Most VAM studies find that teachers account for about 1% to 14% of the variability in test scores, and that the majority of opportunities for quality improvement are found in the system-level conditions. Ranking teachers by their VAM scores can have unintended consequences that reduce quality. (American Statistical Association, 2014, p. 2)

The above statement is not only an argument for reduced use of test scores in teacher evaluation, it is an invitation for states and districts to temper teacher evaluations accordingly. Given that high stakes reading tests are designed to make inferences about students' reading development, and that these tests offer only partial descriptions of that development, what are we to make of their use in inferring (and making judgments of) teacher effectiveness? Teacher evaluations that use high stakes test scores must be augmented with accurate accounts of how teachers influence the affective lives of their students.

In summary, tests measure cognition: the development of reading strategies and skills and content area knowledge gain in reading. They do not measure the development (or lack of development) of affective factors that operate regularly, and with influence, during acts of reading. Tests provide an incomplete account of student readers' development. Reading tests have, at best, partial construct validity. Psychometric theory posits that assessments marked by bias should be used with great caution, or not used at all. That tests exhibiting such bias are used to deem teachers as "effective" or "ineffective" is inappropriate, and contributes to assessment malpractice.

Conclusions

In this chapter I sketched the reasons for the persistence of using students' reading test scores in teacher evaluation schemes. Federal education policy, the privileged status of tests of cognitive strategies and skills, habits of mind, and vested interests all act to reinforce this questionable practice. I focused on the fact that high stakes tests do not provide information on critical affective factors that are part of every student reader's development. Motivation and engagement and self-efficacy are powerful forces in any act of reading, but they are ignored by tests. Thus, test scores do not offer insights into student affect or a teacher's influence on that affect. Evaluating teachers with such incomplete data on their work is inappropriate.

Next, I questioned the practice of using reading tests to measure teachers' contributions, noting that such practice is based on a series of inferences that are difficult to justify. Reading test scores are also used in value-added models (VAMs) to attempt to determine what contributions a teacher makes to student reading development, but the VAM process is fraught with difficulty, and this is in addition to the fact that tests offer only partial information on teachers' work.

Take Action

- Determine what measures of student affect are appropriate for providing a more complete portrait of student accomplishment and teacher achievement, in addition to standardized tests.
- Observation of students provides much valuable data related to student affect. Become familiar with checklists, observation scales, and questionnaires that

focus on affect, including motivation and engagement and self-efficacy, and determine which will complement the partial account of student growth that is provided by test scores.

- Create a construct-valid teacher evaluation. What is needed to provide adequate coverage of students' development in reading skills and strategies? In content area knowledge gain? In developing positive affect towards reading, including high self-efficacy and consistent motivation to read?

References

Afflerbach, P. (in press). *Handbook of individual differences in reading: Reader, text, and context.* New York: Routledge.

Afflerbach, P., Cho, B.-Y., Kim, J.-Y., Crassas, M.E., & Doyle, B. (2013). Reading: What else matters besides strategies and skills? *The Reading Teacher, 66,* 440–448.

Alexander, L., James, T., & Glaser, R. (1987). The Nation's Report Card: Improving the assessment of student achievement. Cambridge, MA: National Academy of Education.

American Statistical Association. (2014). ASA statement on using value-added models for educational assessment. Alexandria, VA: Author.

Bandura, A. (2006). Toward a psychology of human agency. *Perspectives on Psychological Science, 1*(2), 164–180.

California Department of Education. (2014). *California Assessment of Student Performance and Progress.* Sacramento, CA: Author. Retrieved from: http://www.cde.ca.gov/ta/tg/ca/

Guthrie, J., & Klauda, S. (in press). Engagement and motivational processes in reading. In P. Afflerbach (Ed.), *Handbook of individual differences in reading: Reader, text, and context.* New York: Routledge.

Guthrie, J., Wigfield, A., & You, W. (2012). Instructional contexts for engagement and achievement in reading. In S.L. Christenson, A.L. Reschly, & C. Wylie (Eds.), *Handbook of research on student engagement* (pp. 601–634). New York: Springer.

Investopedia. (n.d.) *Path dependency.* Retrieved from: http://www.investopedia.com/terms/p/path-dependency.asp

Mucherah, W., & Yoder, A. (2008). Motivation for reading and middle school students' performance on standardized testing in reading. *Reading Psychology, 29,* 214–235.

National Institute of Child Health and Human Development. (2000). *Report of the National Reading Panel. Teaching children to read: An evidence-based assessment of the scientific research literature on reading and its implications for reading instruction* (NIH Publication No. 00-4769). Washington, DC: U.S. Government Printing Office.

Ohanion, S. (2005). The list. Retrieved from: http://susanohanian.org/show_commentary.php?id=357

Pellegrino, J., Chudowsky, N., & Glaser, R. (2001). *Knowing what students know: The science and design of educational assessment.* Washington, DC: National Academy Press.

Shell, D., Colvin, C., & Bruning, R. (1995). Self-efficacy, attributions, and outcome expectancy mechanisms in reading and writing achievement: Grade-level and achievement-level differences. *Journal of Educational Psychology, 87,* 386–398.

Stanovich, K. (1986). Matthew effects in reading: Some consequences of individual differences in the acquisition of literacy. *Reading Research Quarterly, 21,* 360–407.

4

CONSIDERATIONS FOR EVALUATING INSTRUCTION FOR ENGLISH LANGUAGE LEARNERS

Sultan Turkan

Introduction

This chapter presents a discussion about validity issues in utilizing commonly available teacher evaluation measures for assessing quality in teaching literacy to English language learners (ELLs). The following questions guide the discussion in this chapter: What does effective teaching of literacy for ELLs mean? To what extent can currently available observation instruments be used to generate valid inferences about the instruction of ELLs?

What Is Effective Literacy Teaching for ELLs?

Effective literacy instruction for ELLs can be characterized by several features that might be shared with generic descriptions of effective literacy teaching. Generic descriptions of effective literacy teaching appear to be closely linked to the two views of reading that are prevalent in second language acquisition theory: word recognition and sociopsycholinguistic views (Freeman & Freeman, 2003). This first is a word recognition view of reading, which defines the task of reading as identifying words. This task involves connecting the words in print with the oral vocabulary. When viewed through this lens, the task of teaching reading is to help students make the connections between the print and oral vocabulary. The second is a sociopsycholinguistic view, which approaches the task of reading as meaning-making. With that in mind, Freeman and Freeman explain that "readers use their background knowledge and cues from the text to make sense of print" (p. 37). While either view might centralize "comprehension" as the goal of reading, the instructional practices differ depending on which approach or view is taken towards reading.

Because the philosophies and pedagogies associated with each of these views (and others) contrast, there may not be one uniform way of defining effective literacy teaching for ELLs. For example, within the sociopsycholinguistic view, effective literacy instruction for ELLs means engaging students in making meaning with written texts through reading and writing (Vacca & Vacca, 2008). This might involve extensive discussions, creative writing, and choice of text for independent reading, as the goal of literacy instruction is to generate meaning in socially and culturally relevant ways. Thus observation instruments should have indicators that explicitly value language experience, talk about text, engagement in independent reading and writing to a specific audience.

In contrast, the word recognition view of reading would involve more explicit vocabulary, syntax, and grammar development—practices that may not be valued or reflected in observation instruments that are designed to support practices associated with the sociopsycholinguistic view. For example, Calderón (2007) and others (e.g., Herrera et al., 2010) have argued for addressing the lexical challenges that ELLs face while reading texts. Calderón emphasized the importance of teachers' identification of lexical challenges and development as a foundation for reading in the content areas, including English Language Arts. Based on the work of Beck, McKeown, and Kucan (2002), Calderón suggested that teachers distinguish words as belonging to one of three tiers. Tier I words are common, everyday words. If students do not know a Tier I word, the word will most likely represent a concept that students already know in their native language, but for which they have no label in English. Calderón used *butterfly* as a Tier I word that ELLs may not know but for which they probably have the concept. Teachers could teach the English word for this concept by, for example, pointing to a picture of a butterfly. Tier II words are more academic terms that are used across disciplines. As one teacher in Calderón's article (2007) put it, these words provide "ways of talking about school stuff" (p. 31). In the word recognition view, the central challenge is not meaning-making at large, but vocabulary development in particular, with a focus on learning individual words. Thus instruction organized from this perspective may have a great deal more explicit vocabulary instruction and attention to the mechanics of language than those organized from a sociopsycholinguistic view.

Beyond a specific emphasis on vocabulary development or overall meaning-making, Waxman and Tellez (2002) identify six general instructional practices that support all learners, but are linked to academic benefits among ELL students in particular.

1. Creating cooperative learning environments: small group activities that provide opportunities for students to develop social bonds as these lead to the kinds of interactions that promote language development.
2. Using multiple representations of words: using visuals, sounds, pictures, and multimedia is important in order to help students make connections between words and their meanings as they acquire vocabulary.

3. Building on students' prior knowledge: it is important to make use of the knowledge that students already have by incorporating students' cultural, linguistic, and literary knowledge into lessons without assuming that all students have the same content knowledge or experience with the subject of the text.
4. Engaging students in extended dialogues orally or in writing: this includes engaging students in extended silent reading and discussions about text (engaging with text), discussions of mathematics (i.e., not just in the context of an ELA class). Other scholars (see August & Shanahan, 2006; Genesee et al., 2006) argue that developing ELLs' oral language makes it possible for them to have access to academic content.
5. Acknowledging values and incorporating students' own values, norms, and concerns: this links to drawing on students' prior knowledge as the teachers use students' existing knowledge base for new learning and take students' cultural and linguistic needs into consideration.
6. Promoting students to use cognitive learning strategies: another area of effective instruction is that teachers provide and promote cognitive learning strategies (meta-cognitive skills) of students. For example, specific teaching of reading strategies can promote reading comprehension through using scaffolding and reciprocal teaching approaches.

According to DelliCarpini (2011), regardless of whether a reader is an ELL or not, effective readers utilize various strategies to enhance their comprehension. Observation instruments aimed at identifying and supporting effective literacy instruction to ELLs should explicitly reflect some or all of these practices if they are to be used to identify or improve instruction for ELLs.

Thus far, I have presented themes in the research literature regarding what it means to effectively teach literacy to ELLs. However, as noted in Chapter 2, these themes are not explicitly represented in any commercially available evaluation instrument that might be used to assess teacher quality. That is, the focus on ELLs in any literacy teaching evaluation instrument is not informed by the specific paradigms that define quality literacy teaching of ELLs. In the section that follows, a review of existing measures of teaching is presented to address how they address the teaching of literacy to ELLs.

Measures for Evaluating Literacy Instruction

A recent review of state practices shows that observation instruments are among the most commonly used tools for evaluating teachers (Holdeheide et al., 2010). In the review by Holdeheide et al. (2010), the second most frequently used method was through evaluating the teachers' perceived or measured progress on the specific professional goals. The other cited and used measures were as follows: classroom artifacts, portfolios, and self-report measures. Interestingly, this review showed that states did not appear to fully embrace the use of value-added scores.

Holdeheide et al. argue that while value-added scores have attracted attention by state and national policy makers in linking the academic growth of students to their teachers in order to evaluate and improve teacher effectiveness in U.S. K-12 schools, there is no value-added model proven to be empirically valid to use with ELL specialists and mainstream teachers of ELLs.

In the following section, three evaluation measures are selected to demonstrate the type of analysis educators should apply to any/all evaluation tools. These measures are intended as examples: two generic and one subject-specific. Of specific relevance are the following instruments: Danielson's Framework For Teaching (FFT), The Classroom Assessment Scoring System (CLASS), and the Protocol for Language Arts Teaching Observation (PLATO). The next section presents a brief description about the theoretical and empirical properties of each of the three measures.

Taken together, the three instruments represent some of the range of available observation instruments. For example, the FFT can be applied across grades and content areas; CLASS can be applied across content areas, but has separate versions for different grade ranges; and PLATO is subject-specific, but can be applied across grades. After briefly describing each tool, I present an analysis of their validity when applied to classrooms with a large number of ELLs.

First, the FFT is an observation instrument intended for use in all content classrooms. FFT covers four domains: (1) Planning and Preparation—six components; (2) Classroom Environment—five components; (3) Instruction—five components; and (4) Professional Responsibilities—six components. Only the second and third domains are in an observed lesson. Each of the performance descriptors is rated on four performance levels: satisfactory, basic, proficient, distinguished. FFT is grounded on a constructivist theory of teaching and learning.

The constructivist theory posits that the teacher's role is to guide and engage the learners in a process of reasoning based on content-related experiences that enhance conceptual understanding (Danielson, 2007). Further, the FFT framework assumes that different individuals experience learning materials and concepts differently depending on their background knowledge and cognitive readiness, irrespective of the teacher's actions and quality of instructional practice. Despite this emphasis on learners' varying experiences with the instructional content, Danielson includes only broad indicators in relation to teaching ELLs. For example, Danielson's framework suggests that a teacher needs to make accommodations for special populations, and tailor instruction to individual student needs, backgrounds, cultures, and the like. Also, it is expected that teachers should be knowledgeable about students' language proficiency. Specifically, under Domain 1b: Demonstrating Knowledge and Preparation, the framework identifies that a teacher at the Distinguished level "displays understanding of individual students' skills, knowledge and language proficiency and has a strategy for maintaining such information" (Danielson, 2007, p. 35). However, there is no specificity as to what this would mean or how it would be manifested when the teacher enacts these skills in the classrooms.

As this example demonstrates, the instrument stresses throughout that teachers have to be attentive and responsive to the needs of each individual student in the classroom by stating teacher behavior descriptors such as: "Sensitivity to individual students must be extended to include appropriate accommodations for students with special needs." Speaking specifically about students with disabilities, Danielson writes "and with greater inclusion of students with disabilities in regular classrooms, all teachers require at least some understanding of special needs." However, these descriptors are not sufficient to comprehensively address the evaluation of the teaching of content to special student populations such as ELLs and students with disabilities. Also, even if the descriptors were adequate, it is important to note that unless the raters know what teachers' knowledge of language proficiency is, the implementation of the descriptors would not be valid.

Second, the Classroom Assessment Scoring System (CLASS) is also intended for use in all content classrooms. CLASS includes nine dimensions across three domains of effective teacher-student interactions: (1) Emotional Support; (2) Classroom Organization; and (3) Instructional Support. Under each domain, three dimensions of effective teacher-student interactions are targeted: for example, under Emotional Support, the CLASS instrument captures practices that are "focused on social and emotional functioning in a classroom setting" (Pianta, LaParo, & Hamre, 2008, p. 11). This domain is considered especially critical for children at risk of academic difficulty. Under this domain, the following dimensions are included: Classroom Climate, Regard for Student Perspectives, and Teacher Sensitivity. Classroom Climate is differentiated by positive or negative climate. The domain of Classroom Organization covers the dimensions of Behavior Management, Productivity, and Instructional Learning Formats. The third domain, Instructional Support, includes the following dimensions: (1) Concept Development; (2) Quality of Feedback; and (3) Language Modeling. Each of these dimensions are measured on a 7-point Likert scale, ranging from 1 or 2 (low-quality interactions), to 3, 4, or 5 (mid-range quality), to 6 or 7, indicating high-quality interactions.

The only rationale for using CLASS with linguistically diverse learners is provided in the report by Vitiello (2013) claiming, based on an earlier study (Vitiello, 2012), that CLASS can be used reliably in dual-language classrooms where instruction is typically both in English and Spanish. While the quality of interactions between students and teachers is noted as an important criterion to validate the use of CLASS with diverse learners like ELLs, there is no specific construct definition as to how quality of interactions with ELLs would be different from teachers' interactions with other non-ELL students.

Third, Protocol for Language Arts Teaching Observations (PLATO) is another instrument that is also used in research studies but most specifically in Language

Arts classrooms. The initial version of the instrument covered 12 elements: (1) Purpose; (2) Representation to Content; (3) Connections to Prior Knowledge; (4) Connections to Personal and/or Cultural Experience; (5) Models/Modeling; (6) Explicit Strategy Instruction; (7) Guided Practice; (8) Classroom Discourse; (9) Text-Based Instruction; (10) Accommodations for Language-Learning; (11) Behavior Management; and (12) Time Management. Each of these elements is measured on a 7-point scale. That is, each element included indicators of interactions with low scores (1 and 2), medium (3, 4, 5), and high scores (6 and 7). While the element of accommodations for language learning does not find explicit coverage in the current version of the PLATO, some administrators might still be interested in capturing quality teaching ELA to ELLs using the initial version of the protocol as an informal guide.

The only elements that indirectly or directly are concerned with ELL teaching are "Connections to Personal and/or Cultural Experience" and "Accommodations for Language Learning." Grossman et al. (2010) explain that accommodations teachers provide in the classroom might include scaffolding for academic language development and explicit vocabulary support. They specifically add that accommodations might include "teachers taking into account individuals' levels of language proficiency, strategic use of primary language, grouping strategies, differentiated materials and assessments, as well as graphic organizers and visual displays" (p. 8). However, it is not documented anywhere what theoretical framework drives the orientation to the "accommodation" of ELLs on PLATO, or what this might look like in practice.

The only research that is cited in relation to academic language is by Delpit (1988) and Schleppegrell (2004). The way these two citations are interpreted in PLATO is that teachers should engage in ELLs' academic language development to bridge the gap between this and the "students' home discourse" (Grossman et al., 2010, p. 8). In the absence of any other discussion regarding ELL teaching in publications related to PLATO, while it may be reasonable to infer from these references that language used in school will vary from the language used at home, it is naive to assert that "introducing academic language in classrooms" can bridge the gap between home and school.

Academic language is the default language of schooling in ELA classrooms, or any other content classroom. In a sense, it is not "introducing academic language" that is emphasized in the cited literature on effective instruction for ELLs as much as it is "developing," modeling, and "scaffolding" academic language development. However, the authors do not elaborate on what counts as "academic language development" within the PLATO instrument. The only explication Grossman et al. offer regarding the focus on academic language in PLATO is that the evaluator would examine whether the teacher introduces ELA-specific vocabulary and terms and to what extent the teacher supports the use of the particular vocabulary.

Further, PLATO includes the concept of "accommodation" for ELLs, rather than inclusion. The accommodation practices highlighted in this observation instrument are mostly concerned with indicators of differentiated instruction such as teachers' use of students' primary language, grouping strategies, graphic organizers and visual displays, and their consideration of students' levels of language proficiency. In the pilot study reported in Grossman et al. (2010), it appears that approximately 80% of the teacher participants scored mostly 1 or 2 on a 7-point Likert scale on ELL accommodations. The modal score on ELL accommodations was 1. That is, the most common score teachers received on ELL accommodations was 1, which is considerably low on a 7-point Likert scale. Also, another finding that is not discussed by the authors is that high value-added quartile teachers scored lower on ELL accommodations than the teachers with low value-added quartiles. There is no significant difference between the two high and low value-added quartile teachers in relation to ELL accommodations (p = .72). This insignificance is important to note when the authors report statistical significance between high and low scoring teachers in other elements such as explicit strategy instruction, guided practice, and intellectual challenge. This might suggest that "better" teachers do not score any higher or differently than "not so good teachers" when it comes to instructional practices that support ELLs.

Validity Research across the Three Instruments

There is limited research on validity issues involved in using the three instruments to evaluate the effectiveness of teaching ELA to ELLs. General validity investigations for each of the instruments have been conducted. For example, the validity studies of the FFT have shown that FFT scores correlate with student achievement gains (e.g., Gallagher, 2004; Holtzapple, 2003; Kimball et al., 2004; Milanowski, 2004). However, this finding was not consistent across grades and subject areas. Furthermore, one critical aspect of any instrument's validity is its reliability; that is, the instrument should yield consistent scores across raters and under similar conditions. The reliability information influences how many lessons and the length of each lesson segment should be rated in order to obtain the most stable and consistent scores indicating teaching quality. In other words, the differences in teachers' performances on the instrument should be mostly explained by the teacher differences, not rater characteristics, or other contextual factors such as the curriculum (e.g., number of lessons and length of each lesson segment) and the like. In fact, the only evidence reliability investigation that has been conducted to date came from the Measures of Effective Teaching (MET) study (Bill & Melinda Gates Foundation, 2012, 2013). The MET study (2012) showed that FFT explained the variance due to the teachers by 37%. Variance due to rater differences was only 6%; however, 43% of the variance was not explained. This might mean that the raters did not differ in their rating much. Nonetheless, the fact that a considerable degree of reliability was due to unexplained factors warrants further investigation.

More central to this chapter is the validity considerations in using FFT with teachers of English as a Second Language (ESL) or teachers teaching in predominantly ELL classrooms. While there is some validity research on using FFT with special education teachers (Nougaret et al., 2005; Sindelar, Daunic, & Rennells, 2004 as cited in Jones & Brownell, 2014), there is no single study to date that would provide evidence of the validity of scores for high-stakes decisions for using FFT with content or ESL teachers of ELLs. As Holdeheide et al. (2010) allude to, mainstream and non-subject-specific observation protocols, like FFT, should go beyond addressing teachers' ability to meet the needs of "diverse" learners. Rather, they should address teachers' skills and strategies in culturally and linguistic responsive teaching striking a balance between "acquisition of English with the affirmation of students home culture and language" (Holdeheide et al., 2010, p. 18).

CLASS, on the other hand, seems to have made some progress in examining the validity of inferences made of teaching evaluations that are conducted in classrooms serving ELLs predominantly. For example, Hamre et al. (2007) examined the factor structure of the CLASS instrument and, as it is mentioned in Downer et al. (2012), Latino and ELL students were included as part of the larger sample of students. In this examination, three distinct emotional, organizational, and instructional domains of the early version of CLASS focusing on preschool to third grade fit the teacher observation data. The observations were collected from over 4,000 preschool to fifth grade classrooms in rural, suburban, and urban environments with diverse student populations. However, there is no mention in Hamre et al.'s piece that the three-factor model fit better with a certain student body with uniform social and academic characteristics than another group of students. Thus, the findings of this study cannot be used to imply any generalizations that the instrument would assess the three factors equally well in settings with predominantly ELL students. However, the studies by Downer et al. (2012) and Lopez (2012) fill in this gap by explicitly examining the psychometric properties of the CLASS in classrooms serving ethnically and linguistically diverse learners.

In this study, the classrooms were classified into high-, mid-, and no–Dual Language Learner (DLL) categories depending on the proportion of students who were reported as DLL. Also, the number of Latino/Latina children in the classrooms was identified by a categorization of high-, mid-, and no-Latino classrooms. The resulting numbers of DLLs and Latinos were not equal. However, the three-factor model of the CLASS instrument assessing the three domains (Emotional Support, Classroom Organization, and Instructional Support) did not vary across the three DLL and three Latino/Latina student groups. That is, the function of Latino or DLL composition did not significantly matter for the factorial representation of the CLASS instrument. One caveat is that factor analysis is only one form of validity evidence, and other sources of validity evidence need to be collected. All in all, though, one could see that CLASS research seems to have examined how differently the instrument functions when there are ELLs in the classroom more so than other instruments reviewed here. This might be because the theoretical grounding of the CLASS draws on developmental theory suggesting that interactions between students and teacher determine the extent to which student learning occurs. Hence, the focus of CLASS on students warrants examining further how the CLASS instrument captures what purports to evaluate in the presence of certain groups of students such as ELLs.

As for the PLATO, the only investigation of validity evidence comes from the MET report (Bill & Melinda Gates Foundation, 2012) suggesting that PLATO shows a better correlation with the teacher underlying value-added scores than other observation instruments in the context of ELA classrooms. In relation to the student gains, teachers in the top and bottom quartiles account for the student effort more in PLATO when compared to the other instruments (CLASS and FFT). In this finding, there is no mention about the particular characteristics of the students that the gain scores were based on. Likewise, the finding in Grossman et al. (2010) that teachers scored lowest on the domain of ELL accommodation is not elaborated by any information about the percent of ELLs or their proficiency levels. This fine-grain information would be important to have to evaluate to what extent high-performing ELA teachers do well on the domain of ELL accommodations and how many of these teachers have large numbers of ELLs in their classrooms. Also, Grossman et al. examines the relationship between teachers' PLATO and value-added scores. However, the finding that is reported does not elaborate which student populations are accounted for in the value-added scores.

The issues around variance attributable to raters are worthwhile to consider in all three instruments. However, as the MET findings imply, the subject-specific instruments like PLATO tend to yield less variance that results from "main" rater effects because raters need relatively high levels of subject knowledge to rate the domains of effective ELA instruction, in particular *modeling* and *strategy use* and *instruction*.

Validity Limitations across the Three Instruments

Overall, the information and discussion presented above show that none of the three instruments reviewed here were designed to account for the effective teaching of any specific groups of students in the classroom. This section unpacks the issue of reinforcing validity for each of the three instruments by drawing on Kane's argument-based model of validation. Kane's argument-based model of validation (2006) involves two arguments: the interpretive and the validity argument. The interpretive argument refers to the network of four inferences that are made based on the test taker's performance on a test or instrument. The validity argument "evaluates the plausibility of the proposed interpretive argument" (Kane, 1992, p. 10). The four inferences involved in the validity argument include: (1) scoring, (2) generalization, (3) extrapolation, and (4) interpretation.

Scoring inference essentially involves a process of examining the extent to which the test or instrument measures what it purports to measure. Research along these lines would look into the three areas of improvement: appropriateness, accuracy, and quality. While examining appropriateness, the focus would be on including the appropriate criteria for what the test or instrument is intended to assess. In the case of evaluating instruction for ELLs, this would mean including indicators that address specific features of effective ELL instruction. In examining accuracy, the researchers would investigate how accurately and consistently the scores are assigned to the performance of the test takers. Quality control in relation to instrument administration is also key to the degree of confidence in the scoring inference in that the control procedures should provide evidence that there is no rater bias, and that raters were trained.

Generalization inference involves an investigation as to whether the instrument or test is representative of a wide variety of the possible instances or contexts in which the test taker would need to perform the skills and knowledge base assessed by the instrument. For example, each tool is validated with a specific population of students, which may not be representative of the population or composition of classes across country (e.g., Lopez, 2011, 2012). ELLs are such a heterogeneous population that empirical research must find evidence that classroom observations as measured through the particular instrument are representative of possible encounters with a diverse pool of ELL profiles and their academic challenges.

Extrapolation inference refers to examining the degree to which the test takers' performance on an instrument correlates with the performance on other instruments that are designed to assess similar target skills. For example, in a 2013 report, Terry et al. demonstrated that the Early Literacy Language Classroom Observation tool (ELLCO) predicted student outcomes for African-American and Hispanic students, while CLASS did not. Similarly, Lopez (2011) has demonstrated that classroom quality indicators included in CLASS fail to capture some of the behaviors associated with literacy achievement in classrooms with more Hispanic students, but can explain the variance in student achievement in non-Hispanic classrooms. This may indicate that such tools are biased towards certain demographic groups and therefore cannot explain their performance on other measures.

Lastly, **interpretation inferences** examine the degree to which the scores are relevant to the decision(s) that the scores would be used for. Given the lack of direct connection between currently available observation instruments and the research base on effective ELL instruction, there is reason to exercise caution when making interpretation inferences using tools for teacher evaluation in settings with large numbers of ELLs. Drawing on Kane's interpretive argument theory and the network of four inferences, this section presents a discussion about the limitations of the three focus instruments. The following question guides this discussion: what validity limitations would need to be overcome if FFT, CLASS, and PLATO were to be used for evaluating effective teaching of ELLs?

In light of the scoring inference, the first limitation that is shared across the three instruments is that they do not address the most salient aspects of quality teaching ELA to ELLs. In other words, the degree to which these instruments are *appropriate* to use for the purposes of assessing and scoring effective ELA instruction for ELLs is not addressed. For example, FFT takes a constructivist approach to defining quality teaching. However, it does not cover any dimensions that unpack how the teachers should approach constructivist teaching with ELLs. CLASS is another instrument that is used across content areas and strictly focused on teacher-student interactions.

Even though this instrument focuses on students and the quality of interactions with teachers around content, dimensions of effective teaching are not specified vis-à-vis specific student populations such as ELLs. Hence, just like FFT, CLASS does not specify particular dimensions of effective ELL teaching that would support an inference that the scores derived from this instrument would be *appropriate* for the purposes of assessing or evaluating teachers of ELLs. However, there is some evidence that the underlying factor structure targeted by CLASS functions invariably across the groups of dual language learners and Latino/Latina students.

Amongst the three instruments, PLATO is the only one that recognizes the dimension of how characteristics of student population might play a role in the quality of instruction. PLATO therefore specifies two dimensions related to effective ELL teaching (i.e., connections to personal/cultural experience and accommodations for language learning) as part of its definition on what it means to teach ELA. However, it does not offer substantial evidence to support any scoring inference that the scoring models are *appropriate, accurate,* and unbiased to use for assessing the teaching of ELA to ELLs.

In relation to the generalization inference, the main limitation across the three instruments is simply that they do not include guidance for deciding whether the sample of lessons observed by any of the three instruments represents all the potential lessons that teachers of ELLs would enact in ELA classrooms. For example, given the wide range of practices that could be associated with effective literacy instruction for ELLs, it is difficult to make decisions about the sample of teaching (how many observations for how long) and density of ELL-specific practices that should be used to reliably indicate quality.

Likewise, if guided by the extrapolation inference needed to build a strong interpretive argument, all three instruments would need to provide evidence that teachers' performance on the instruments correlates with other definitions of ELL teaching quality as measured by other instruments. To prove that FFT, CLASS, and PLATO could be used to measure effective teaching of ELLs, studies could be conducted to examine how the performance on these instruments correlates with the performance on other measures that are designed to measure teaching of ELLs. Since the number of standardized instruments used for measuring effective teaching of ELA is limited and those that measure effective teaching of ELA to ELLs are even more limited (one more recent instrument is Classroom Qualities for English Learners [CQEL], 2014), it would be challenging to collect evidence supporting that the performance on these measures correlates with the measures assessing quality of teaching ELLs.

As for the interpretation inference, none of the three instruments provide strong evidence that they should be used to make specific interpretations or high-stakes decisions about the quality of literacy instruction for ELLs. Evidence collected to support the interpretation inference should generate compelling evidence that supports the use of scores for those purposes; the particular uses of the scores as targeted by the instruments have to be appropriate for the identified uses. For example, PLATO researchers would need to examine the degree to which PLATO predicts student outcomes in classrooms with a large proportion of ELLs. Researchers could examine whether ESL licensed teachers would also be equally effective to teach ELLs based on their PLATO scores. Along the same lines, since the initial version of PLATO in particular includes two dimensions on teaching ELLs, it would be important to examine whether using PLATO would actually serve the function to improve the teaching of literacy to ELLs.

Take Action

This review and discussion of the validity issues in using widely common teacher evaluation measures for assessing quality in teaching literacy to ELLs revealed that the existing generic or ELA-specific observation instruments do not conceive ELL teaching as part of their definition of quality teaching of reading and literacy. In this context, there is little room for policy makers or administrators to use any of these instruments for any consequential purposes such as teacher licensure or retention. However, administrators could consider using some of these instruments for formative purposes, as is discussed in Chapter 8 of this volume. Unless any of the three instruments incorporates teaching ELLs as part of their construct definition (see the following chapter for a discussion of this), their use for making any high-stakes claims about effective teaching of reading and literacy to ELLs would compromise validity.

In the absence of a uniform body of empirical work defining quality teaching of ELA to ELLs, it is the individual responsibility of the practitioners to maintain a focus on the needs of ELLs when considering or executing instructional quality. One implication of this discussion for teachers might be that a partnership of teachers and researchers consider the features of ELL instruction discussed above that may not be explicitly outlined in observation rubrics. Additionally, given the shortage of teachers and administrators with ELL-specific training, administrators could invest in professional development or incentives aimed at supporting educators in identifying elements of effective instruction for ELLs beyond descriptions of instruction in current rubrics. If this work spreads amongst the ELA teachers, then practice-based construct definitions for what it means to teach ELA to ELLs could ground the development of observation instruments that are valid and relevant to the actual work of teaching ELA to ELLs.

References

August, D., & Shanahan, T. (Eds.). (2006). *Developing literacy in second-language learners: Report of the National Literacy Panel on language-minority children and youth.* Mahwah, NJ: Lawrence Erlbaum.

Beck, I., McKeown, M., & Kucan, L. (2002). *Bringing words to life.* New York: Guilford Press.

Bill & Melinda Gates Foundation. (2012). *Gathering feedback for teaching: Combining high quality observations with student surveys and achievement gains.* Seattle, WA: Author.

Bill & Melinda Gates Foundation. (2013). *Ensuring fair and reliable measures of effective teaching: Culminating findings from the MET project's three-year study.* Seattle, WA: Author.

Calderón, M. (2007). *Teaching reading to English language learners, grades 6–12: A framework for improving achievement in the content areas.* Thousand Oaks, CA: Corwin Press.

Classroom Qualities for English Learners (CQEL). (2014). Retrieved from https://people.stanford.edu/claudeg/cqell/about

Danielson, C. (2007). *Enhancing professional practice: A framework for teaching* (2nd ed.). Alexandria, VA: Association for Supervision and Curriculum Development.

DelliCarpini, M. (2011). Supporting ELLs before, during, and after reading. *English Journal, 100*(5), 108–112.

Delpit, L. (1988). The silenced dialogue: Power and pedagogy in educating other people's children. *Harvard Educational Review, 58,* 280–298.

Downer, J.T., Lopez, M.L., Grimm, K.J., Hamagami, A., & Pianta, R.C. (2012). Observations of teacher-child interactions in classrooms serving Latinos and dual language learners: Applicability of the Classroom Assessment Scoring System in diverse settings. *Early Childhood Research Quarterly, 27,* 21–32.

Freeman, D., & Freeman, Y. (2003). Teaching English learners to read: Learning or acquisition? In G. Garcie (Ed.), *Reaching the highest level of English literacy* (pp. 34–54). Newark, NJ: International Reading Association.

Gallagher, H.A. (2004). Vaughn Elementary's innovative teacher evaluation system: Are teacher evaluation scores related to growth in student achievement? *Peabody Journal of Education, 79,* 79–107.

Genesee, F., Lindholm-Leary, K., Saunders, W., & Christian, D. (2006). *Educating English language learners.* New York: Cambridge University Press.

Grossman, P., Loeb, S., Cohen, J., Hammerness, K., Wyckoff, J., Boyd, D., & Lankford, H. (2010). Measure for measure: Measures of instructional practice in middle school English language arts and teachers. *NBER Working Paper Series.* 1–37.

Hamre, B.K., Pianta, R.C., Mashburn, A.J., & Downer, J.T. (2007). Building a science of classrooms: Application of the CLASS Framework in over 4,000 U.S. early childhood and elementary classrooms. Retrieved from http://www.fcdus. org/sites/default/files/ BuildingAScienceOfClassroomsPiantaHamre.pdf

Herrera, S.G., Perez, D.R., & Escamilla, K. (2010). *Teaching reading to English language learners: Differentiated literacies.* Boston: Allyn & Bacon.

Holdheide, L., Goe, L., Croft, A., & Reschly, D. (2010). *Challenges in evaluating special education teachers and English language learner specialists* (Research & Policy Brief). Washington, DC: National Comprehensive Center for Teacher Quality. http://www.tqsource.org/ publications/July2010Brief.pdf

Holtzapple, E. (2003). Criterion-related validity evidence for a standards-based teacher evaluation system. *Journal of Personnel Evaluation in Education, 17*, 207–219.

Jones, N.D., & Brownell, M.T. (2014). Examining the use of classroom observations in the evaluation of special education teachers. *Assessment for Effective Intervention, 39*(2), 112–124.

Kane, M.T. (1992) An argument-based approach to validity. *Psychological Bulletin, 112*, 527–535.

Kane, M.T. (2006). Validation. In R.L. Brennan (Ed.), *Educational measurement* (pp. 17–64). New York: Praeger.

Kimball, S., White, B., Milanowski, A., & Borman, G. (2004). Examining the relationship between teacher evaluation and student assessment results in Washoe County. *Peabody Journal of Education, 79*, 54–78.

Lopez, F. (2011). The nongeneralizability of classroom dynamics as predictors of achievement for Hispanic students in upper elementary grades. *Hispanic Journal of Behavioral Sciences, 33*(3), 350–376.

Lopez, F. (2012). Moderators of language acquisition models and reading achievement for English language learners: The role of emotional warmth and instructional support. *Teachers College Record, 114*, 1–30.

Milanowski, A. (2004). *Relationships among dimension scores of standards-based teacher evaluation systems, and the stability of evaluation score: Student achievement relationships over time.* Madison: Wisconsin Center for Education Research, Consortium for Policy Research in Education, University of Wisconsin-Madison.

Nougaret, A., Scruggs, T., & Mastropieri, M. (2005). Does teacher education produce better special education teachers? *Exceptional Children, 71*, 217–229.

Pianta, R.C., La Paro, K.M., & Hamre, B.K. (2008). *Classroom Assessment Scoring System: Manual K–3.* Baltimore: Paul H. Brookes.

Schleppegrell, M. (2004). *The Language of schooling: A functional linguistics perspective.* Mahwah, NJ: Lawrence Erlbaum Associates.

Terry, N.P., Mills, M.T., Bingham, G.E., Mansour, S., & Marencin, N. (2013). Oral narrative performance of African American prekindergartners who speak nonmainstream American English. *Language, Speech, and Hearing Services in Schools, 44*(3), 291–305.

Vacca, R.T., & Vacca, J.L. (2008). *Content area reading: Literacy and learning across the curriculum* (9th ed.). Boston: Pearson.

Vitiello, V.E. (2012, June). *Inter-rater agreement on the Pre-K CLASS in English-only and multilingual classrooms.* Poster presented at the 11th National Head Start Research Conference, Washington, DC.

Vitiello, V.E. (2013). Dual language learners and the CLASS measure: Research and recommendations. *Teachstone Training*, 2–13.

Waxman, H.C., & Tellez, K. (2002). *Research synthesis on effective teaching practices for English language learners.* Philadelphia, PA: Temple University.

5

THE PRACTICE AND EVALUATION OF CULTURALLY RESPONSIVE LITERACY FOR ENGLISH LANGUAGE LEARNERS IN THE TWENTY-FIRST CENTURY

Alyson Lavigne and Tammy Oberg De La Garza

The racial, cultural, ethnic, and linguistic demographics in the United States have dramatically shifted in the past 20 years, becoming more diverse. Latinos are the largest, fastest growing racial/ethnic group in U.S. classrooms (Humes, Jones, & Ramirez, 2011), and by 2050, Latino student enrollment will represent the largest group in K-12 education (Fry & Gonzales, 2008). As population demographics in the nation and U.S. classrooms become increasingly diverse, school leaders and administrators are responsible for establishing policies, developing teachers, and demonstrating values that support the achievement of all students (Austin, Brown, & Forde, 2006). In culturally responsive institutions, students' cultural and linguistic differences that have been historically perceived as liabilities are instead perceived as strengths and utilized to promote student achievement. In this chapter, we examine research-based and culturally responsive literacy practices (CRLPs) that target the academic development of multicultural and multilingual students. We assess to what degree current observation instruments capture CRLPs, and present a new supervision tool for administrators to use in supporting and extending teachers' use of culturally responsive instructional practices to enhance the achievement of all students.

School leaders are keenly aware that diverse learners are a historically underserved group who experience sustained school failure (Artiles, Kozleski, Trent, Osher, & Ortiz, 2010). This trend is particularly true for Latino students because despite rising rates of college enrollment, academic achievement of Latinos remains low while the high-school dropout rates are among the highest in the nation (Buchanan, 2005; Pew Research Center, 2013). It would seem logical to rationalize their academic struggle with limited proficiency in English; however, longitudinal research reveals that Latino immigrants actually outperform their

U.S.-born, English-speaking children, grandchildren, and great-grandchildren in grades, test scores, and dropout rates (Buriel, 1987; Buriel & Cardoza, 1988; Hao & Woo, 2012; Suárez-Orozco, 2001;Vigil & Long, 1981). Educational leaders and researchers are instead starting to reconcile that the problem lies within the confines of school—that U.S. schools are organized in ways that strip culturally and linguistically diverse youth of significant social and cultural resources in ways that challenge their ability to identify with school or subsequent success (Jay, 2003; Urrieta, 2005; Valenzuela, 1999). Conversely, there is substantial research that demonstrates high levels of academic success for students whose language, culture, and identity remain intact throughout their school careers (Christian, 1994; Lessow-Hurley, 1991; Lindholm-Leary, 2001; Thomas & Collier, 2003). It is important now, more than ever, that school leaders and administrators shape institutional policy and instruction in ways that support rather than hinder the academic success of culturally and linguistically diverse learners.

Adding to this urgency for change is the emergence of Common Core State Standards (CCSS, 2012), a corporate school-reform initiative aligning national standards—standardizing what K-12 students should know in literacy and math by the end of each grade. The CCSS sets high levels of expectations and outcomes for all students: mainstream, urban, and culturally diverse populations. The CCSS vision is to prepare students to think, understand complex concepts, and become lifelong learners. Some critics declare that it is realistically impossible to achieve national equality because of the diversity in culture, ethnicity, and language (Bomer & Maloch, 2011); but lowering or raising expectations for certain groups of people would only further marginalize and extend social inequalities that currently exist. Developing instruction that is intellectually engaging is critical (Rebora, 2013), and designing it to meet the needs of diverse learners will be vital if schools and districts want to keep pace with national standards in education. It is critical that school leaders keep the needs of all students at the forefront of school policies and practices by ensuring that teachers employ daily culturally responsive instruction and literacy practices.

Culturally Responsive Literacy Practices for the Twenty-first Century

Culturally Responsive Instruction

Culturally responsive pedagogy (CRP) is defined as teaching practices that are embedded in the cultural characteristics that make students different from one another and the teacher (Rychly & Graves, 2012). In CRP, teachers are expected to "respond to the cultures actually present in the classroom." Teachers "connect new information to students' background knowledge, and present the information in ways that respond to students' natural ways of learning" (Rychly & Graves,

2012, p. 45) and enable students to experience academic success (Ladson-Billings, 2009). Culturally responsive teachers possess a solid understanding of their students' cultures and experiences, demonstrate cultural sensitivity, and utilize cross-cultural communication skills and practices to demonstrate genuine care for their students in ways that foster students' cultural competence in their home and school lives (Garcia & Dominquez, 1997; Ladson-Billings, 2009; Obiakor & Utley, 2001).

Culturally responsive pedagogy is much more than just a special week or month highlighting leaders of color and it goes beyond the stereotypical "Four F's" of culture—food, fun, folklore, and fashion. CRP is grounded in a systematic integration of works from diverse individuals (in the broadest sense of the word) throughout a school year and across content areas (Griner & Stewart, 2013). Students learn from each other and from shared personal experiences, and engage in critical thinking through service learning, problem solving, vignettes, and/or student-created projects to address needs and answer student-centered questions (Morey & Kilano, 1997). Self-reflection and assessment are characteristic of this level of instruction. In the grander picture, CRP acknowledges the legitimacy of the cultural heritages of different ethnic groups. This includes acknowledging culture both as legacies that affect students' dispositions, affect, and approaches to learning and as worthy content to be taught in the formal curriculum (Gay, 2000).

Teachers who engage in culturally responsive *literacy* instruction systematically embed these elements of CRP into practices that include students' reading, writing, language, and speaking skills. They also emphasize high expectations and outcomes, academically rich curricula and materials, active and cooperative student learning, and instructional technologies that extend learning. Teachers may also be acutely aware of students' language interaction patterns (e.g., overlapping speech, eye contact, reluctance to participate, shout-outs), and that these patterns may or may not be culturally embedded, but may dictate students' participation levels and opportunities to learn (McIntyre & Hulan, 2013). Likewise, students' native language should be viewed as an asset and used to develop academic English proficiency as well as support their overall achievement (López, 2014). Although there has been significant and recent attention to CRP, school faculty and staff often lack explicit examples of the best practices within CRP (Fiedler et al., 2008). To respond to this need, this section explores intersections of research-based literacy instruction and critical elements of culturally responsive teaching to address the needs of all learners in our nation's classrooms. We present examples of CRLPs that can be used across the grades, with sensitivity to the changing student demographics of the United States.

Culturally Responsive Literacy Practices

Culturally responsive literacy instruction is a combination of research-based literacy practices with components of appropriate, culturally relevant practices. Literacy instruction should foster a genuine appreciation for quality literature through the development of skills necessary to access meaning of complex texts: phonemic awareness/phonics, word study, fluency, comprehension, and writing (Fountas & Pinnell, 1996; Snow, Burns, & Griffin, 1998). Table 5.1 organizes commonly utilized research-based literacy practices with culturally relevant approaches and observable characteristics of each.

TABLE 5.1 Research-based literacy practices, culturally relevant literacy, and observable teaching practices

Research-Based Literacy Practices	Culturally Relevant Literacy Practice Elements	Observable Teaching Practice/Characteristics (Example)
Gradual Release of Responsibility (GRR): introduced skill is modeled, followed by student-shared practice of the skill, and finally independent skill employment	Teacher understands and taps into the individual and unique paths of students' prior knowledge, culture, experiences, language and interests when introducing a new skill/strategy. In community, students practice the strategy several times before utilizing it independently.	Introduce visualization strategy: teacher reads a vivid description and students visualize a family gathering, complete with the aroma of tamales, sound of ranchera music, taste of chile, crunch of tortilla chips, and bright colors of salsa.
Classroom Libraries: collections of books in the classroom, which are available for students to select and read in school as well as at home.	Classroom library and curricular materials should foster and extend academic language in both English and native languages and be utilized as a tool in eroding stereotypes of culturally diverse students.	One library's labeled bins display a wide variety of Latino authors and illustrators, books in Spanish/English, different reading levels, and books about experiences in the Dominican Republic, Mexico, Cuba, Puerto Rico, etc.
Read Aloud: exposes students daily to good reading behaviors, provides exposure to a range of literature, extends vocabularies and understanding of complex language patterns, supports independent reading, activates imagination and creativity, and can encourage a lifelong enjoyment of reading.	Teacher chooses texts and poses questions during reading that promote reflection on and appreciation of culture.	During the reading of *Too Many Tamales* by Jose Alvarez, teacher invites students to share their family traditions?" in small groups.

(Continued)

TABLE 5.1 (Continued)

Research-Based Literacy Practices	Culturally Relevant Literacy Practice Elements	Observable Teaching Practice/Characteristics (Example)
Comprehension Strategy Instruction: teaching readers to be metacognitive about employing the following reading comprehension strategies can extend and enhance their understanding of fiction and non-fiction texts: making connections, questioning, visualizing, predicting, inferring, summarizing, and synthesizing.	Teacher introduces strategies using texts that are connected to students' backgrounds, follows GRR, and invites discussion with peers in English or native language.	While introducing the Making Connections strategy, teacher uses the book *Carmen Speaks English*, and asks students to make connections by thinking of a time when they were uncomfortable with the way their speech sounded.
Guided Reading: small group reading instruction that is leveled, differentiated, and follows GRR to meet students' needs and extend their reading and writing proficiency.	Engaging their cultural identities; students are frequently encouraged to informally share connections and ask questions of each other and the teacher in this relaxed setting.	Teacher listens attentively while a group of four reads lines of text from *The Revolution of Evelyn Serrano* by Sonia Manzano. Students ask questions in English and Spanish that are answered by either teacher or peers.
Writing Workshop: organizational structure where the teacher provides instructional support for individualized process. Students independently transition through stages of prewriting, first draft, revision, editing, and publishing on self-selected topics or those prescribed by teacher.	The classroom atmosphere is student-centered, cooperative in nature, and sets a stage for collective belonging, where the individual is responsible for supporting the group through peer conferencing, editing, group goal setting, and group monitoring.	After a mini-lesson on sentence punctuation, students move through various stations with their writing. Teacher briefly confers with several students about their writing, asking, "What are you working on as a writer today?"

Do Current Classroom Observation Rubrics Capture CRLPs?

In the first part of the chapter, we established the role of culturally responsive literacy practices in U.S. schools. We now turn to address whether current classroom observation rubrics capture CRLPs. We also explore how evaluators and those observing teachers can better assess CRLPs and provide appropriate feedback to help teachers improve their use of these practices. To address these issues, first we examine two popular observation rubrics used in teacher evaluation: the Framework for Teaching (Danielson, 2013) and the Causal Teacher Evaluation Model (Marzano, 2013). We critically assess if and how the practices illustrated in the first half of the chapter are captured with these two instruments, and propose supplemental materials and modifications that help to better address CRLPs. We close the chapter with coaching tools and **teacher self-evaluation practices** which support continued growth of teachers and their practices in this critical area.

Observation Instruments: A Brief Overview

The Danielson Framework for Teaching. The 2013 edition of the Framework for Teaching (Danielson, 2013) is a generic observation instrument designed for application across the disciplines. Grounded in a constructivist approach to learning and teaching, the Framework for Teaching is purported to integrate research-based instruction with Interstate Teacher Assessment and Support Consortium (INTASC) standards. The framework is composed of 22 components (with 76 smaller elements) organized into four domains. Each component is rated on a 4-point scale. See Table 5.2 for a summary of the domains and components.

TABLE 5.2 The Danielson Framework for Teaching: Summary of domains and components*

Domain 1: Planning and Preparation
    1a: Demonstrating Knowledge of Content and Pedagogy
    1b: Demonstrating Knowledge of Students
    1c: Setting Instructional Outcomes
    1d: Demonstrating Knowledge of Resources
    1e: Designing Coherent Instruction
    1f: Designing Student Assessments

Domain 2: The Classroom Environment
    2a: Creating an Environment of Respect and Rapport
    2b: Establishing a Culture for Learning
    2c: Managing Classroom Procedures
    2d: Managing Student Behavior
    2e: Organizing Physical Space

Domain 3: Instruction
    3a: Communicating with Students
    3b: Using Questioning and Discussion Techniques
    3c: Engaging Students in Learning

(*Continued*)

TABLE 5.2 (Continued)

3d: Using Assessment in Instruction
3e: Demonstrating Flexibility and Responsiveness

Domain 4: Professional Responsibilities
　4a: Reflecting on Teaching
　4b: Maintaining Accurate Records
　4c: Communicating with Families
　4d: Participating in the Professional Community
　4e: Growing and Developing Professionally
　4f: Showing Professionalism

＊ Table adapted from the Framework for Teaching (Danielson, 2013)

TABLE 5.3 Marzano Causal Teacher Evaluation Model＊

Domain 1: Classroom Strategies and Behaviors
　Routine Segments (5 elements)
　Content Segments (18 elements)
　On the Spot Segments (18 elements)

Domain 2: Planning and Preparing
　Lesson and Units (3 elements)
　Use of Materials and Technology (2 elements)
　Special Needs of Students (3 elements)

Domain 3: Reflecting on Teaching
　Evaluating Personal Performance (3 elements)
　Professional Growth Plan (2 elements)

Domain 4: Collegiality and Professionalism
　Promoting a Positive Environment (2 elements)
　Promoting Exchange of Ideas (2 elements)
　Promoting District and School Development (2 elements)

＊ Table adapted from http://www.marzanoevaluation.com/evaluation/four_domains/

The Marzano Causal Teacher Evaluation Model. The Marzano Causal Teacher Evaluation Model (Marzano, 2013) is based on a number of research- and theory-based works published by Marzano and colleagues (see Marzano, 2003; Marzano, 2006; Marzano, 2007; Marzano, Frontier, & Livingston, 2011; Marzano, Marzano, & Pickering, 2003; Marzano, Pickering, & Pollock, 2001). Like the Framework for Teaching, Marzano's Causal Teacher Evaluation Model is composed of four domains, and includes 60 elements. Each element is rated on a 4-point scale. See Table 5.3 for an overview of the four domains.

Critiquing Current Observation Instruments

In order for observation rubrics to address CRLPs, particularly for ELLs, culture and language need to be explicitly mentioned in item or rating level rubric descriptions. Subsequently, in assessing the observation rubrics, we first looked for use of the terms "culture"' and "language." For the purpose of this analysis, we chose to investigate those domains most closely aligned with instruction. Hence, for the Danielson Framework for Teaching, we chose Domains 1 and 3 (Planning and Preparation and Instruction), and for the Marzano Teacher Evaluation Model, we chose Domains 1 and 2 (Classroom Strategies and Behaviors and Planning and Preparing).

Culture and Language in Selected Observation Instrument Domains

To examine the presence of "culture" and "language" we searched for instances in which language was used to refer to language background, not language use or use of academic language. In general, we found that the instruments do capture many effective literacy practices outlined in Table 5.1, but these practices are not described in the context of instructing and planning to instruct culturally and linguistically diverse students. In the Framework for Teaching (Danielson, 2013) we chose to examine two domains—Domain 1 (Planning and Preparation) and Domain 3 (Instruction). From the 11 items in these two domains, we were able to identify one item that explicitly addresses students' cultural and linguistic backgrounds (Domain 1: Planning and Preparation, 1b: Demonstrating Knowledge of Students). In Marzano's Causal Teacher Evaluation Model (Marzano, 2013), we examined the 49 elements that fall under Domain 1 (Classroom Strategies and Behaviors) and Domain 2 (Planning and Preparing) and were able to identify only one element that addresses culture or language—Element 6 (Planning and Preparing for the Needs of English Language Learners).

Essentially, the presence of "culture" and "language" in the selected domains of these observation instruments is limited and, upon further exploration, sometimes superficial. While present students' culture and language appears in domains that assess teachers' plans to teach, they do not appear in the actual execution of lesson plans. Although a teacher may have well-designed intentions and plans prior to a lesson, it is important to assess what actually happens in the classroom. Furthermore, for CRLPs to be powerful, they must extend beyond one or two elements of planning and should be integrated into every element of a child's learning experience so that students receive a clear message that their culture and language are valued in school.

One might ask: how can evaluators and observers overcome the limitations of common observation instruments? We suggest evaluators and others responsible with the task of observing teachers consider making minor language adjustments to existing rubric items. For example, in Marzano's Causal Teacher Evaluation

Model, Domain 1 (Classroom Strategies and Behaviors), although there is no explicit use of "language" and "culture" in the descriptions, there are two elements that loosely suggest teachers should attend to the backgrounds of the students in the classroom. In Element 31, Providing Opportunities for Students to Talk about Themselves, teachers prompt students to make connections between what is being learned in class and their interests. Although this may evolve into discussions related to language and culture, teachers are not prompted to address this as part of making learning meaningful for students. We see Element 31 as an ample opportunity for teachers to support students in making culturally responsive home-to-school and self-to-text connections. In Element 36, Understanding Students' Interests and Backgrounds, the teacher is expected to use "students' interests and backgrounds to produce a climate of acceptance and community." It is not clear that teachers' inquiry about students' lives should include culture or language, but rather the "events in their lives" (see Table 5.4).

TABLE 5.4 Modifications of Marzano's Teacher Evaluation Model Domain 1

Element 31: Providing opportunities for students to talk about themselves*				
Innovating (4)	Applying (3)	Developing (2)	Beginning (1)	Not Using (0)
	• Provides students with opportunities to relate what is being addressed in class to their language, culture, and personal interests • Monitors impact on student engagement	• Provides students with opportunities to relate what is being addressed in class to their language, culture, and personal interests		
Element 36: Understanding students' interests and backgrounds*				
Innovating (4)	Applying (3)	Developing (2)	Beginning (1)	Not Using (0)
	• Uses students' interests and backgrounds (including culture and language) during interactions • Monitors classroom sense of community	• Uses students' interests and backgrounds (including culture and language) during interactions		

*Retrieved from http://www.marzanoevaluation.com/evaluation/four_domains/; modifications noted in bold

Similar adjustments can be made to the Framework for Teaching. For example, Domain 3 (Instruction), 3a: Communicating with Students, does address language, specifically teachers' modeling of expressive, vivid, accurate language use. Although these practices would help rather than hinder English language development for ELLs, Communicating with Students does not address the possible challenges non-native speakers may face and how the teacher can use both English and native language to respond to and reduce these challenges. Hence, extending existing rubric language to be more inclusive and explicit of diverse learners could make an enormous contribution to the learning opportunities afforded to students (see Table 5.5).

Beyond the examples presented in Table 5.1, and the slight modifications noted in Table 5.4 and 5.5, we extend our discussion of how evaluators can copebelow by providing explicit rubrics in order to strengthen the assessment of CRLPs, particularly in the domains of planning and preparing and instruction.

TABLE 5.5 Modification of Domain 3 of the Framework for Teaching: Instruction*

3a: Communicating With Students			
1	2	3	4
• Instructional purpose of the lesson is unclear • Directions and procedures are confusing • Explanation of the content contains major errors • Explanation does not include any explanation of strategies students might use • The teacher's academic vocabulary is inappropriate or vague, resulting in student confusion • The teacher does not use research-based language strategies in communication with English Language Learners			• Lesson objective is linked to the larger curriculum • Directions, procedures, and explanation of content are clear • Teacher develops conceptual understanding through scaffolding and students' interests • Students explain concepts to one another and suggest strategies • The teacher's language is expressive and extends students' vocabularies • Students use appropriate academic vocabulary • The teacher regularly and successfully uses research-based language strategies to communicate with English Language Learners

* Adapted from the Danielson Framework for Teaching (Danielson, 2013); modifications noted in bold

Take Action

Modifications and Supplementary Suggestions

Many districts have the opportunity to create their own observation rubrics or modify existing ones. With this in mind, and the achievement outcomes of culturally and linguistically diverse students, we offer two possible ways districts (and more directly, evaluators) can modify existing frameworks for observation. We integrate the work of Griner and Stewart (2013) and others with our own proposed CRLPs, and provide two rubrics that can supplement existing tools. For consistency, we used the format of the Framework for Teaching and the Marzano Causal Teacher Evaluation Model (4-point rating categories and related domains) to create two rubrics—one that can be used for assessing and providing feedback about planning and preparation and a second one that addresses instruction (see Table 5.6).

We also provide a series of questions that observers, evaluators, and coaches can use to help assess teachers' use of CRLPs. We believe these questions can support scripting as part of establishing a culturally responsive narrative of a teacher's practice. We also believe that these questions can be fruitful in informing pre- and post-observation conversations and teachers' reflection on their use of CRLPs. By implementing one or both of these approaches, evaluators can play their own role as change agents for equitable schooling experiences for all.

Discussing Culturally Responsive Literacy Practices with Teachers

In having valuable conversations with teachers about their use of CRLPs, it might be helpful to start with a set of broader questions. For example, some questions to guide pre- and post-conversations might be: (1) How do your lesson plans address the needs of culturally and linguistically diverse learners? (2) To what extent did your instruction reflect those plans? (3) Were your plans successful? Did the culturally and linguistically diverse learners meet the intended objectives? What is your evidence? (4) What would be some additional and alternative ways to address the needs of these learners? Below is a more comprehensive list of questions that complement the rubrics provided in Table 5.4. The hope is that these questions help evaluators assess and refine teachers' understanding and use of CRLPs and, more broadly, teachers' ability to play on students' cultural and linguistic strengths to enhance diverse learner outcomes. For specific questions related to high expectations, we direct readers to Lavigne and Good (2015).

Planning and Preparation

1. Does the lesson plan incorporate authentic learning opportunities for all students?
2. Does the lesson plan reflect the use of texts (for both the teacher and students) in English and students' native language(s)?

TABLE 5.6 Culturally responsive literacy practices rubric

CRLP	1 Does Not Meet Expectation	2 Partially Meets Expectation	3 Meets Expectation	4 Exceeds Expectation
Planning & Preparation				
High Expectations and Outcomes	• Lesson does not demonstrate teacher's high expectations that all students are capable of becoming readers and writers. • Lesson is not differentiated to meet the needs of ELL, bilingual, and diverse student body. • Lesson is not designed to engage students in authentic and meaningful ways. • Lesson does not provide opportunities for students to see relevance in lesson via connection to culture, language, values, and experiences. • Lesson objectives are not aligned with student strengths/weaknesses to provide opportunities for academic success.	• Lesson minimally demonstrates teacher's high expectations that all students are capable of becoming readers and writers. • Lesson is partially differentiated to meet the needs of ELL, bilingual, and diverse student body. • Lesson is minimally designed to engage students in authentic and meaningful ways. • Lesson provides limited opportunities for students to see relevance in lesson via connection to culture, language, values, and experiences. • Lesson objectives are partially aligned with student strengths/weaknesses to provide opportunities for academic success.	• Lesson demonstrates teacher's high expectations that all students are capable of becoming readers and writers. • Lesson is adequately differentiated to meet the needs of ELL, bilingual, and diverse student body. • Lesson is designed to engage all students in authentic and meaningful ways. • Lesson provides opportunities for students to see relevance in lesson via connection to culture, language, values, and experiences. • Lesson objectives are aligned with student strengths/weaknesses to provide opportunities for academic success.	• Lesson demonstrates and communicates teacher's high expectations that all students are capable of becoming excellent and lifelong readers and writers. • Lesson is effectively differentiated to meet the needs of ELL, bilingual, and diverse student body. • Lesson is creatively designed to engage students in authentic and meaningful ways. • Lesson provides multiple opportunities for students to see relevance in lesson via connection to culture, language, values, and experiences. • Lesson objectives are thoughtfully aligned with student strengths/weaknesses to provide ample opportunities for academic success.

(Continued)

TABLE 5.6 (Continued)

CRLP	1 Does Not Meet Expectation	2 Partially Meets Expectation	3 Meets Expectation	4 Exceeds Expectation
Planning & Preparation				
Rich Curricula and Materials	• Lessons fail to incorporate opportunities to engage with texts in English and native language(s). • Lessons are not designed around high quality culturally relevant texts/content that reflect students' culture and values. • Lessons are designed to develop bi/multicultural competence in home and school life.	• Lessons minimally incorporate opportunities to engage with texts in English and native language(s). • Lessons are partially designed around high quality culturally relevant texts/content that reflect students' culture and values. • Lessons are designed to develop bi/multicultural competence in home and school life.	• Lessons adequately incorporate opportunities to engage with texts in English and native language(s). • Lessons are designed around high quality culturally relevant texts/content that reflect students' culture and values. • Lessons are designed to develop bi/multicultural competence in home and school life.	• Lessons thoughtfully incorporate opportunities to engage with texts in English and native language(s). • Lessons are creatively designed around high quality culturally relevant texts/content that reflect students' culture and values. • Lessons are designed to develop bi/multicultural competence in home and school life.
Active and Cooperative Student Learning	• Lesson is not designed to incorporate culturally relevant pedagogy for participation. • Lesson fails to incorporate materials in native language(s) for students who aren't proficient in academic English. • Lesson fails to present opportunities for students to learn from each other and shared experiences.	• Lesson is partially designed to incorporate culturally relevant pedagogy for participation. • Lesson incorporates minimal materials in native language(s) for students who aren't proficient in academic English. • Lesson presents limited opportunities for students to learn from each other and shared experiences.	• Lesson is adequately designed to incorporate culturally relevant pedagogy for participation. • Lesson adequately incorporates materials in native language(s) for students who aren't proficient in academic English.	• Lesson is effectively designed to incorporate culturally relevant pedagogy for participation. • Lesson thoughtfully incorporates materials in native language(s) for students who aren't proficient in academic English. • Lesson presents multiple opportunities for students to learn from each other and shared experiences.

• Lesson is not designed to engage students in critical thinking, problem solving, and/or student-created projects. • Lesson is not designed to encourage students to generate and answer student-centered questions.	• Lesson is designed to minimally engage students in critical thinking, problem solving, and/or student-created projects. • Lesson is designed to minimally encourage students to generate and answer student-centered questions.	• Lesson presents adequate opportunities for students to learn from each other and shared experiences. • Lesson is designed to engage students in critical thinking, problem solving, and/or student-created projects. • Lesson is designed to encourage students to generate and answer student-centered questions.	• Lesson is designed to creatively engage students in critical thinking, problem solving, and/or student-created projects. • Lesson is thoughtfully designed to encourage students to generate and answer student-centered questions.
Instructional Technologies that Extend Learning			
• Teacher has not prepared any tools such as graphic organizer or outline to help ELLs navigate oral lesson in English. • No Internet/computer use to incorporate lesson with students' cultural experiences and lives. • Internet/computer is not used to access culturally relevant stories, vignettes, and/or examples of culturally relevant text.	• Teacher has prepared minimal tools such as graphic organizer or outline to help ELLs navigate oral lesson in English. • Internet/computer use partially or superficially incorporates lesson with students' cultural experiences and lives. • Internet/computer is somewhat or superficially used to access culturally relevant stories, vignettes, and/or examples of culturally relevant text.	• Teacher has prepared tools such as graphic organizer and/or outline to help ELLs navigate oral lesson in English. • Internet/computer use adequately incorporates lesson with students' cultural experiences and lives. • Internet/computer is used to access culturally relevant stories, vignettes, and/or examples of culturally relevant text.	• Teacher has thoroughly prepared tools such as graphic organizer and outline to help ELLs navigate oral lesson in English. • Internet/computer use thoughtfully incorporates lesson with students' cultural experiences and lives. • Internet/computer is thoughtfully and creatively used to access culturally relevant stories, vignettes, and/or examples of culturally relevant text.

(Continued)

TABLE 5.6 (Continued)

CRLP	1 Does Not Meet Expectation	2 Partially Meets Expectation	3 Meets Expectation	4 Exceeds Expectation
Planning & Preparation				
Self-Reflection and Assessment	• Lesson is not designed to rely on student self-reflection that reveals opportunities for teacher to bridge new information with students' background knowledge. • Efficacy of the lesson is not determined by any elements of student self-assessment and/or group assessment.	• Lesson is designed to rely on limited student self-reflection that reveals opportunities for teacher to bridge new information with students' background knowledge. • Efficacy of the lesson is superficially determined by elements of student self-assessment and/or group assessment.	• Lesson is designed to rely on student self-reflection that reveals opportunities for teacher to bridge new information with students' background knowledge. • Efficacy of the lesson is determined in part by elements of student self-assessment and/or group assessment.	• Lesson is designed to rely on authentic and thoughtful student self-reflection that reveals a wide variety of opportunities for teacher to bridge new information with students' background knowledge. • Efficacy of the lesson is determined authentically and effectively by elements of student self- and/or group assessment.
Instruction				
Read Aloud	• Text selection is not relatable to students. • Text is not available to students in English and native language. • The delivery of the read aloud is not engaging or does not reflect elements of storytelling (i.e., eye contact, drama, expression, gestures). • Students do not engage with the text through	• Text selection is somewhat relatable to students. • Text is not available to students in English and/or native language. • Minimally engaging delivery of narrative similar or dissimilar to storytelling (i.e., eye contact, drama, expression, gestures). • Students minimally engage with the text through	• Text selection is adequately relatable to students. • Text is available to students in English and/or native language. • Engaging delivery of narrative similar to storytelling (i.e., eye contact, expression, gestures, drama). • Students adequately engage with the text through comprehension strategy	• Text selection is readily relatable to students. • Text is available to students in English and native language. • Creative and engaging delivery of narrative similar to many elements of storytelling (i.e., eye contact, expression, gestures, drama). • Students thoughtfully engage with the text through comprehension strategy selection

	Students do not engage in peer discussion before, during, or after read aloud.	Students minimally engage in peer discussion before, during, and/or after read aloud.	Students engage in peer discussion before, during, and after read aloud.	Students actively engage in peer discussion before, during, and after read aloud.
Comprehension Strategy Instruction • make connections • question • visualize • make predictions • inference • summarize • synthesize	• Strategies are not modeled using culturally relevant texts. • Strategies are not practiced by students in English or native languages. • Students do not have opportunities to practice skills in pairs or small groups. • Students do not have opportunities to decide which strategies to employ to comprehend different texts.	• Strategies are minimally modeled using culturally relevant texts. • Strategies are minimally practiced by students in English or native languages. • Students have limited opportunities to practice skills in pairs or small groups. • Students have limited opportunities to decide which strategies to employ to comprehend different texts.	• Strategies are adequately modeled using culturally relevant texts. • Strategies are practiced by students in English and/or native languages. • Students have opportunities to practice skills in pairs or small groups. • Students have opportunities to decide which strategies to employ to comprehend different texts.	• Strategies are thoroughly modeled using culturally relevant texts. • Strategies are thoroughly practiced by students in English and/or native languages. • Students have ample opportunities to practice skills in pairs or small groups. • Students have ample opportunities to decide which strategies to employ to comprehend different texts.
Guided Reading	• Small groups of students are not organized by specific needs. • Students do not collaborate or contribute to discussion; failing to take ownership in activating background knowledge.	• Small groups of students are partially organized by specific needs. • Students minimally collaborate or contribute to discussion; minimally taking ownership in activating background knowledge.	• Small groups of students are organized by specific needs. • Students collaborate and contribute to discussion; taking ownership in activating background knowledge.	• Small groups of students are thoughtfully organized by specific needs. • Students thoughtfully and authentically collaborate and contribute to discussion; taking ownership in activating background knowledge.

(Continued)

TABLE 5.6 (Continued)

CRLP	1 Does Not Meet Expectation	2 Partially Meets Expectation	3 Meets Expectation	4 Exceeds Expectation
Instruction				
	• Lesson fails to bridge new information to students' knowledge, experience, and/or language from home and school lives. • Students do not engage in shared practice to strengthen and extend skills in pairs or small groups.	• Lesson minimally bridges new information to students' knowledge, experience, and language from home and school lives. • Students minimally engage in shared practice to strengthen and extend skills in pairs or small groups.	• Lesson bridges new information to students' knowledge, experience, and language from home and school lives. • Students engage in shared practice to strengthen and extend skills in pairs and/or small groups.	• Lesson effectively bridges new information to students' knowledge, experience, and language from home and school lives. • Students actively engage in shared and authentic practice to strengthen and extend skills in pairs and/or small groups.
Writing Process/ Writing Workshop	• Students do not collaborate with peers in shared practice of editing/revising. • Students do not consult with each other throughout the writing process. • Students take no ownership or do not feel responsible for individual and group progress. • Students do not share their finished product or receive feedback from peers.	• Students minimally collaborate with peers in shared practice of editing/ revising. • Students minimally consult with each other throughout the writing process. • Students take limited ownership or feel minimally responsible for individual and group progress. • Students have limited opportunities to share their finished product and/or receive feedback from peers.	• Students collaborate with peers in shared practice of editing/revising. • Students consult with each other throughout the writing process. • Students take ownership and feel responsible for individual and group progress. • Students share their finished product and receive feedback from peers.	• Students thoughtfully collaborate with peers in shared practice of editing/revising. • Students thoughtfully consult with each other throughout the writing process. • Students take authentic ownership and feel genuinely responsible for individual and group progress. • Students have ample opportunities to share their finished product and receive feedback from peers.

3. Does the lesson plan attend to issues of equity, justice, and/or diversity?
4. Does the lesson plan include the use of multicultural literature when modeling research-based literacy strategies?
5. Does the lesson plan include student grouping sensitive to the cultural and linguistic assets of students?
6. Does the lesson plan attend to students' language interaction patterns, in general, and as culturally embedded?
7. Does the lesson plan build a bridge between students' home and school lives?
8. Does the lesson plan scaffold goals with student knowledge in ways that support student academic success?
9. Is the lesson plan designed to develop cultural competence in both the students' home and school lives?

Instruction

1. Are all students engaged in authentic learning opportunities?
2. Are students encouraged and supported to reach high expectations for reading, writing, and speaking in English and native language(s)?
3. Are texts available in English and other languages?
4. Does the teacher use texts in English and other languages during the observation segment?
5. Do students use texts in English and other languages during the observation segment?
6. Do students participate, critically engage with literacy, and seek social and political consciousness?
7. Does the teacher use multicultural literature when modeling research-based literacy strategies?
8. Does the teacher educate students about diversity through modeling research-based literacy strategies?
9. Are groups organized to utilize the cultural and linguistic assets of students in ways that enhance learning for each group?
10. Does the teacher attend to students' language interaction patterns, in general, and as culturally embedded?

Conclusion

In this chapter, our goal was to provide teachers and those who evaluate teachers with a set of practices that integrate research-based literacy practices with culturally responsive pedagogy—culturally responsive literacy instruction. Our intent was to move beyond the simplistic conceptions of CRP (Sleeter, 2011), and provide meaningful practices that can be systematically woven into curriculum. We do not believe that these practices will solve the marginalization of diverse youth in schools, but we do believe they are one step in reducing the inequitable schooling opportunities experienced by culturally and linguistically diverse leaners. Rather than stripping youth of their culture and language, these practices seek to empower administrators, teachers, and students to use culture and language as the gateway to enhanced learning outcomes. We also believe that integrating CRLPs into the evaluation process will promote more intentional conversations and modifications in instructional practices and school culture for children who have historically been underserved by schools.

References

Artiles, A., Kozleski, E., Trent, S., Osher, D., & Ortiz, A. (2010). Justifying and explaining disproportionality, 1968–2000: A critique of underlying views of culture. *Exceptional Children, 76*, 279–299.

Austin, H., Brown, A., & Forde, T. (2006). *Addressing diversity in schools: Culturally responsive pedagogy.* Washington, DC: National Center for Culturally Responsive Systems and U.S. Office of Special Education.

Bomer, R., & Maloch, B. (2011). Relating policy to research and practice: The common core standards. *Language Arts, 89*(1), 38–43.

Buchanan, B. (2005, October). *Dropping out, dropping chances; dropping out comes at high personal cost.* Greensboro, NC: News & Record.

Buriel, R. (1987). *Academic performance of foreign- and native-born Mexican Americans: A comparison of first-, second-, and third-generation students and parents.* Report to the Inter-University Program for Latino Research, Social Science Research Council.

Buriel, R., & Cardoza, D. (1988). Sociocultural correlates of achievement among three generations of Mexican American high school seniors. *American Educational Research Journal, 25*, 177–192. doi:10.3102/00028312025002177

Christian, D. (1994). Two-way bilingual education: Students learning through two languages. Washington, DC: National Center for Research on Cultural Diversity and Second Language Learning.

Common Core State Standards Initiative. (2012). English language arts standards: Introduction. Key design consideration. Retrieved from: http://www.corestandards.org/ela-literacy/introduction/key-design-consideration

Danielson, C. (2013). *The framework for teaching evaluation instrument.* Princeton, NJ: Danielson Group.

Fiedler, C., Chiang, B., Van Haren, B., Joregensen, J., Halber, S., & Boreson, L. (2008). Culturally responsive practices in schools: A checklist to address disproportionality in special education. *Exceptional Children, 40*, 52–59.

Fountas, I.C., & Pinnell, G.S. (1996). *Guided reading: Good first teaching for all children.* Portsmouth, NH: Heinemann.

Fry, R., & Gonzales, F. (2008). *One-in-five and growing fast: A profile of Hispanic public school students.* Washington, DC: Pew Research Center. Retrieved from: http://pewhispanic.org/reports/report.php?ReportID=92

Garcia, S., & Dominquez, L. (1997). Cultural contexts that influence learning and academic performance. *Child and Adolescent Psychiatric Clinics of North America, 6*(3), 621–655.

Gay, G. (2000). *Culturally responsive teaching: Theory, research, and practice.* New York: Teachers College Press.

Griner, A.C., & Steward, M.L. (2013). Addressing the achievement gap and disproportion-ality through the use of culturally responsive teaching practices. *Urban Education, 48,* 585–621.

Hao, L., & Woo, H.S. (2012). Distinct trajectories in the transition to adulthood: Are children of immigrants advantaged? *Child Development, 83*(5), 1623–1639.

Humes, K.R., Jones, N.A., & Ramirez, R.R. (2011). *Overview of race and Hispanic origin: 2010. 2010 Census briefs.* Washington, DC: U.S. Census Bureau.

Jay, M. (2003). Critical race theory, multiculturalism, education, and the hidden curriculum of hegemony. *Multicultural Perspectives, 5*(4), 3–9.

Ladson-Billings, G. (2009). *The dream-keepers: Successful teachers of African American children* (2nd ed.). San Francisco, CA: Jossey-Bass.

Lavigne, A.L., & Good, T.L. (2015). *Improving teaching through observation and feedback: Beyond state and federal mandates.* New York: Routledge.

Lessow-Hurley, J. (1991). *A commonsense guide to bilingual education.* Alexandria, VA: Association for Supervision and Curriculum Development.

Lindholm-Leary, K.J. (2001). *Dual language education.* Tonawanda, NY: Multilingual Matters.

López, F. (2014, April). *Addressing the Need for Explicit Evidence on the Role of Culturally Responsive Teaching and Achievement among Latino Youth: Preliminary findings for the Spencer/National Academy of Education Postdoctoral Fellowship.* Poster presented at the 2014 annual meeting of the American Educational Research Association, Philadelphia, PA.

Marzano, R.J. (2003). *What works in schools.* Alexandria, VA: ASCD.

Marzano, R.J. (2006). *Classroom assessment and grading that work.* Alexandria, VA: ASCD.

Marzano, R.J. (2007). *The art and science of teaching.* Alexandria, VA: ASCD.

Marzano, R.J. (2013). *The Marzano teacher evaluation model.* Retrieved from: http://tpep-wa.org/wp-content/uploads/Marzano_Teacher_Evaluation_Model.pdf

Marzano, R.J., Frontier, T., & Livingston, D. (2011). *Effective supervision: Supporting the art and science of teaching.* Alexandria, VA: ASCD.

Marzano, R.J., Marzano, J.S., & Pickering, D.J. (2003). *Classroom management that works.* Alexandria, VA: ASCD.

Marzano, R.J., Pickering, D.J., & Pollock, J.E. (2001). *Classroom instruction that works.* Alexandria, VA: ASCD.

McIntyre, E., & Hulan, N. (2013). Research-based, culturally responsive reading practice in elementary classrooms: A yearlong study. *Literacy Research and Instruction, 52,* 28–51.

Morey, A., & Kilano, M. (1997). *Multicultural course transformation in higher education: A broader truth.* Needham Heights, MA: Allyn and Bacon.

Obiakor, F.E., & Utley, C.A. (2001). Culturally responsive teacher preparation programming for the twenty-first century. In F.E. Obiakor & C.A. Utley (Eds.), *Special education, multicultural education and school reform* (pp. 188–207). Springfield, IL: Charles C. Thomas.

Pew Research Center. (2013). *High school drop out rate at record low: Hispanic high school graduates pass whites in college enrollment.* Retrieved from http://www.pewhispanic.org/files/2013/05/PHC_college_enrollment_2013–05.pdf

Rebora, A. (2013). *Charlotte Danielson on Teaching and the Common Core.* Education Week Teacher.

Rychly, L., & Graves, E. (2012). Teacher characteristics for culturally responsive pedagogy. *Multicultural Perspectives, 14*(1), 44–49.

Sleeter, C. (2011). An agenda to strengthen culturally responsive pedagogy. *English Teaching Practice and Critique, 10,* 7–23.

Snow, C.E., Burns, M.S., & Griffin, P. (1998). *Preventing reading difficulties in young children.* Washington, DC: National Academy Press.

Suárez-Orozco, C. (2001). Psychocultural factors in the adaptation of immigrant youth: Gendered responses. In M. Agosín (Ed.), *Women and human rights: A global perspective* (pp. 170–188). Picataway, NJ: Rutgers University Press.

Thomas, W. P., & Collier, V. (2003). *A national study of school effectiveness for language minority students' long-term academic achievement.* Washington, DC: Center for Research on Education, Diversity & Excellence. Retrieved from http://www.usc.edu/dept/education/CMMR/CollierThomasExReport.pdf

Urrieta, L. (2005). "Playing the game" versus "selling out": Chicanas' and Chicanos' relationship to whitestream schools. In B.K. Alexander, G.L. Anderson, & B.P. Gallegos (Eds.), *Performance theories in education: Power, pedagogy, and the politics of identity* (pp. 127–153). Mahwah, NJ: Lawrence Erlbaum and Associates.

Valenzuela, A. (1999). *Subtractive schooling: U.S.-Mexican youth and the politics of caring.* Albany: SUNY Press.

Vigil, J. & Long, J. (1981). Unidirectional or nativist acculturation: Chicano paths to school achievement. *Human Organization, 40,* 273–277.

6

THE DEVELOPMENT OF A CLASSROOM OBSERVATION SYSTEM FOR FIRST-GRADE WRITING INSTRUCTION[1]

David Coker, Elizabeth N. Farley-Ripple, Huijing Wen, and Allison Jackson

Introduction

For our work as researchers interested in writing development and instruction, observational research is a powerful tool. Classroom observations provide a glimpse into the complex interactions that occur during instruction. They offer insight into how teaching and learning can be enhanced or degraded by factors as varied as classroom management, student autonomy, instructional approach, motivation, or even available resources. As a result, classroom observations offer unparalleled sources of information, but they are also complex and unwieldy.

In this chapter, we provide a description of our recent work constructing and implementing an observation system for first-grade writing instruction. We discuss how it was initially conceived and tested and also address the challenges associated with the development of a valid and reliable observational system. Additionally, we provide some preliminary results and discuss the appropriate uses for observational data. It is our hope that administrators interested in classroom observation can deepen their understanding of the strengths and challenges associated with classroom observations.

The Need to Understand Writing Instruction

The importance of writing is widely recognized in contemporary American society. Writing provides an essential means of communication in both academic and professional settings. Students who lack proficient writing skills find themselves at a disadvantage in their academic and social lives (National Commission on Writing, 2003). The academic significance of writing is evident in the Common

Core State Standards (CCSS). These new standards have specified what students should be able to write and how they should engage in writing as early as kindergarten. For example, beginning in kindergarten, students are expected to be able to compose (with support) in three different genres (narrative, opinion, and informational). For teachers in most schools, these new standards offer new and more challenging expectations.

Despite the importance of writing, students in the U.S. have not demonstrated strong writing skills. In the last national assessment of elementary school students' writing, over 70% of fourth-grade students did not meet the benchmark for proficient writing for the National Assessment of Educational Progress (Persky, Daane, & Jin, 2003).

Adding to the difficulty associated with writing instruction and achievement is the complex nature of writing development. Researchers agree that writing development is influenced by an interaction of many factors including transcription skills, language skill, procedural knowledge, text knowledge, and motivation (Berninger & Chanquoy, 2012). Thus, it generally takes strong instruction and years of practice for a novice writer to develop the skills and competencies of an expert. In order to meet the needs of young writers, instruction must target the areas important for writing development. Naturally, this poses a formidable challenge for classroom teachers; however, it also raises difficult questions for administrators who must provide instructional leadership.

In an age when administrators are held accountable for student achievement, they must wrestle with the challenges of evaluating instruction. Although administrators may conduct classroom observations with slightly different goals than researchers, both groups need a valid and reliable observation system to capture what is happening in the classroom. Accurate observations are at the heart of researchers' analyses and administrator's evaluations.

The Importance of Research

Our research team was interested in observational research to learn more about early writing instruction. Before we could begin observing teachers, we quickly realized that we would need to design our own system, since there were no ready-to-use systems designed for our purposes. The first step in the development of the observational system was to look closely at the existing research on early writing instruction. It was crucial that our observational system would be sensitive to the instructional practices that help students write better.

Reviewing the research, we found that there is fairly broad evidence that instruction in spelling and handwriting in first and second grades is related to improvements in these skills and in higher writing quality (Berninger et al., 1997; Berninger et al., 1998; Graham, Harris, & Fink, 2000; Graham, Harris, & Fink-Chorzempa, 2002; Jones & Christensen, 1999). Providing effective skills instruction in handwriting and spelling in the early grades has been recommended as a way to prevent the need for remediation efforts in later grades (Berninger & Amtmann, 2003).

Other effective instructional practices include teaching the writing process, modeling how to write, asking students substantive questions, giving students opportunities to write extended texts, keeping students engaged, and teaching writing frequently (Bohn, Roehrig, & Pressley, 2004; Taylor, Pearson, Peterson, & Rodriguez, 2003; Wharton-McDonald, Pressley, & Hampston, 1998). In these decade-long investigations of literacy instruction, researchers found that children's writing improves through instruction and practice that happens every day over multiple years.

Other useful empirical evidence on early writing instruction comes from surveys conducted with teachers. Cutler and Graham (2008) found that primary-grade teachers devoted considerable instructional time to grammar and lower-level skill instruction. Teachers also reported using a combination of process and traditional skills approaches. It was also reported that most instruction took place in whole class settings with small group and individual instruction being offered when necessary. In another survey study on instructional adaptations, Graham, Harris, Fink-Chrozempa, and MacArthur (2003) found that teachers reported using more instructional time for lower-level skills than composing. They also reported that they conferenced more with struggling writers than with average writers. Both survey studies also asked teachers about how much time was devoted to writing instruction. The results indicated that writing took only a small portion of daily literacy instruction time (20–30 minutes).

All these observational and survey studies contributed to our understanding of writing instruction in early grades. Yet, due to the methodological limitations and gaps in the literature, many questions remain. Our reading of the available research helped us identify important components to include in our observational system. We were eager to conduct observations in first grade that would provide a deeper understanding of the amount and nature of writing instruction.

Development of the Observational System

One of the first steps in the development of our observational system was to review other observational studies. We located a number of observational studies of literacy instruction in primary-grade classrooms (e.g., Baker, Gersten, Haager, & Dingle, 2006; Bitter, O'Day, Gubbins, & Socias, 2009; Connor et al., 2004, 2009; Foorman et al., 2006; Hoffman et al., 2004; Taylor et al., 2003). However, the observation systems used in these studies were primarily designed to capture reading instruction.

For our purposes it was necessary to develop an observational system that was sensitive to writing as well as reading instruction. The observational systems that we consulted had few writing-specific codes, so we relied on our reading of writing research to guide our decisions about which codes to include. As reading and writing are interrelated literacy activities, we thought that it was important to also include reading instruction and behavior in our observations. Our system includes reading codes that were borrowed from the Center for the Improvement of Early Reading Achievement (CIERA) system developed by Taylor and colleagues (Taylor & Pearson, 2000; Taylor et al., 2003). In total, our system includes nine reading-focused codes (e.g., Comprehension, Read Aloud, Vocabulary, Word Recognition) and 16 writing-focused codes (e.g., Editing, Prewriting, Punctuation, Spelling, Handwriting).

In addition to capturing the overall literacy instructional focus (i.e., reading and writing), we also thought that capturing what students were doing in relation to reading and writing was important. We developed a category called the *Nature of Student Activity*, which included 10 possible codes encompassing reading, writing, and speaking (e.g., correct/copied written response, drawing, oral response, reading chorally). Given that student activities in reading and writing may vary at the level of language used, we further expanded the *Nature of Student Activity* codes into five language-level options including Individual Letters, Individual Words, Sentence, Connected Text, and Marking Response (for multiple-choice tasks). During instances when students were demonstrating different levels of language, the highest level of language was selected. For example, imagine a classroom where six students were writing about text during small-group work. Of those six, four students wrote only one sentence while the other two students wrote four sentences. When coding, observers should code "Writing About Text" in the *Nature of Student Activity* and code "Connected Text" as the level of language since this was the highest level of language used by students in the group.

Drawing on previous research on classroom observation and important factors in writing instruction, our observational system included a number of codes sensitive to writing and reading instruction. The system employs a hierarchical coding scheme with 111 individual codes organized into seven categories: Grouping of Students, Management of Instruction, Broad Instructional Focus, Specific Writing and Reading Foci, Materials, Teacher Instruction, and the Nature of Student Activity.

Refining the Observational System

The final observational instrument that was used to describe classroom instruction is an iPad-based application. The observational instrument took a year to develop and refine through two stages. The first stage involved an iterative process of testing and revising our coding manuals using a traditional paper and pencil system. During the second stage we used the observation system as the basis for the researcher-developed iPad application named iSeeNCode.

In the first stage, the paper observation system was tested in several ways to assess whether the codes were able to capture what was happening in the classroom. Initially we watched videos of first-grade instruction to test our observational system. The videos had been collected to provide examples of effective instruction in local schools. After exhausting these resources, we realized that it would be wise to code a wider range of instructional practices, and not just those considered effective. By searching YouTube and other video hosting sites on the Internet, we located a number of videos of first-grade instruction that had been posted by teachers. Many of these were useful, but we realized that testing our observational system by only coding videos could not substitute for real classroom observations.

As a next step, we field-tested the observational system in first-grade classrooms of patient, cooperating teachers. Observations were conducted numerous times to determine if the codes were capturing reading and writing activities and if additional codes were necessary. For each observation, two or three coders simultaneously coded the classroom activities. After the session, the coders compared their codes to assess the level of agreement. This process helped us identify points of confusion in individual codes, and in many cases we revised the descriptions of codes to ensure clarity for observers. Refining the observation system took approximately six months.

Several changes were made based on the observations. For example, it was discovered that the observation system did not have a code that could accurately capture the nature of students' writing when they were completing multiple-choice worksheets. To address this, Marking Response was added to the level of language options in the Nature of Student Activity. Shortly after adding this new option, Writing Numbers was also added to capture when students were writing numbers during math practice.

After we were satisfied that the coding system was sensitive to both teacher and student behaviors important for writing instruction in the pilot classrooms, the system was converted into an iPad application named "iSeeNCode." A colleague with extensive experience and skill writing iPad-based applications designed and wrote the application. Based on our needs, the developer included a number of features in iSeeNCode to facilitate data collection, data entry, and data organization.

One of the most useful features is the arrangement of the codes in separate categories (Figure 6.1). When an observer taps on an individual category, the subordinate codes automatically appear with icons on the side and brief descriptions. This streamlined organization simplifies the process of locating and selecting individual codes. When we were testing the paper-and-pencil version of the system, we realized how challenging it was for observers to find the appropriate codes when they had to flip through a multipage description of the codes. The

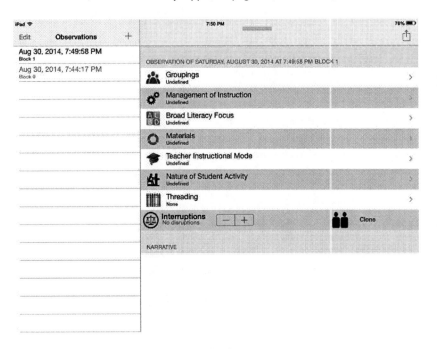

FIGURE 6.1   Main screen of the iSeeNCode observation system

application saves observers from memorizing all the codes or constantly referencing the manual during the two-minute coding session.

Another practical feature of this application is its automatic timing of the five-minute observation blocks. The observation system relies on time-sampled coding. In each five-minute block, observers watch classroom instruction and take field notes for the first three minutes, and then they code for two minutes. iSeeNCode has a timing bar at the top of the screen to provide information about how much time is left in the five-minute block. During the three-minute observation period the timing bar is green, and then it switches to red during the two-minute coding period. Furthermore, the application automatically prompts observers when it is time to observe and when they should begin coding. This feature allows observers to focus on the observation because the work of tracking time is automated.

iSeeNCode also contains powerful features to facilitate data management. As observers enter codes, the data are instantly imported into a spreadsheet. Observers can view the spreadsheet to verify the codes they have entered, and the data can be exported easily for analysis. With all the above-mentioned features, the iSeeNCode iPad application facilitates the entire process of data collection and data organization. It presents the codes clearly, keeps observers on track, organizes the data, and expedites data analysis.

After we had trained the observers to use iSeeNCode, it was used in a number of trial observation sessions. During these trials, some small bugs were discovered and were then corrected by the developer. The research team engaged in several iterations of this process until we were confident that the application met our needs. At that point, we were ready to use it for live data collection.

Challenges for Development and Use

The development or selection of any observation instrument comes with a number of practical challenges. In this section, we focus on issues of reliability and validity as well as the organization of data for ease of use.

Validity and Reliability

In the development of any instrument, issues of validity and reliability are central. These concepts are more often heard in the context of research or assessment or found in technical appendices, but in reality there are important practical implications for the selection or development of any instrument.

A particularly important dimension of validity is content validity—that is, does the instrument measure what you want it to? In the context of writing instruction, we were concerned with whether our instrument captured what happened in classrooms so that we could make valid inferences about the nature of writing instruction. In making decisions about literacy instruction in school or district contexts, it is equally important that the observation instrument developed or selected permits valid, or accurate, inferences. Three important sources of information can be used to ensure that any instrument you develop or select has content validity:

1. Research on literacy instruction;
2. What actually happens in classrooms in your school/district;
3. What you want to be happening in classrooms in your school/district.

In our own instrument we addressed content validity by establishing a framework grounded in the research literature, specifically including practices that have been shown to improve students' outcomes in reading and writing. We also extensively tested this instrument to be sure that the observational system would be able to capture the instructional practices actually used in first-grade classrooms. This ensured that the data we collected captured the realities of literacy instruction, not just the elements we expected to see. The last source of information listed above is more pertinent to specific school or district improvement contexts and is related to curricular and instructional *alignment*. In our work, we sought to find out what writing instruction looks like, with little expectation of what it *should* look like.

In contrast, school and district leaders may have adopted a specific instructional approach or writing curriculum, in which case decision-makers would want to be sure that the key features of that program are included in the instrument, whether or not they are actually being used in classrooms.

The three sources of information that could serve as a basis for content validity may result in a rather lengthy set of practices to be included in the instrument. This raises a challenge with respect to organizing and managing data. Our experience using the iPad as a data collection device made the coding more feasible as well as more reliable because the tool was simple and limited observers' ability to make errors or to have missing data. But after the observation, the organization of data is still complex—with many data points for each observation, multiplied by the number of observations. This makes analysis for decision making cumbersome and unfocused—a challenge we faced at the close of data collection. Based on this experience, we recommend identifying a handful of data points that are priorities for literacy instruction in your school or district. For example, in our work we started with a few key pieces of information we felt were foundational to our understanding writing instruction: the amount of time spent on writing (total and as a proportion of the day), the specific focus of writing instruction (e.g., spelling, prewriting), and variability between teachers and observations. These three pieces of information were relatively simple to extract from a mountain of data, and they gave us a broad picture that helped inform our next steps. Planning ahead for these priority data points will help focus data organization and analysis and enable timely information on which to base decisions.

Reliability is an additional consideration when selecting or developing an observation instrument. In our work, we faced two challenges with respect to reliability. First, we needed to establish inter-rater reliability—the degree to which two or more independent observers would agree on what they saw and how they coded it in our instrument. Simply put, we wanted to be confident that the observation data collected would have been nearly identical irrespective of who conducted the observation. Inter-rater reliability applies in a practical sense as well. In a typical school, there may be many more staff than can be observed by a single leader, coach, department chair, or other administrator. For the data to be reliable, observers must share a common understanding about what these practices look like and agree on how to code practices within the instrument.

A crucial first step in addressing inter-rater reliability is ensuring that all of the observers are trained to use the observation system. The observers for this project were experienced classroom teachers and administrators who had recently retired. They participated in a three-day training session to learn about the project and to practice using iSeeNCode. At the end of each day of the training, the observers and the first author double-coded videos of classroom instruction. Then we calculated the agreement between each observer and the first author. In subsequent sessions, we addressed problem areas and worked to improve the observers' accuracy. Once the observers demonstrated at least 80% accuracy coding the videos, we tested their reliability live coding in the participating classrooms. Before the coders were cleared to collect data, they had to achieve at least 80% reliability in a classroom coding session.

Two approaches we adopted could be used to help establish inter-rater reliability in school contexts. One would be to have the group of individuals responsible for observations conduct an observation together, then compare their results to each other's to see how similar or dissimilar they are. When there are disagreements, observers can discuss their understanding of the practice and its occurrence in the lesson until their joint observations lead to a high degree of agreement. The second approach is similar, except that it relies on calibration with an expert opinion. For example, a literacy coach or other expert might be able to engage in observations alongside individuals typically responsible for conducting observations. Then, rather than comparing observers' data with each other, each observer's data would be compared to data collected by the expert. Disagreements would be reconciled by working with the expert to better understand the practices observed. These two approaches help to establish inter-rater reliability for an observation instrument, and they may also generate shared understandings of practice within the school or district, which may be valuable in improvement efforts.

Reliability can also be understood as reliability within the subject observed. In our research, we observed each teacher four times throughout the year. Our data show substantial variability between observations of the same teacher in the amount of time, specific literacy focus, and instructional strategies used during the course of the year (see Figures 6.2 and 6.3). This may suggest that teachers use different instructional approaches depending on the day, lesson, student needs, or point in the year. Correspondingly, if we drew inferences about literacy instruction from a single observation of a teacher, our findings would simply be inaccurate. In order to draw reliable conclusions about literacy instruction in a school or district, it will be important to consider when and how often observations are conducted to ensure decisions are not based on a single observation.

In the next section, we discuss potential uses of data from an observation instrument focused on literacy instruction. It is important to note that these uses depend on the validity and reliability of the instrument. Without establishing the validity in terms of content and alignment, or reliability in terms of inter-rater reliability and reliability within subject, inferences drawn from these data may be inaccurate and may lead to erroneous or even inappropriate decisions that affect teaching and learning.

Interpreting Observational Data

In this section, we consider some of the uses of observational data. Specifically we describe how our own data are being used, and we present some of our findings. These findings offer insight into the strengths and the limitations of observational data.

When we were developing this project, one of the primary goals was fairly simple. We were interested in learning more about writing instruction in first-grade classrooms. As described earlier in this chapter, the research literature on early instruction is fairly thin, so there was not a large body of work that addressed this question. Results from surveys (e.g., Cutler & Graham, 2008, Graham et al., 1993) and observational research (e.g., Wharton-McDonald, Pressley, & Hampston, 1998) guided the development of our work. Since these other studies did not address our specific questions, we elected to observe a group of typical first-grade teachers in an effort to learn more about writing instruction.

Observational data is particularly helpful in situations when little is known about an instructional approach, as in our case. One advantage of this kind of data is that it can reveal the general instructional trends that are occurring. These trends provide researchers (and administrators) with a broad understanding of what may be happening in classrooms.

For example, Table 6.1 provides some results from the observations conducted in 50 first-grade classrooms. These results are averaged across the four observations that occurred during a school year. By looking at the average number of five-minute blocks devoted to writing instruction (5.4), we learn that teachers engaged in writing instruction for about 27 minutes a day, on average. This finding is not surprising considering that nearly all schools in the study scheduled a half an hour a day for writing instruction.

Compared to a recent kindergarten observational study that found students averaged 6.1 minutes in the fall and 10.5 minutes in the spring for writing

TABLE 6.1 Descriptive statistics from four observations conducted in 50 first-grade classrooms

	Mean	*SD*	*Min*	*Max*
Writing Instruction (Number of 5-minute blocks per day)	5.2	4.3	0	24
Writing Instruction (Percentage of total blocks per day)	9.4	7.8	0	49
Student Writing (Number of 5-minute blocks per day)	25.6	7.6	11	45
Student Writing (Percentage of total blocks per day)	45.3	12.5	19	79
Total Writing Activity (Number of 5-minute blocks per day)	27.8	7.6	13	45
Total Writing Activity (Percentage of total blocks per day)	49.1	12.5	24	80

instruction and practice (Puranik, Al Otaiba, Sidler, & Greulich, 2014), the first graders in our study averaged nearly three times as much time just for writing instruction. This suggests that the first-grade teachers in our sample are devoting more time to writing. It is logical to expect first-grade teachers to provide more writing instruction than kindergarten teachers as the academic demands in first grade are higher. Another explanation for the difference is that in Puranik et al.'s (2014) study, observations only occurred during the 90-minute literacy block, rather than the whole day as ours did. Perhaps if the observers in Puranik et al.'s (2014) study had remained in the classroom for the whole day, they would have seen more writing instruction.

By looking at the trends across the observations, we can get a sense of how much time teachers devote to writing. However, what may be more interesting is the amount of variability around the average. The variability is helpful because it reveals how much classrooms (or teachers) differ from each other.

In these data, the variability is quite large. For example, the standard deviations in Table 6.1 are nearly as large as the averages, which suggest that there are substantive differences among individual teachers in our sample. If we consider the amount of time for writing instruction again, the standard deviation (4.0) reveals that many teachers are providing more or less time to writing instruction than the average. The amount of variability suggests that teachers are not all doing exactly the same thing in their classrooms. This finding was also not surprising to us because previous research also found wide variability in teachers' writing instruction (Cutler & Graham, 2008; Puranik et al., 2014).

To learn a little bit more about the sources of the variability in the observations, we used hierarchical linear modeling (HLM). This method allows us to see how much of the variability in the target variables was associated with differences among the four observations, the classrooms (or teachers), and the schools (Figures 6.2 and 6.3). Figure 6.2 displays how much of the variability in each target variable is associated with the observation, the classroom, and the school out of the entire instructional day. Figure 6.3 also shows sources of variability, but it focuses only on the time blocks that included either writing instruction or practice.

It was immediately obvious that for all of the variables we examined, most of the variability was found at the level of the observation. For example, for the amount of time for writing instruction, 88.6% of the variability was associated with differences in the four observations that occurred during the school year. This was a startling figure because it suggests that there is considerable variability in the amount of time devoted to writing instruction across the school year. One possible explanation could be that our observations were not reliable from time point to time point. Instead of having consistent amounts of time devoted to writing instruction, there were differences depending on the time of the year when the observations occurred. This could mean that the observation system or

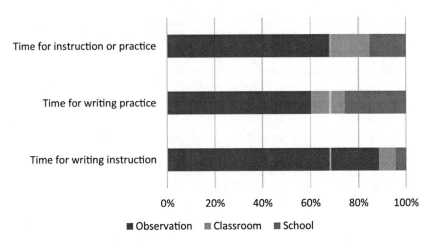

FIGURE 6.2 Proportion of variability attributable to observation, classroom, and school out of all blocks

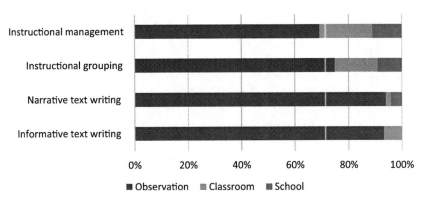

FIGURE 6.3 Proportion of variability attributable to observation, classroom, and school out of writing blocks

the trained observers were unable to accurately identify when writing instruction was occurring, so that the estimates had a lot of mistakes (or error) in them. As we discussed earlier, reliability is important for observational systems, so the possibility that the system was inaccurate was troubling. However, the safeguards that we used to establish and maintain inter-rater reliability make this an unlikely conclusion.

From an instructional perspective, instructional reliability is not always desirable. In most first-grade classrooms, instruction changes across the school year, and we believe that it should. As students learn and their capacity grows, the nature of instruction and the length of instruction should change. It could be that in some classrooms students receive more instruction early in the year in foundational skills such as handwriting and spelling. Then, later in the year, they have less instruction but more time to practice writing. Conversely, in other classrooms students may have limited instruction early in the year but as students learn more and their ability to attend develops, the instructional periods get longer. Given these possibilities, it is not surprising that there is considerable variability in the amount of instructional time across observation periods.

Considering our interest in writing instruction, we were particularly interested in how much variability was associated with differences among the classrooms or teachers (Figure 6.2). Only 7.0% of the variability in writing instructional time was associated with teacher differences. In terms of time for writing instruction, there did not seem to be a lot of teacher differences. However, when we examined the amount of time students practiced writing, bigger classroom differences were found (14.0%).

We also examined the variability of important instructional variables during the time blocks where any kind of writing occurred (Figure 6.3). Once again, most of the variability was associated with the observation. Small classroom differences in terms of the time devoted to narrative and informational text writing were found. However, larger classroom differences were detected in instructional management (e.g., who was leading the lesson; 19.8%) and how students were grouped (16.0%). These results point to potentially important differences among teachers in their approaches to writing instruction. As our project moves forward, we plan to investigate whether these classroom differences can help us predict students' writing performance.

Uses of Observational Data

Observational data like these can be used in a number of ways by researchers and school administrators. Some of these uses are warranted, but others are less appropriate and should be avoided.

In our work, the central goal was to learn about writing instruction. Most researchers who have engaged in observational work draw on the available research to focus their observations. We constructed our observation system so that it was sensitive to instructional features that we thought would be important. As we move forward with the project, data from the observations will help us learn about the nature of first-grade writing instruction and how specific features of instruction are related to students' writing achievement. These kinds of questions are reasonable ones to ask given the nature of the data.

Other questions that administrators might reasonably ask are not appropriate for these kinds of data. For example, our observational data should not be used to evaluate teachers' writing instruction. One reason that observational data would be inappropriate for teacher evaluation is that writing expectations for students are in a state of flux. With the widespread adoption of the Common Core State Standards, many states have seen their writing standards change considerably. In our home state of Delaware, the standards have introduced new end-of-the-year expectations for first graders to write in three different genres: narrative, opinion, and informational writing. These new standards have changed the writing land-scape in first grade. As a result, teachers are adapting their approaches to instruction to meet these new standards. Using the observational data to make instructional evaluations would be premature until those changes are finalized.

Another complication in evaluating writing instruction is the writing knowl-edge base. Earlier in the chapter we described how writing researchers have made progress identifying effective instructional approaches (e.g., Graham et al., 2012; Graham & Perin, 2007). Despite this progress, there is still much that is not known about teaching writing. Given these limitations, evaluating writing instruction needs to be done with great care. Administrators should use evaluative criteria built on solid evidence. When observing writing instruction for evaluative purposes, admin-istrators should use observational protocols that include well-supported criteria.

Finally, we believe that evaluating instruction without providing support is both unfair and unproductive. Many teachers in our project have received neither professional development nor curricular support for writing instruction. Until they have been given high-quality instructional guidance, it is unreasonable to evaluate their teaching.

Take Action

Classroom observations can provide valuable information for both administrators and researchers. As we described in this chapter, researchers depend on observa-tions to investigate questions about classroom practice. Administrators also rely on classroom observations to evaluate teacher performance and to ascertain that specific curricular and instructional guidelines are met.

During the development of our classroom observational system, we had a number of resources, such as extended time and expert advice, that are not usu-ally available to school administrators. However, our work may be instructive to administrators interested in developing their own observational protocols. As administrators approach the task of creating an observational system, special attention needs to be devoted to reliability and validity. If these dimensions are neglected in an observational system, the data produced may have little value.

Finally, it is important to recognize that the way a system is used should drive how it is structured. For example, our project was designed to investigate what occurred during writing instruction. Since relatively little is known about early writing instruction, our system needed to be flexible enough to capture a wide range of activities that might occur. However, an observation system designed to evaluate whether teachers were employing a set of established best practices or instructional moves should be much more streamlined. As administrators approach the challenge of creating an observational protocol, they will need to balance their specific needs with the important technical requirements.

Note

1 The research reported here was supported by the Institute of Education Sciences, U.S. Department of Education, through Grant R305A110484 to the University of Delaware. The opinions expressed are those of the authors and do not represent views of the institute or the U.S. Department of Education.

References

Baker, S.K., Gersten, R., Haager, D., & Dingle, M. (2006). Teaching practice and the reading growth of first-grade English learners: Validation of an observation instrument. *The Elementary School Journal, 107*(2), 199–219.

Berninger, V., & Chanquoy, L. (2012). What writing is and how it changes across early and middle childhood development: A multidisciplinary perspective. In E.L. Grigorenko, E. Mambrino, & D.D. Preiss (Eds). *Writing: A mosaic of new perspectives* (pp. 65–84). New York: Psychology Press.

Berninger, V.W., & Amtmann, D. (2003). Preventing written expression disabilities through early and continuing assessment and intervention for handwriting and/or spelling problems: Research into practice. In H.L. Swanson, K.R. Harris, & S. Graham (Eds.), *Handbook of learning disabilities* (pp. 345–363). New York: Guilford Press.

Berninger, V.W., Vaughan, K.B., Abbott, R.D., Abbott, S.P., Rogan, L.W., Brooks, A., Reed, E., & Graham, S. (1997). Treatment of handwriting problems in beginning writers: Transfer from handwriting to composition. *Journal of Educational Psychology, 89*(4), 652–66.

Berninger, V.W., Vaughan, K., Abbott, R.D., Brooks, A., Abbott, S.P., Rogan, L., Reed, E., & Graham, S. (1998). Early intervention for spelling problems: Teaching functional spelling units of varying size with a multiple-connections framework. *Journal of Educational Psychology, 90*, 587–605.

Bitter, C., O'Day, J., Gubbins, P., & Socias, M. (2009). What works to improve student literacy achievement? An examination of instructional practices in a balanced literacy approach. *Journal of Education for Students Placed at Risk, 14*(1), 17–44.

Bohn, C.M., Roehrig, A.D., & Pressley, M. (2004). The first days of school in the classrooms of two more effective and four less effective primary-grades teachers. *Elementary School Journal, 104*(4), 269.

Connor, C.M., Morrison, F.J., Fishman, B., Ponitz, C.C., Glasney, S., Underwood, P.S., Piasta, S.B., Crowe, E.C., & Schatschneider, C. (2009). The ISI classroom observation system: Examining the literacy instruction provided to individual students. *Educational Researcher, 38*(2), 85–99.

Connor, C.M., Morrison, F.J., & Katch, E.L. (2004). Beyond the reading wars: The effect of classroom instruction by child interactions on early reading. *Scientific Studies of Reading, 8*(4), 305–336.

Cutler, L., & Graham, S. (2008). Primary grade writing instruction: A national survey. *Journal of Educational Psychology, 100*(4), 907–919.

Foorman, B., Schatschneider, C., Eakin, M.N., Fletcher, J.M., Moats, L.C., & Francis, D.J. (2006). The impact of instructional practices in grades 1 and 2 on reading and spelling achievement in high poverty schools. *Contemporary Educational Psychology, 31*, 1–29.

Graham, S., Harris, K.R., & Chorzempa, B.F. (2002). Contributions of spelling instruction to the spelling, writing, and reading of poor spellers. *Journal of Educational Psychology, 94*, 669–686.

Graham, S., Harris, K.R., & Fink, B. (2000). Is handwriting causally related to learning to write? Treatment of handwriting problems in beginning writers. *Journal of Educational Psychology, 92*(4), 620–33.

Graham, S., Harris, K.R., Fink-Chorzempa, B., & MacArthur, C.A. (2003). Primary grade teachers' instructional adaptations for struggling writers: A national survey. *Journal of Educational Psychology, 95*, 279–292.

Graham, S., McKeown, D., Kiuhara, S., & Harris, K. (2012). A meta-analysis of writing instruction for students in the elementary grades. *Journal of Educational Psychology, 104*(3), 879–896.

Graham, S., & Perin, D. (2007). A meta-analysis of writing instruction for adolescent students. *Journal of Educational Psychology, 99*, 445–476.

Graham, S., Schwartz, S., & MacArthur, C. (1993). Knowledge of writing and the composing process, attitude toward writing, and self-efficacy for students with and without learning disabilities. *Journal of Learning Disabilities, 26*, 237–249.

Hoffman, J.V., Sailors, M., Duffy, G.R., & Beretvas, S.N. (2004). The effective elementary classroom literacy environment: Examining the validity of the TEXIN3 observation system. *Journal of Literacy Research, 36*(3), 303–334.

Jones, D., & Christensen, C. (1999). The relationship between automaticity in handwriting and students' ability to generate written text. *Journal of Educational Psychology, 91*, 44–49.

National Commission on Writing in America's Schools and Colleges. (2003). *The neglected R: The need for a writing revolution.* New York: College Board.

Puranik, C., Al Otaiba, S., Folsom, J., & Greulich, L. (2014). Exploring the amount and type of writing instruction during language arts instruction in kindergarten classrooms. *Reading and Writing: An Interdisciplinary Journal, 27*(2), 213–236.

Taylor, B.M., & Pearson, P.D. (2000). *The CIERA school change classroom observation scheme.* Minneapolis: University of Minnesota.

Taylor, B.M., Pearson, P.D., Peterson, D.S., & Rodriguez, M.C. (2003). Reading growth in high-poverty classrooms: The influence of teacher practices that encourage cognitive engagement in literacy learning. *The Elementary School Journal, 104*(4), 3–28.

Persky, H.R., Daane, M.C., & Jin, Y. (2003). *The nation's report card: Writing 2002, NCES 2003.* Washington, DC: National Center for Educational Statistics.

Wharton-McDonald, R., Pressley, M., & Hampston, J.M. (1998). Literacy instruction in nine first-grade classrooms: Teacher characteristics and student achievement. *Elementary School Journal, 99*(2), 101–128.

Examples of Alternative Systems/Approaches for Evaluating Literacy Instruction

We asked Mr. Garry, principal of South Side School in Bristol, Connecticut, what had changed for his school after the first year of a new teacher evaluation policy. He told us:

> We are "all in" for literacy—this year and next, and hopefully the next. And this is one of the things I am most proud of this year. Call it the echo of a very challenging year where many things did not make sense. As a result, this year we are retaking our castle! We are working to create a coherent plan that supports teacher and student literacy learning.

Section II provides examples of tools, frameworks, and observation instruments for school leaders hoping to support and infuse effective literacy instruction within their teacher evaluation routines and practices.

7. *Using the School Change Observation Scheme to Support Effective Literacy Instruction.* Debra S. Peterson, University of Minnesota
8. *Assessing Literacy Teaching: Using the Text Environment as a Window into the Examination of Literacy Practices.* Misty Sailors, University of Texas at San Antonio; James Hoffman, University of Texas at Austin
9. *The Use of Formative Assessment to Improve Instruction of English Learners and Evaluation of Literacy Practices.* Francesca López, The University of Arizona; Patrick Proctor, Boston College; Martin Scanlon, Marquette University
10. *What Does Effective Teaching Look Like?: The Observations of Effective Teaching in Reading (OET-Reading) Systems.* Carol MacDonald Connor, Sarah Ingebrand, and Nicole Sparapani, Arizona State University

7

USING THE SCHOOL CHANGE OBSERVATION SCHEME TO SUPPORT EFFECTIVE LITERACY INSTRUCTION

Debra S. Peterson

The purpose of this chapter is to present examples from four studies that used classroom observation data for professional learning, reflection, and collaborative change. The support systems built into the reform process were critical components and they facilitated the effective use of the observation data for instructional change and increased student performance. In these studies schools serving students from diverse linguistic, cultural, and socioeconomic backgrounds were able to demonstrate accelerated student growth on a variety of standardized reading assessments. A description of the various components of professional support will be provided and potential action steps suggested for administrators, teacher leaders, and classroom teachers as they consider the use of observation data for evaluation and professional learning.

The School Change Framework

The School Change Framework (Taylor, Pearson, Peterson, & Rodriguez, 2005) was developed to guide individual schools and districts as they created their own reading reform efforts. Based on research on effective schools and accomplished teachers, the framework identified key components that schools should consider when implementing reading reform. These included:

- Shared leadership between administration and teachers so that all educators feel they have a voice in the school-wide decisions related to reading instruction (Fullan, 2005; Leithwood, Louis, Anderson, & Wahlstrom, 2004).
- Professional development that is ongoing, job-embedded, collaborative, and focused on practices validated by research (Dillon, O'Brien, Sato, & Kelly, 2011; DuFour, Eaker, & Many, 2006; Joyce & Showers, 2002; Valli & Hawley, 2007).

- Collaborative reflection on instruction for continuous improvement (Allington & Cunningham, 2007; Cox & Hopkins, 2006; Guthrie et al., 2004; McIntyre, Kyle, & Moore, 2006; Sailors, 2009).
- School-wide use of data on students, teaching, and the school culture for instructional goal setting and decision making (Au, Raphael, & Mooney, 2008).
- Strong partnerships with families and communities as they work toward the success of all students (Senechal, 2006; Weigel, Martin, & Bennett, 2006).

Schools tailored the components of the framework to fit their local contexts and to meet the needs of their students and communities. This included the selection of their own reading curricula, materials, and models (e.g., basal programs, workshop models).

The schools involved in these four studies were geographically and demographically diverse. They were located in rural, small town, large town, suburban, and inner city sites in states ranging from Connecticut, California, North Carolina, Minnesota, Michigan, Iowa, and Florida. They included public, charter, and private schools. All the schools served high percentages of students who received free and reduced-price lunch and whose home languages ranged from Spanish, Hmong, Karen, Ojibwa, Armenian, and Somali, to list a few. The summary of the participating schools' demographics are listed in Table 7.1.

Schools participated in the School Change project for approximately three years. All schools agreed to assess their students on common measures of reading during the fall and spring of each year. These assessments addressed growth in areas of phonemic awareness (Kindergarten–Grade 1), phonics (K–Gr. 5), fluency (Gr. 1–5), comprehension, and vocabulary (K–Gr. 5). The teachers and administrators also participated in individual interviews and completed self-study surveys twice each year. Teachers of reading, including specialists (i.e., Title 1, English Learners, Special Education teachers) were observed during reading instruction for one hour three times a year. The notes and codes from an observation were sent directly to each individual teacher along with reflection questions, and summaries of more and less effective teaching practices. Teachers were encouraged to reflect on their observation data with a trusted colleague like a literacy coach or grade level peer. In Study 4, 20 out of 23 schools reported that teachers discussed grade level and school level classroom observation data at whole group and grade level meetings (Peterson, Taylor, Burnham, & Schock, 2008; Taylor & Peterson, 2006c, 2007a). Discussions revolved around topics that emerged from the data, such as how to teach comprehension as a strategy and not just as a skill or how to engage students in writing and asking their own higher-level questions in student-led discussions.

The School Change Observation Scheme (Taylor, 2003) is a research-based tool designed to support reading reform by providing teachers with data related

TABLE 7.1 Demographics of schools across studies

	STUDY 1 (Taylor, Pearson, Peterson, & Rodriguez, 2003, 2005)	STUDY 2 (Taylor & Peterson, 2003, 2006a, 2007b; Taylor, Peterson, Marx, & Chein, 2007)	STUDY 3 (Taylor & Peterson, 2006b)	STUDY 4 (Peterson, Taylor, Burnham, & Schock, 2008; Taylor & Peterson, 2006c, 2007a)
Number of Schools	13	23	27	24
Percentage of Students on Free and Reduced Price Lunch	M. 81 (S.D. 12)	M. 74 (S.D. 20)	M. 73 (S.D. 16)	M. 62 (S.D. 18)
Percentage of English Learners	M. 20 (S.D. 17)	M. 21 (S.D. 15)	M. 23 (S.D. 22)	M. 24 (S.D. 19)

to their reading instruction. The observation scheme includes detailed field notes of the observed instruction along with codes defining the behaviors and activities recorded. The tool provides information related to these elements of instruction: grouping practices, literacy activities, materials, interaction styles, expected student responses to the literacy activities, and students' engagement rates. The codes and definitions for each level are presented in Appendix A.

In all four of the studies described here, scheduled observations were conducted by trained elementary teachers three times a year. During an observation, the data collector would type a description of what was happening in the classroom for five minutes, stop to quickly count the number of students who appeared to be on task and code the instruction that just occurred.

The observer then continued to type for another five minutes. This rotation continued throughout the hour-long observation. On average, there would be 8–10 five-minute segments recorded during an hour observation.

Codes from the observations were used to conduct statistical analyses, hierarchical linear modeling (Raudenbush & Bryk, 2002), to identify instructional practices that were positively or negatively related to students' growth in reading. Qualitative analyses of the narrative field notes served to provide detailed descriptions of what these positive and negative practices looked like in day-to-day instruction. These patterns were shared with school staff three times a year.

In individual interviews conducted twice a year with all the teachers, they repeatedly discussed their use of the observation data to set professional goals and make changes in their instruction (Taylor & Peterson, 2007a). Their perceptions were further supported by the analysis of school artifacts including: professional learning action plans completed by each Professional Learning Community (PLC), transcripts of coaching conversations between literacy coaches

TABLE 7.2 Increase in percent of 5-minute segments in which activity was observed

	Year 1	Year 2
Grade 2	17%	21%
Higher Level Talk and Writing about Text		
Grade 2	4%	16%
Comprehension Strategy Instruction		
Grade 3	22%	26%
Higher Level Talk and Writing about Text		
Grade 3	11%	18%
Comprehension Strategy Instruction		

and individual teachers, and transcriptions of PLC or data retreat conversations. Changes in the observation data over time also documented the fact that teachers were changing their instruction. To illustrate this point, an example from Study 4 is presented in Table 7.2. From year one to year two, second and third grade teachers' observations showed an increase in the amount of higher level talk and writing about text and comprehension strategy instruction they were providing to students. These changes reflect the percent of five-minute segments during an observation in which the targeted instructional strategies were observed.

Essential Components of Professional Development

Research has suggested that evaluation alone might be insufficient to substantially change instruction in ways that will result in increased student learning and achievement. Goe and Bell (2008) stated, "Scores from a value-added model may provide information about a teacher's contribution to student learning, but it would be less helpful in providing teachers with guidance on how to improve their performance" (p. 52). Evaluation that provides observational data on instruction along with professional development and ongoing support is more likely to stimulate substantive changes than evaluation alone (Curtis, 2011; Doubek & Cooper, 2007; Duffy, 2004; Kennedy, 2010; Kennedy & Shiel, 2010; Timperley & Parr, 2007). To support teachers, administrators, and coaches in the use and interpretation of the observation data, a variety of professional development opportunities were provided through The School Change Framework. These examples of support are described here so that schools and districts using classroom observation data for teacher evaluation and school improvement can consider which support structures might best be used with their staff. They might include:

- **Training on the observation scheme.** Training on the definitions and procedures of the observation scheme were provided by a senior researcher to administrators, teachers, and literacy coaches two to three times a year.

The purpose of these training sessions was to equip the teachers and literacy coaches with the knowledge needed to understand and interpret their personal observation feedback. During these trainings, participants had many opportunities to discuss and clarify terms. These discussions helped the participants form a common understanding of effective instruction. For example, one common topic was teacher modeling. The observation scheme defined "modeling" as explicit demonstration of how to apply a skill or strategy while reading, writing, or talking about a text. Many teachers thought they were modeling if they merely told students to use a skill or strategy. Developing a school-wide understanding of key terms and instructional practices was an important component in their professional learning and it provided a basis for them to establish a unified focus for change. When a special education teacher was asked to describe the communication and collaboration at her school, she stated, "We are doing this building-wide and it helps us to be on the same page, and when kids go from grade to grade [they see] that we are using the same terminology and are consistent from year to year." Whatever observation tool or rating scale might be used to document and evaluate instructional practices, there is benefit in collaborative, school-wide, professional conversations about what the data mean, what they measure, and what alternative practices might look like in daily instruction. This is aligned with the research on teacher evaluation highlighting the importance of setting clear definitions of what constitutes effective instruction across a school or district (Curtis, 2011; Goe, Bell, & Little, 2008).

- **Professional Learning Communities.** All staff, including administrators, met for an hour three times a month throughout each school year in teacher-led study groups, or Professional Learning Communities. In their PLCs, they analyzed data and set professional learning goals by writing group action plans, read and discussed research articles, shared videos of their instruction, and analyzed student work (Peterson, 2013; Taylor, 2012). Teachers studied a topic over multiple months so that they had many opportunities to apply and refine new practices in their instruction. PLC topics included: comprehension strategy instruction, explicit instruction in phonics and the application of word recognition strategies, higher-level talk and writing about text, effective fluency instruction, etc. Groups were encouraged to use protocols to guide their discussions and reflection. It was also suggested that they balance grade-level and cross-grade groups to facilitate a sense of collective efficacy across the school culture. The PLCs provided ongoing, collaborative professional learning that was intentionally applied to decisions related to reading programs, materials, and instructional practices (Taylor, Pearson, Peterson, & Rodriguez, 2005). Many schools and districts around the country are currently using PLCs or study groups with varying levels of effectiveness (e.g., NIET, 2013). One factor that may impact the effectiveness of PLCs is the inclusion of data on teaching. This is often a missing piece in the process (Peterson, Taylor, Burnham, & Schock, 2008) and can prove to be a powerful tool for reflection and change. When teachers examine concrete evidence about changes in their instruction and compare that to changes in student work or progress monitoring data, then they can more easily refine their instructional practices based on the strengths and needs of their particular students. When they examine student data alone, they may be uncertain about which elements of instruction are proving effective or which ones are not. Evidence of instructional change might include: lesson plans, video clips of instruction, informal or formal observational data, examples of teacher-developed rubrics or anchor charts, and student work samples.

- **Whole school meetings.** School staff met for an hour once a month throughout each school year for cross-grade sharing of data, celebration of successes, and discussion of school-wide issues related to reading instruction. Topics were identified based on the trends seen across the school's observation data and students' progress monitoring data. These topics included: differentiation, reading in the content areas, alignment of core curriculum and interventions, supporting English Learners, etc. (Peterson, 2013; Taylor, 2012). These meetings were designed to contribute to a sense of shared leadership and collective efficacy among the entire school staff and to build consistency of instruction from grade to grade. Again, most schools conduct whole staff meetings, but often these address issues of day-to-day management of the school schedule and building, and do not focus on school-wide instructional practices and student data. Whole school meetings focused on supporting instructional change should include: an agenda for the meeting with an explicit purpose statement related to the goal for the meeting and how it connects to instruction and student progress, a celebration of successes based on current assessment data, cross-grade discussions around the instructional topic, an analysis of research on best practices, and specific plans for action steps by grade-level teams.

- **Coaching conversations.** Literacy coaches in our studies were general education elementary teachers with advanced degrees or additional licenses in reading. Coaches were trained by a senior researcher to ask questions to help teachers reflect on their observation data and set goals for changes or refinements to their instruction (Peterson, Taylor, Burnham, & Schock, 2008). These reflection questions were based on the Cognitive Engagement Model (Taylor, Pearson, Peterson, & Rodriguez, 2003) which asks teachers to consider:

1. To what extent am I involving my students in higher-order talk and writing about text?
2. To what extent am I teaching comprehension and word recognition as strategies, not just as skills?
3. To what extent am I teaching from a student-support stance (i.e., modeling, coaching, listening, and giving feedback) rather than from a teacher-directed stance (i.e., telling and recitation)?
4. To what extent are my students engaged in active responding (i.e., reading, writing, working with a partner, or manipulating) rather than passive responding (i.e., listening, reading turn-taking, oral turn-taking)?

5. To what extent did I clearly state the purpose of my lesson to the students? Did I explain how this lesson will move all students forward?

Coaches supported teachers in the goals they set for instructional change by modeling instructional strategies, co-planning and co-teaching lessons, and informally observing instruction. Coaches also encouraged teachers to apply what they were learning in their PLCs to their daily instruction. The observation data and the study of research articles helped teachers to determine what kinds of changes they could be making to their instruction, and the coaches provided the support and expertise on how those changes could be implemented (Taylor, Peterson, Pearson, & Rodriguez, 2002). Other researchers have documented the impact that coaching models can have on instructional change because they provide the individualized, ongoing support that teachers need to refine their practice (Bean et al., 2010; Biancarosa, Bryk, & Dexter, 2010; Matsumura et al., 2010; Sailors & Price, 2010). Coaching models might include practices like co-planning and co-teaching, modeling of a new technique or strategy by the coach followed by the implementation of the new technique by the classroom teacher with the guidance of the coach, analysis of videos of the teacher's instruction with the coach, informal and formal classroom observations including coaching conversations, and individualized follow-up support.

- **Professional development in cross-schools meetings.** Schools also had the opportunity to meet across schools for professional development days. At these meetings, participants attended presentations by national researchers on effective reading instruction and effective reading reform. Schools shared how they were translating the research-based practices and policies to their specific situations and local communities through poster sessions and panel discussions. Teachers shared videos of their instruction and led discussions with their cross-school colleagues about effective reading instruction in a variety of workshops or break-out sessions (Peterson, 2013). The professional learning that occurred at these meetings served to challenge local expectations for student success and to inspire teachers to make changes to their instruction. Cross-school meetings could occur between elementary and secondary schools within the same district, with schools from neighboring areas, or with schools from across the region or state. Schools might take turns hosting "gallery walks" where they can highlight the effective strategies that they are using through photo displays, Microsoft PowerPoint presentations, slide shows, and student work displays. They might video record students and teachers talking about the progress they are making and share their videos across school sites. Colleagues from other schools could also be invited to participate in PLCs using a video chat or video-conferencing platform.
- **Data meetings.** Grade-level teams, including the specialists, met at least three times a year to analyze their progress monitoring data and to discuss the growth

their students were demonstrating in all areas of reading (Taylor, 2012). They discussed possible adaptations to the core curriculum that might be advantageous for the students who were not making progress, and they made adjustments to the interventions or supplemental supports that were available to those students. They also identified instructional changes that had contributed to positive growth for students so they could celebrate and build upon those successes. These meetings fostered a sense of collective efficacy and collaborative reflection among the general education teachers and the specialists. As schools implement multi-tiered systems of support like Response to Intervention (Fuchs, Fuchs, & Vaughn, 2008), many of them have been incorporating regular grade-level data meetings to analyze and interpret student assessment data. Incorporating the discussion of classroom observation data or other evidence of instructional practice could increase the effectiveness of these sessions because teachers are directly examining the connection between what they do and how students are growing. One way to ensure the effectiveness of data meetings is to provide protocols or guiding questions to facilitate teacher reflection and discussion (Saunders, Goldenberg, & Gallimore, 2009). For example, if a grade-level team is trying to see growth in their students' ability to summarize informational texts, they might examine their lesson plans, video clips of instruction, and observation data to answer the following questions:

1. What are the components of effective summaries of informational text? Is there a common understanding across the grade level including the specialists? What evidence do we see of this? If there is not a common understanding, what resources or professional development might we need to help us refine our understanding?
2. How were the components of effective summaries communicated and modeled for students? What evidence do we see of this? How do we know that students learned what we taught them about summarizing informational text? What else might be done?
3. What are our action steps between now and our next meeting for teaching summarizing? What evidence of instructional change and student progress will we collect?

These examples are not presented here to suggest that schools and districts must provide all these opportunities for professional learning and support to their teachers and administrators. Realistically, most sites will not have the resources, time, or personnel necessary to provide this depth of professional support. The point of these examples is to stress the importance of support structures when implementing reform efforts. Evaluations of instructional skill and competence may not in and of themselves lead to changes in instruction or increases in students' reading achievement. Making substantive changes to reading instruction, changes that will positively impact students' achievement, is a difficult and laborious process. Gaffney and Anderson (2000) describe this persistent problem as the "research to practice gap" (p. 68) and they outline the multiple difficulties involved in changing instructional practices. Evaluating teachers without providing the professional learning and collaborative support they need to change only leads to defeated and demoralized educators.

Take Action

These studies are relevant to teachers, literacy coaches, administrators, and policymakers who are exploring the interaction between teacher evaluation, reading reform, and student achievement because they describe the complex processes and levels of support required to fuel school-wide reading reform. Collecting data on instruction and student performance may be non-productive unless schools provide the time and structures necessary for deep reflection and collaborative learning. To that end, the following action steps are recommended:

For Administrators

- Use classroom observations and the analysis of student assessment data for collaborative reflection and change. Pigott and Barr (2000) suggest that program evaluation is best conducted in a formative way where the stakeholders have a chance to participate in the policies and practices designed to increase program and school effectiveness.
- Collect data from multiple sources. Research has shown that leadership and other school-level factors contribute to student learning (Fullan, 2005; Leithwood, Louis, Anderson, & Wahlstrom, 2004; Saunders, Goldenberg, & Gallimore, 2009). Data on school-level factors should be collected and analyzed along with information about the effectiveness of teachers' instruction. Tools for data collection might include self-study surveys soliciting teachers' perceptions of the school climate and culture, or parent focus groups where families can share their perceptions of the school's effectiveness.
- Explicitly examine the alignment between the core reading program, student assessments, reading interventions, and the evaluation tool being used to determine teacher effectiveness. The validity of the evaluation system relies on the fact that the students were taught what they needed to know, that they received additional support or differentiation as needed, that the assessments actually measured what students learned, and that the teacher evaluation tool was designed to capture the behaviors and practices directly related to the students' learning outcomes. For example, if the school or district is concerned about the growth of their students in reading, then their evaluation tools should be able to document reading-specific instructional strategies and practices. The information gained from more general observation tools may be harder to translate into practical application.

- Time, resources, and personnel are needed to maintain ongoing support and continuous improvement of school-wide reading programs and instruction (Curtis, 2011; Dillon, O'Brien, Sato, & Kelly, 2011; Jerald & Van Hook, 2011). These might include ongoing training for observers to maintain a high level of valid and reliable data on instruction (Hoffman, Maloch, & Sailors, 2011), hiring trained literacy coaches and providing time for collegial conversations about data and instruction, targeted follow-up support through co-planning and co-teaching, and integration of data analysis and professional learning.

For Literacy Coaches and Teacher Leaders

- Help teachers reflect on their observation data through coaching conversations. Use data as the basis for the goals they set for instructional change and professional learning (Peterson, Taylor, Burnham, & Schock, 2008).
- Mentor colleagues through co-planning and co-teaching. Once teachers know what to change, they also need support in how to create that change (Taylor, Peterson, Pearson, & Rodriguez, 2002).
- Lead by example, be the first ones to enact change (Leithwood, Louis, Anderson, & Wahlstrom, 2004).

For Classroom Teachers

- Demonstrate a willingness to reflect on data on instruction and on student progress by working collaboratively with coaches, grade-level colleagues, and specialists to refine instruction. When interviewed about the reform effort in her school, a reading specialist reported, "I am more conscious of my goals. I try to do more writing and have students be more active in responding by providing opportunities for each child to respond. This change is a result of reading research and study group discussions. I use the feedback from observations and the video sharing in study groups."
- Discontinue activities or practices that are not supported by research or are ineffective in moving students forward. When a third grade teacher was asked if her teaching of reading had changed during the year, she responded, "Definitely! After looking at my observation data, I needed to release more responsibility to my students. I could move away from recitation and oral turn-taking to more students actively responding."

Conclusion

The purpose of this chapter was to provide examples of how schools used data on instruction to positively impact students' growth and achievement. The teachers, literacy coaches, and administrators in these four studies worked with tremendous persistence and dedication to change their contexts from cultures of blame and defeat to ones of collaboration and success. They seriously examined the data on their own instruction and practices, and made tough, intentional changes. These changes led to accelerated growth (i.e., more than a year's growth in a year's time) in their students' standardized test scores. The variety and depth of professional learning and support that occurred in these four projects were crucial components of their ability to make substantive changes. Schools and districts that are committed to student achievement may want to consider the depth and level of support they are providing to teachers, coaches, and administrators as they implement their evaluation and reform efforts.

Appendix A: Classroom Observation Levels, Codes, and Definitions

Level 1: Who	Code	Definitions
Classroom teacher	c	Classroom teacher
Reading specialist	s	Reading teacher, Title 1 teacher, reading resource teacher, special education teacher, speech and language teacher, ESL teacher, bilingual teacher, etc.
Aide	a	Paraprofessional or instructional aide
No one	n	No one is in the room, or no one is directly working with the children (e.g., the children are working in their seats independently and no one is circulating)
Not applicable	9	No instruction is occurring

Level 2: Grouping	Code	Definition
Whole class/Large group	w	All of the children in the class (except for 1 or 2 individuals working with someone else), or a group of more than 10 children. If there are 10 or less in the room, code this as a small group.
Small Group	s	Children are working in 2 or more groups. If there are more than 10 children in a group, call this large group.
Pairs	p	Children are working in pairs
Individual	i	Children are working independently
Other	o	Some other grouping practice is in place
Not applicable	9	None of the above seem to apply; no instruction is taking place

Level 3: Major focus	Code	Definition
Reading	r	Reading, word recognition, reading comprehension, writing in response to reading (where this is the major purpose for the writing), literature study, reading vocabulary
Composition/ Writing	w	Writing for the purpose of expressing or communicating ideas (but not writing in which major purpose is to respond to reading); learning how to write; writer's workshop, creative writing, report writing
Other language	l	Aspect of language arts other than the above; grammar, mechanics, oral expression, etc.
Other	o	Focus is academic but not on literacy
Not applicable	9	None of the above seem to apply; focus is not academic

Level 4: Activity	Code	Definition
Reading connected text	r	Students are engaged in reading text; this includes silent reading, choral reading, oral turn-taking reading
Listening to connected text	l	Students are engaged in listening to text; if teacher is reading to students, code as l, even if the students are to be following along
Vocabulary	v	Students are engaged in discussing/working on a word meaning(s)
Meaning of text/ comprehension— lower level	m1 m2	Students are engaged in talk (m1) or writing (m2) about the meaning of text which is at a lower level of thinking or lower level of text interpretation. The writing may be a journal entry about the text requiring a lower level of thinking or may be a fill-in-the blank worksheet that is on the text meaning (rather than on a comprehension skill or vocabulary words).
Meaning of text/ comprehension— higher level	m3 m4	Students are involved in talk (m3) or writing (m4) about the meaning of text which is engaging them in higher level thinking. This is talk or writing about text that is challenging to the children and is at either a high level of text interpretation or goes beyond the text: generalization, application, evaluation, aesthetic response. Needless to say, a child must go beyond a yes or no answer (e.g., in the case of an opinion or aesthetic response).

Level 4: Activity	Code	Definition
Comprehension skill	c	Students are engaged in a comprehension activity (other than a comprehension strategy) which is at a lower level of thinking (e.g., traditional skill work such as identifying main idea, cause-effect, fact-opinion). The activity is designed to foster their capacity to understand comprehension skills. This differs from "m1" in that it is more likely to be a decontextualized lesson than tied to questions about a particular text.
Comprehension strategy	cs	Students are engaged in use of a comprehension strategy that will transfer to other reading and in which this notion of transfer IS (typically) mentioned. A strategy is a routine designed to improve children's overall comprehension especially for new passages. Common examples include reciprocal teaching and questioning the author. The key to distinguishing between a skill and a strategy is the emphasis on a transferable routine. For example, predicting done for the sake of completing a worksheet would be a "c," but done with the explicit idea that readers can and should use it when they read would be a "cs." A teacher will specifically discuss transfer or signal transfer through a comment such as, "Good readers summarize as they read to keep them remembering the important ideas."
Writing	w	Students are engaged in writing ideas (not just writing words); focus is on composition, not meaning of text (which would be m2 or m4).
Word ID	wi	Students are focusing on identifying words. For example, the teacher or someone else is telling them a word when they get stuck during reading or the teacher is reviewing words prior to reading.
Sight words	sw	Students are drilling on sight words. (Word wall would be coded as "sw.")
Phonics	p1 p2 p3 p4	Students are focusing on symbol/sound correspondences (p1), letter-by-letter decoding (p2), or decoding by onset and rime or analogy (p3), but this is not tied to decoding of words while reading. If students are decoding multisyllabic words, code as "p4" (e.g., "Making words" would be coded as "p2," but also code as "p3" if word sorting by phonograms is done).
Word recognition strategy(ies)	wr	Students are focusing on use of 1 or more strategies to figure out words while reading, typically prompted by the teacher.

(*Continued*)

(*Continued*)

Level 4: Activity	Code	Definition
Phonemic awareness	pa	Students are identifying the sounds in words or blending sounds together (an oral activity). The purpose is to develop phonemic awareness, not letter-sound knowledge (e.g., Sound Box technique would be coded as "pa" since the focus is on learning the sounds in words).
Letter ID	li	Students are focusing on letter name identification
Spelling	s	Students are focusing on how to spell word(s)
Other	o	Literacy focus other than one of the above
Not applicable	9	None of the above apply

Level 5: Material	Code	Definition
Narrative	n	Narrative trade book (e.g., narrative picture book, novel, poem, other trade book)
Informational	i	Informational trade book, reference book (encyclopedia, etc.), newspapers, magazines, Weekly Readers
Student writing	w	Student writing (more than words or disconnected sentences) is being used (finished or in progress)
Board/chart	b	Board, chart, or card is being used (e.g., blackboard, pocket chart, hanging chart, flashcards)
Worksheet	s	Worksheet, workbook page, sheet of paper, individual whiteboards for one-word or one-sentence answers
Other	o	Something other than the above is being used, for example, dictionary
Not applicable	9	None of the above seem to apply

Level 6: Interaction Style	Code	Definition
Telling	t	Telling or giving children information, explaining how to do something
Modeling	m	The teacher is coded as explicitly showing/demonstrating the steps of how to do something or how to do a process as opposed to simply explaining it (e.g., a teacher models fluent reading after she models word-by-word readings, and she talks about the difference. A teacher reading her own book as kids are reading would *not* be coded as modeling since she is not being explicit).

Level 6: Interaction Style	Code	Definition
Recitation	r	The teacher is coded as engaging the students in answering questions, or responding, usually low-level q-a-q-a. The purpose primarily appears to be getting the children to answer the questions asked rather than engaging them in a formal discussion or fostering independence in terms of answering questions with more complete thinking.
Coaching/ scaffolding	c	The teacher is coded as prompting/providing support which will transfer to other situations as students are attempting to perform a strategy or activity or to answer a question. The teacher's apparent purpose is to foster independence to get a more complete action or to help students elaborate on an answer (rather than to simply get a student to answer a question).
Listening/ watching	l	Teacher is listening or watching **and** giving feedback as students are engaged in activity. Do not code as listening if the listening is only a part of recitation.
Reading aloud	ra	Teacher is reading aloud to students.
Assessment	a	Engaging in questioning/explaining/providing of directions for the purpose of assessing student performance. Typically this would involve record keeping.
Other	o	Interaction style other than what is listed above. Listening or watching without giving feedback would be coded as "other."

Level 7: Type of expected pupil response	Code	Definition
Reading	r	Students are to be reading. Code as "r" if students are reading individually or in pairs.
Reading turn-taking	r-tt	Students in group are to be reading by taking turns
Orally responding	or	Students are to be orally responding. Oral responding is coded when there is choral responding, partners sharing ideas, or a majority of children in the group responding at the same time.
Oral turn-taking	or-t	Students in a group either wait to be called on or wait to take turns as they orally respond. Recitation most likely would have been coded at level 6.
Listening	l	Students in a group are to be listening (and no student is reading or orally responding). Typically this is coded when the teacher is telling children information (at level 6) or is reading aloud to the children (at level 4 and 6).

(Continued)

(Continued)

Level 7: Type of expected pupil response	Code	Definition
Writing	w	Students are to be writing words, sentences, or paragraphs
Manipulating	m	Students are to be manipulating, using their hands (other than writing; e.g., code as "m" if children are coloring or completing a multiple choice activity).
Other	o	Some form of responding other than what is listed above is expected
Not applicable	9	None of the above seem to apply

References

Allington, R.L., & Cunningham, P.M. (2007). *Schools that work: Where all children read and write* (3rd ed.). Boston: Allyn & Bacon/Pearson.

Au, K.H., Raphael, T.E., & Mooney, K. (2008). Improving reading achievement in elementary schools: Guiding change in a time of standards. In S. Wepner & D. Strickland (Eds.), *Supervision of reading programs* (4th ed.; pp. 71–89). New York: Teachers College Press.

Biancarosa, G., Bryk, A.S., & Dexter, E.R. (2010). Assessing the value-added effects of Literacy Collaborative professional development on student learning. *The Elementary School Journal, 11*(1), 7–34.

Bean, R.M., Draper, J.A., Hall, V., Vandermolen, J., & Zigmond, N. (2010). Coaches and coaching in Reading First schools: A reality check. *Elementary School Journal, 111*, 87–114.

Cox, B.E., & Hopkins, C.J. (2006). Building on theoretical principles gleaned from Reading Recovery to inform classroom practice. *Reading Research Quarterly, 41*(2), 254–267.

Curtis, R. (2011). *Achievement First: Developing a teacher performance management system that recognizes excellence.* Washington, DC: The Aspen Institute. Retrieved January 13, 2014 from: http://www.aspeninstitute.org/sites/default/files/content/docs/education%20and%20society%20program/AI_Achievement%20First_performance%20mangmt.pdf

Dillon, D.R., O'Brien, D.G., Sato, M., & Kelly, C.M. (2011). Professional development and teacher education in reading instruction. In M. Kamil, P. D. Pearson, E. Moje, & P. Afflerbach (Eds.), *Handbook of reading research, Vol. IV.* New York: Routledge.

Doubek, M.B., & Cooper, E.J. (2007). Closing the gap through professional development: Implications for reading research. *Reading Research Quarterly, 42*(3), 411–415.

Duffy, G.G. (2004). Teachers who improve reading achievement: What research says about what they do and how to develop them. In D. Strickland & M. Kamil (Eds.), *Improving reading achievement through professional development* (pp. 3–22). Norwood, MA: Christopher-Gordon Publishers.

DuFour, R., Eaker, R., & Many, T. (2006). *Learning by doing: A handbook for professional development communities at work.* Bloomington, IN: Solution Tree Press.

Fuchs, D., Fuchs, L., & Vaughn, S. (Eds.). (2008). *Response to intervention: A framework for reading educators.* Newark, DE: International Reading Association.

Fullan, M. (2005). *Leadership and sustainability: System thinkers in action.* Thousand Oaks, CA: Corwin.

Gaffney, J., & Anderson, R.C. (2000). Trends in reading research in the United States: Changing intellectual currents over three decades. In M. Kamil, P. Mosenthal, P. D. Pearson, & R. Barr (Eds.), *Handbook of reading research, Vol. III,* 53–76. Mahwah, NJ: Erlbaum.

Goe, L., Bell, C., & Little, O. (2008). *Approaches to evaluating teacher effectiveness: A research synthesis.* Washington, DC: National Comprehensive Center for Teacher Quality.

Guthrie, J.T., Wigfield, A., Barbosa, P., Perencevich, K.C., Taboada, A., Davis, M.H., Scafiddi, N., & Tonks, S. (2004). Increasing reading comprehension and engagement through concept-oriented reading instruction. *Journal of Educational Psychology, 96*(3), 403–423.

Hoffman, J., Maloch, B., & Sailors, M. (2011). Researching the teaching of reading through direct observation. In M. Kamil, P. D. Pearson, E. Moje, & P. Afflerbach (Eds.), *Handbook of reading research, Vol. IV,* 3–33. New York: Routledge.

Jerald, C.D., & Van Hook, K. (2011). *More than measurement: The TAP Systems lessons learned for designing better teacher evaluation systems.* Santa Monica, CA: National Institute for Excellence in Teaching.

Joyce, B.R., & Showers, B. (2002). *Student achievement through staff development* (3rd ed.). Alexandria, VA: Association for Supervision and Curriculum Development.

Kennedy, E. (2010). Improving literacy achievement in a high-poverty school: Empowering classroom teachers through professional development. *Reading Research Quarterly, 45*(4), 384–387.

Kennedy, E., & Shiel, G. (2010). Raising literacy levels with collaborative on-site professional development in an urban disadvantaged school. *The Reading Teacher, 63*(5), 372–383.

Leithwood, K., Louis, K.S., Anderson, S., & Wahlstrom, K. (2004). *How leadership influences student learning.* New York: The Wallace Foundation.

Matsumura, L.C., Garnier, H.E., Correnti, R., Junker, B., & Bickel, D.D. (2010). Investigating the effectiveness of a comprehensive literacy coaching program in schools with high teacher mobility. *Elementary School Journal, 111,* 35–62.

McIntyre, E., Kyle, D., & Moore, G. (2006). A primary-grade teacher's guidance toward small-group dialogue. *Reading Research Quarterly, 41*(1), 36–66.

National Institute for Excellence in Teaching. (2013). *Beyond job-embedded: Ensuring good professional development gets results in Knox County schools.* Retrieved February 3, 2014 from: eric.ed.gov/?id=ED533379

Peterson, D.S. (2013). Professional learning: Professional learning communities (PLCs), whole school meetings and cross-school sharing. In B.M. Taylor & N.K. Duke (Eds.), *Handbook on effective literacy instruction.* New York: Guilford.

Peterson, D.S., Taylor, B.M., Burnham, B., & Schock, R. (2008). Reflective coaching conversations: A missing piece. *The Reading Teacher, 62*(6), 500–509.

Pigott, T., & Barr, R. (2000). Designing programmatic interventions. In M. Kamil, P. Mosenthal, P. D. Pearson, & R. Barr (Eds.), *Handbook of reading research, Vol. III* (pp. 99–108). Mahwah, NJ: Erlbaum.

Raudenbush, S.W., & Bryk, A.S. (2002). *Hierarchical linear models* (2nd ed.). Thousand Oaks, CA: Sage Publications.

Sailors, M. (2009). Improving comprehension instruction through quality professional development. In S. Israel & G. Duffy (Eds.), *Handbook of research on reading comprehension.* New York: Routledge.

Sailors, M., & Price, L. (2010). Professional development that supports the teaching of cognitive reading instruction. *Elementary School Journal, 110*, 301–322.

Saunders, W.M., Goldenberg, C.N., & Gallimore, R. (2009). Increasing achievement by focusing grade-level teams on improving classroom learning: A prospective quasi-experimental study of Title I schools. *American Educational Research Journal, 46*(4), 1006–1033.

Senechal, M. (2006). Testing the home literacy model: Parent involvement in kindergarten is differentially related to grade 4 reading comprehension, fluency, spelling, and reading for pleasure. *Scientific Studies of Reading, 10*, 59–87.

Taylor, B. (2003). *School Change Observation Scheme*. Minneapolis, MN: University of Minnesota.

Taylor, B. (2012). *Catching schools: An action guide to school-wide reading improvement*. Portsmouth, NH: Heinemann.

Taylor, B.M., Pearson, P.D., Peterson, D.S., & Rodriguez, M.C. (2003). Reading growth in high-poverty classrooms: The influence of teacher practices that encourage cognitive engagement in literacy learning. *The Elementary School Journal, 104*(1), 3–28.

Taylor, B.M., Pearson, P.D., Peterson, D.S., & Rodriguez, M.C. (2005). The CIERA School Change Framework: An evidence-based approach to professional development and school reading improvement. *Reading Research Quarterly, 40*(1), 40–69.

Taylor, B.M., & Peterson, D.S. (2003). *Year 1 report of the Minnesota REA School Change project*. St. Paul, MN: University of Minnesota, Minnesota Center for Reading Research.

Taylor, B.M., & Peterson, D.S. (2006a). *The impact of the school change framework in twenty-three Minnesota REA schools*. St. Paul, MN: University of Minnesota, Minnesota Center for Reading Research.

Taylor, B.M., & Peterson, D.S. (2006b). *Year 3 report of the Minnesota Reading First Cohort 1 School Change project*. St. Paul, MN: University of Minnesota, Minnesota Center for Reading Research.

Taylor, B.M., & Peterson, D.S. (2006c). *Year 1 report of the Minnesota Reading First Cohort 2 School Change project*. St. Paul, MN: University of Minnesota: Minnesota Center for Reading Research.

Taylor, B.M., & Peterson, D.S. (2007a). *Year 2 report of the Minnesota Reading First Cohort 2 School Change project*. St. Paul, MN: University of Minnesota: Minnesota Center for Reading Research.

Taylor, B.M., & Peterson, D.S. (2007b). Steps for school-wide reading improvement. In Taylor & Ysseldyke (Eds.) *Educational interventions for struggling readers, K-6*. New York: Teachers College Press.

Taylor, B.M., Peterson, D.S., Marx, M., & Chein, M. (2007). Scaling up reading reform in high-poverty elementary schools. In B. Taylor & J. Ysseldyke (Eds.), *Educational interventions for struggling readers, K-6*. New York: Teachers College Press.

Taylor, B.M., Peterson, D.S., Pearson, P.D., & Rodriguez, M.C. (2002). Looking inside classrooms: Reflecting on the "how" as well as the "what" in effective reading instruction. *The Reading Teacher, 56*(3), 270–279.

Timperley, H.S., & Parr, J.M. (2007). Closing the achievement gap through evidence-based inquiry at multiple levels of the education system. *Journal of Advanced Academics, 19*(1), 90–115.

Valli, L., & Hawley, W.D. (2007). Designing and implementing school-based professional development. In W. Hawley & D. Rollie (Eds.), *The keys to effective schools: Educational reform as continuous improvement* (2nd ed., pp. 86–96). Thousand Oaks, CA: Sage/Corwin Publishers.

Weigel, D.J., Martin, S.S., & Bennett, K.K. (2006). Contributions of the home literacy environment to preschool-aged children's emerging literacy and language skills. *Early Childhood Language Development and Care, 176*, 357–378.

8

ASSESSING LITERACY TEACHING

Using the Text Environment as a Window into the Examination of Literacy Practices

James Hoffman and Misty Sailors

In the late nineteenth century, Joseph Mayer Rice set out on a yearlong journey across America to observe teaching in public elementary schools. Rice's goal was to describe the state of public education with particular reference to the teaching of reading, writing, and mathematics. Rice observed in classrooms across the country, assessing the quality of teaching. While not trained or experienced as an educator, Rice was an early progressive in his regard for the potential for scientific methods to study teaching. Rice was also an advocate for efficiency. Everyone should play their role to maximize productivity and minimize waste. Through the systematic observation of practice, he believed, we could allow science to guide reform. Rice's tools consisted of his pen and his notebook where he recorded what he saw and heard through observations and his interviews. With only a few exceptions, Rice found the quality of teaching in schools appalling. Rice documents incident after incident of teachers not working hard, making errors in content, and drilling students over mindless matters into numbness. Rather than blame teachers, Rice represented teachers as victims of a system that was corrupt and inefficient. District superintendents, school boards, and campus administrators were as much to blame for failures of education as the teachers.

By today's standards for rigor in observation and assessment, Rice would have been challenged in his claims. But Rice's efforts stand as a testimony and a reminder regarding the assessment of teaching. Walk into any elementary classroom during instructional time and what do you see? Of course, answers will vary as a function of the teacher, the students, and the context. Those committed to valid assessment of teaching will commit to multiple samples of teaching and the limiting of inferences around teaching within particular contexts. Answers will also vary as a function of the observers who enter the classroom space and a function of their backgrounds, their purposes, and their agendas. Those committed to the valid assessment of teaching often go to extremes (e.g., rigorous training toward standardization of instruments) to ensure that the influence of the observer is minimized in the assessment of teaching. Answers will also vary as a result of the tools used to guide, interpret, and express the findings associated with an observation. The tools of assessment are both physical (e.g., the checklist, the notepad) and philosophical (e.g., What counts as teaching? What is visible vs. not visible? What is verbal vs. what is non-verbal? What is easily measured vs. what is more abstract, intuitive, emotional, and even aesthetic?). As observers: we see what we expect to see. We see what is allowed to be seen. We see what we want to see. We see what others allow us to see. Answers will vary.

But surely, numbers don't lie. In the mid-twentieth century, with behaviorism in education at its zenith, the assessment of teaching began to rely on counting teacher behaviors. Ned Flanders introduced the FIAC (Flanders Interaction Assessment Categories), which would allow observers to count the frequency of teacher behaviors that were authoritative (e.g., asking questions, lecturing) as opposed to democratic (e.g., students initiating questions), and then related these behaviors to achievement and attitudinal outcomes. Dunkin and Biddle (1974) described this model for research as oriented toward both the "process and product" of teaching. Programs of research during this period (e.g., Brophy and Good, 1986, in the Texas Teacher Effectiveness Studies; Stallings, 1975, in the Follow Through Studies; Evertson & Green, 1986, in the classroom management studies) produced list after list of teacher behaviors associated with raising academic outcomes. Attempts to shift the consideration of teaching to include the "mental lives of teachers" (e.g., teacher planning, interactive decision making) failed the test of observable behaviors. While research around teacher thinking gathered momentum within the theoretical and research communities advocating for socioconstructivist perspectives (Shulman, 1986), in practice, the findings from the socioconstructivist perspective were largely ignored. The findings from the behaviorist tradition were quickly turned into teacher assessment instruments used to evaluate the quality of teaching. These are the same findings used today in most teacher assessments. Numbers may not lie, but do they tell the whole story?

In the midst of the struggle between behaviorists and socioconstructivist perspectives for teacher observation and assessment, Walter Doyle (1983) proposed a quite remarkable shift in perspective. Don't begin by watching the teacher. When you walk into a classroom, focus on what the students are doing (a nod to the behaviorist) and saying (a nice middle ground) and thinking (a nod to the socioconstructivist). Examine the work for the challenges presented to the learner. Examine the work for how it was introduced, engaged with, negotiated, supported, and evaluated. Examine the work for the tensions experienced and the strategizing that took place around these tensions. This notion of "task" and "academic work" fit nicely into the socioconstructivist view on activity and activity systems in the classrooms. Activity systems are directed toward the production of certain "products" that demand the use of tools and colleagues to make progress toward goals. This view of activity is no different in principle for infants as it is for children as it is for adults. The goals get loftier, the tools more sophisticated, and the forms of collaboration more complex, but it is the work we do that defines the moment. No part of the activity system can be analyzed outside of attention to the whole and no analysis of the whole can be fulfilled without attention to how the parts are working. This academic work perspective, or task perspective, or activity perspective requires conversations and close inspection of tool use and inspection of the artifacts of learning.

In this chapter we present a description of a tool that we have used to inspect the literacy practices in elementary and middle school classrooms. Following Doyle, we focus on the child and their work. We focus on the tools, artifacts, and work around and in the literacy environment. We inspect the teaching as it interacts with the learner in the context of activity. We begin this chapter with a general description of the tool, its theoretical roots, and research base. We move to focus specifically on the student talk that surrounds the texts in classrooms as we see these conversations as particularly revealing of the teaching and learning.

Perspective

The view of teaching literacy that guides our work is based on the social practice perspective. From this perspective, literacy is more than just the ability to decode and comprehend texts. Rather, literacy practices are "the general cultural ways of utilizing written language, which people draw upon in their lives. In the simplest sense literacy practices are what people do with literacy" (Barton & Hamilton, 2000, p. 7), making literacy practices inclusive of values, attitudes, feelings, and social relationships. Literacy practices, therefore, include people's awareness of literacy, how they talk about it, and how they make sense of it. Although these processes are internal to the individual, they also connect people to each other (Barton & Hamilton, 2000).

That said, literacy acts arise out of the practices of a community and are instantiated as literacy events, or those acts in which "a piece of writing is integral to the nature of the participants' interactions and their interpretative processes" (Heath, 1983, p. 93). Literacy events give insight into the literacy practices of the community through the documentable texts located there within (Ormerod & Ivanic, 2000). Texts are both a form of verbal and visual representation of practices as well as "permanent and material evidence" (Tusting, 2000, p. 43). In a Vygotskian sense, texts represent mediated action and are representative of individuals and the goal-oriented activity in which the individual engages (Yamagata-Lynch, 2010). Texts (or tools, in a Vygotskian sense) facilitate engagement in an activity (Engeström, 1993). In keeping with this framework, individuals not only internalize the processes implicated in tool-mediated activities, but also construct and adapt activities in ways that lead to the modification of those tools (Yamagata-Lynch, 2010; Miettinen, 2001). In fact, individuals both shape tools and are shaped by the tools around them (Brandt & Clinton, 2002).

However, tools are but one way to think about literacy practices. Other aspects are not as easily observable. Included in these unobservable aspects of literacy practices are the mental construction, sense-making, purpose-setting, and valuing that go on inside people's heads. The ways in which people think about literacy, their awareness of it, their constructions of it, how they talk about it, and how they make sense of it are all indicative of the literacy practices of a society. When combined, the observable and "interpretivistic aspects" (how the members of the community use, think about, are aware of, construct, talk about, and how those members make sense of the texts; Barton & Hamilton, 2000) become an inference to the larger global patterns of literacy practices within a particular community. These inferences then become indicative of the role literacy plays in the lives of the members of the society (Barton & Hamilton, 1998; Barton, Hamilton, & Ivanic, 2000).

Our work within the social practice perspective led us to design an instrument (Hoffman & Sailors, 2004) that contains an identified set of literacy tools used in classrooms across the U.S., a set of rubrics associated with each literacy tool, and a set of benchmarks, scales, and holistic rating for those literacy tools, how they are used, and what is understood about them. In the next section, we briefly summarize each of the three sections of the instrument and the research that surrounds the use of the instrument.

The TEX-IN3

The TEX-IN3 is an acronym for the three principal components of the instrument: the Text Inventory, the Text-In-Use observation, and the Text Interview. The TEX-IN3 is designed to (a) capture and represent the range and qualities of texts in classrooms; (b) observe teachers and students as they engage with these texts during instruction; and (c) record the understandings of the forms, functions, and uses of these texts by teachers and students.

Text Inventory. The Text Inventory is a description and a valuing of the physical text environment in the classroom. We identified a set of 17 text types that helped us organize the inventory of the texts in the classroom (see Table 8.1, adopted from Hoffman & Sailors, 2002). Within these categories of texts there are several broad dimensions of texts to examine: public and personal; extended and limited; local and commercial; process and product. Once the texts are inventoried, a five-point rubric rates the quality of each of the text types. Two additional rubric ratings are applied during the inventory. The first applies to the overall effectiveness of the text environment. The second holistic rating scale applies to the quality of the

TABLE 8.1 Text types

Text types and examples	Explanation
Assessments: End-of-book tests, spelling and grammar tests, portfolios, etc.	Include tests or testing materials used by the students in the classroom. These may appear as student testing protocols from formal or informal assessments. Assessments are used for a variety of instructional purposes and goals.
Computer/Electronic: Email, Internet access, reading and authoring applications, tests or test preparation, recorded books, news, text messaging systems, etc.	Include any texts that are accessed and used through an electronic medium.
Extended Text Process Charts: Inquiry charts, language charts, math or reading strategies, rubrics, writing process charts, etc.	Appear as connected texts (multi-sentence) that are usually procedural and guide students toward the use of a particular process or strategy.
Games/Puzzles/Manipulatives: Board games (Bingo, Clue), word sorts, magnetic poetry, etc.	Include games designed for student use (often as independent or small group work) and features.
Instructional Aids: Morning messages, labels, vocabulary lists, word banks, color charts, science/math posters, etc.	Often public and often appear as a poster. They are always used to support instruction or represent past instruction. Often these instructional aid charts are used as a visual aid to support direct instruction or mini-lessons.
Journals: Reading response logs, personal and/or writing journals, content logs (inquiry in the subject areas), etc.	Often "local" texts created by the students based primarily on their work and writing. "Spiral folders" where students record their work in response to assignments may be considered in this category.
Leveled Books: Basal readers, "little books," guided reading books and decodable readers, etc.	Often found in "book format," but they differ from trade books because they are created explicitly for instruction and are leveled for difficulty and accessibility.
Limited Text Process Charts: Alphabet charts, word walls, etc.	Include letter/word level texts that are procedural and guide the students in the use of a particular strategy or set of strategies. These are similar to the Extended Text Charts in purpose and design; however, they tend to focus at the letter or word level.
Organizational/Management Charts: Work boards, class rules, local or state curricular objectives, multiplication facts charts, student helper charts, etc.	Often used to manage or organize the social, academic, or curricular work within the classroom. They may be enlarged or small, local or public.
Reference Materials: Thesaurus, globes, maps, atlases, dictionaries, encyclopedias, etc.	Used as resources for finding information (e.g., word spellings, locations, how to do something).

Text types and examples	Explanation
Serials: Scholastic newspapers, *Ranger Rick, Highlights,* classroom news reports, school newsletters, etc.	Often found moving in and out of a classroom on a regular basis.
Social/Personal/Inspirational displays: Child-of-the-week poster, "Readers, Read!," etc.	Used to motivate and inspire. They may come from a commercial source or they might be created locally.
Student/Teacher Published Works: Student-authored books, reports from inquiry projects, text innovations, etc.	Usually locally authored books or publications that are on display and accessible for students to read.
Text books: Content area books (science, social studies, math, handwriting, etc.)	These literacy tools are student texts that are typically identified with a subject/content area that are typically leveled by grade and the difficulty levels increase with each grade level.
Trade Books: "Library books" (picture books, chapter books, poetry, etc.)	Typically found in "book format" and do not have any obvious instructional design features.
Work Product Displays: Writing samples, tests, etc.	Displayed teacher or student work that is being "celebrated" and set forward for others to read and enjoy.
Writing on Paper: Story and sentence starters, reading/math/phonics/spelling worksheets, etc.	Conceptualized on a continuum ranging from tightly constrained text response formats (e.g., check marks, fill in the blank, multiple choice) to entirely open-ended response/writing formats (e.g., blank paper, lined paper).

"local texts" in the classrooms, or those texts that are created by the teacher and/or the student as part of the literacy environment (Maloch, Hoffman, & Patterson, 2004). And, while the rubrics allow for a rating of the physical texts, they don't answer the questions: How, when, and by whom are these texts used? This brings us to the second component of the instrument, the Texts In-Use.

Texts In-Use. The Texts In-Use allowed us to watch the students and the teachers as they engaged with the texts in the classroom, using a relatively low inference observation scheme in which engagements with texts in specific time bands are counted and sorted based on the types of texts engaged with and the context in which they are used. We typically focus our observations on the teacher and three students in the class: a highly skilled reader, an on-grade-level reader, and a below-grade-level reader. The coding scheme is modeled after the work of Jane Stallings (Stallings et al., 1975, for example) and allows us to make a direct connection to the effective teaching literature, where levels of sustained engagement are seen as closely tied to achievement growth. We calculate an "in-use" score from our observations that is considerate of the amount of engaged time weighted by the quality rating for the texts used by students. And, although these observations allow us to begin to understand the literacy practices, there are still aspects of it that we cannot access through direct observation. We simply cannot observe what is inside a student's head. We have to talk to the student to reveal these understandings.

Text Interviews. The third and final component of the TEX-IN3 refers to the Text Interviews. The Text Interviews are intended to capture the beliefs, valuing, and understandings about text in the classroom by the teacher and the students. We start our interviews with the teacher, asking her to both rank and rate the texts in her classroom. We present the teacher with 17 cards, each with the name of a text category. We talk about these briefly in terms of the terminology we are using, pointing out whenever we can how these texts appear in the classroom. We ask her to rank them from most to least important and we ask them to then rate each of them individually in terms of their importance. As the teacher is ranking and rating, we ask her to talk aloud, specifically addressing these questions: Why is it important? Who uses it? How is it used? Based on the interviews, we assign a rating for the teacher's understanding and valuing of each of the text types in her classroom.

Last, but not least, the student interview is conducted in a sort of reading-the-room strategy. Each of the three students is asked to lead the observer on a tour of the print in the room. We identify texts that we saw the students using and ask them to think aloud for us, providing us with such information as: What is this text? What is it for? Who uses it? How is it used? We then talk with the students about other texts in the room, until we have covered at least one of each of the text types. Based on these interviews the observer then assigns a rating to the students' understanding and valuing of each of the text types in their classroom.

Uses of the TEX-IN3

We have successfully used the instrument to document differences in the print environment of elementary and middle school classrooms across the country (Hoffman, Roller et al., 2005) and the role of the text environment in improving reading comprehension (Hoffman, Sailors, Duffy, & Beretvas, 2004). We have also used the instrument to identify the texts that were most associated with reading achievement in high-performing classrooms (Sailors & Hoffman, 2010). Finally, we have written about the instrument as a way of supporting a teacher's reflective teaching practices (Hoffman & Sailors, 2004) and in the use of the tool as a means of professional development for teachers (Sailors, Kumar, Blady, & Willson, 2013).

Conversations around Texts

We have come to believe that a focus on the interview portion of the TEX-IN3 can reveal qualities of the teaching and learning dialogue within classrooms. Furthermore, we assert that students in print-rich classrooms "take up" the language that surrounds the texts in their classrooms as part of the literacy practices that surround them; in many cases, the language that the students "take up" sounds suspiciously like the language of their teacher. Furthermore, we assert that this language becomes a frame around which we can understand how texts in classrooms work for students as they become fully participatory in their literacy community. In the next section of this chapter, we will provide evidence for our assertions.

Evidence

In order to test these assertions, we drew upon interviews from six students, drawn from three print-rich classrooms in three different schools. These classrooms scored exceedingly high on all three measures of the TEX-IN3 and were all located in a large metropolitan area in the Southwest. Table 8.2 illustrates the students who participated in this study with us.

Our data drew from interviews we conducted with these six students. During each interview, we followed the protocol in the TEX-IN3 but allowed for lingering conversations about each of the texts in the classroom. We asked the children to take us on a tour of the classroom, reading the room for us. We asked them questions such as, "What is this text? What is it for? How did it get there? Who uses it? When? Do you use it? When? Is it important? Why? What do you like about it?" We audiotaped each of the interviews and transcribed them, using denaturalized methods (Oliver, Serovich, & Mason, 2005). We organized the data around emergent categories that we heard from the students, formulating these categories with a constant return to the original audio files. Our findings organize themselves around four broad categories, including (a) texts are functional and purposeful; (b) we "do" things with texts; (c) these texts belong to "us"; and (d) we value some texts more than others. We present each in the sections that follow.

TABLE 8.2 Students

Student	Gender	Grade	Ethnicity	Classroom
1	Female	2	African-American	A
2	Female	5	African-American	B
3	Male	5	Hispanic	B
4	Female	2	Hispanic	C
5	Male	2	Hispanic	C
6	Male	2	African-American	C

Texts Are Functional and Purposeful

Texts, for these students, were not only pervasive, they were functional. And, while we did not set out to document the types of texts in these classrooms, we feel compelled to present the variety of texts students discussed during their interviews. The sheer variety of texts they discussed and the excitement with which students discussed them with us simply cannot be ignored. Students showed us and talked to us about their journals, including personal journals, literature response logs, content inquiry logs (math, science, and social studies), and draft writing. Students showed us and talked about the instructional aids (posters and charts that support instruction) in their classrooms, including the chart that displayed their "observations, connections, and wonderings" and told us of the importance of charts such as this one for their learning. Brianna, for example, showed us the word walls in her classroom and explained to us how that the word walls were helpful for "tricky words, like *thought*."

Students showed us and talked to us about the organizational/management charts in their classrooms, including charts that managed the social, academic, and curricular work of these classrooms and students. Students showed us their electronic writing (located on the classroom computers) and procedural charts that helped them navigate new websites. They showed us student-helper charts, work boards, class rules, and charts that documented the number of books read by students. These charts served a purpose in the classroom. For example, Shanna showed us the job chart in her classroom and explained that she is "the line leader [pointing to the chart]" and that her job is to lock the door on their way to lunch and then "give the keys to my teacher to make sure she doesn't get locked out."

Finally, the prominence of trade books cannot be underestimated in these classrooms. Trade books were important to the students we talked to and they appreciated the books, enjoyed them, and actively used them in their learning. For example, Brianna proudly showed us the biographies on display in her classroom. Her favorite biography was the Anne Frank book she picked up and embraced as she explained why it was her favorite: "It was so sad and this one made my mom cry. I also like it because I can use it to study about biographies."

Not only were texts functional, there seemed to be a layering of texts in the classrooms. For example, Shanna explained to us how her journal entries become part of an instructional aid that prominently displays the "observations, wonderings, and connections" of students in the class. She explained, "These are our journals, our journals that we use [pointing to her journal]. I wrote all over mine because I like the book and because I was really into it and sometimes we ask questions in our journal." She went onto explain that her teacher "picks what different kids write down [in their journal] and writes them up there [pointing to the chart]."

Public texts (displayed for all to see and use) and private texts (stored in private spaces, as in a desk or personal reading basket) in the classroom were used often as referent texts. For example, Stephanie told us the bulletin board that declared, "Yum!

I'm thinking about cookies!" that displayed her work (and that of her classmates) was intended for two purposes. First, she said, her teacher had them work at their desks (private) to write down what they were thinking about cookies. Then, they were supposed to practice using quotation marks. Finally, those private texts became public when they were decorated and placed on the bulletin board. The purpose for making those texts public, according to Stephanie, was, "In case you forget where they [quotation marks] go, you can look up there [pointing to the display]."

We "Do" Things with Texts

Not only were the texts functional and purposeful, their presence created a sense of "doing" literacy in these classrooms. For example, David told us about the way in which they use trade books during their science lessons, "Well we look up stuff in here and she reads this stuff to us and after that we study about it . . . like with the globe and the flashlight we learned that at night the sun doesn't go down it . . . the earth turns in circles." Again, we heard this in the conversation with Shanna about the Literature Circle management chart hanging just above the carpeted area in her classroom. She said,

> That right here is Literature Circles. It's like a group reading session. And it's all like we get . . . like *Music of the Dolphins* is what I'm reading and so we just get the book and we lay down and read for a little bit and then when the time is over we sit up and we talk about what our favorite part [was] and we like push each other to get a little bit more, like if we asked 'How did you like the book?' and 'It was good' but we ask them 'Why?' and they can answer the question.

In both of these cases, texts were the reason to engage in acts of literacy while the literacy act was driving the type of text used by the students.

It was clear from our conversations with these students that texts were not only a pervasive part of their daily lives, but their interactions with texts were routine. For example, Alex told us that every Monday he "puts" (self-selects) books in his "book box" so he has "something to read anytime" he "needs it." He explained how he and others select a book:

> You look in the book [picking up a book and starting to look through it] and if there is a lot of words you can't read, it's too hard for you and if you read it really fast, it's too easy for you. And, if you read it just right that means the book is just right for you.

We heard this notion of routine over and over in our interviews. Not only did students tell us they wrote or read "almost all the time," students seemed to revel in the fact that they knew not only what to expect and how to do what they were asked, but also appeared very confident in telling us about those literacy routines.

In addition, there was a sense of audience related to the texts in which the students spoke. This sense was related to themselves as authors and outsiders who came into their classrooms as visitors. For example, when asked why their collection of biographies is important, Brianna told us that "someone might be coming to this city, someone important, and they might walk in and see all these books are real and true and you must know that we are studying about biography." Likewise, Shanna told us that the "Observations, Connections, and Wonderings" chart displayed in her room are there "to show the school what we are learning."

Finally, learning was a result of their interactions with the texts in their classrooms for the students with whom we talked. For example, when discussing the science workstation, which contained both informational books as well as student science journals, Shanna told us it was her favorite. In fact, she said:

> The reason it is my favorite is because I like science a lot and it [the management chart] tell you like an even number and an odd number so my teacher picks what number we are supposed to write and like this side it goes into your brain, I mean on your paper. Here you are you writing stuff but on this side [pointing to the example of an interactive science journal entry hanging above the station] it goes out and into your brain because you are learning so much.

Similarly, Timmy told us that through the publication of his own books, he was able to "learn a lot" because publishing his own book helped him learn about his topic and "learn to investigate."

These Texts Belong to "Us"

While they talked about the importance of the texts in their classroom to their learning, there was a strong sense of "we" and "us" for what they've contributed to their environment across our conversations with the students.

Similarly, there was a strong sense of pride in their accomplishments as readers and writers. Often, when we asked students to talk to us about a particular text, those explanations were preceded by, "Wait! Let me find mine for you!" More often than not, explanations of texts were grounded in examples of their own work, such as the sample Reading the Room work Stephanie completed that morning during centers. Or, the This is My Heart product (model of a heart and its purpose and mechanics) completed by Alexis as a science project. And Timmy's signature on the Class Rules chart hanging prominently above the classroom door. A strong sense of "that's mine" and "it's here for others to read and enjoy and learn from" was a pervasive part of our conversations with these students.

Additionally, these students had a strong sense of self-identity as writers and proudly claimed their contributions to the classroom text environment. They appeared to be cognizant of who they were as readers and writers, where they had come from, and where they were headed. For example, in one of our conversations with Shanna, we were discussing her poem "Where I'm From." We asked her if she liked having her writing hanging on the wall for everyone to see. Her response was indicative of her self-identity:

> After we read "Where I'm From" by George Ella Lyon, we wrote our own poems. Some people did one poem, some people did two. I did one because that's all I felt like and it's all I have for right now but when I'm older, I bet I'll have more than that.

Others echoed similar identities. Stephanie, in fact, bragged to us that her book was sitting on the bookshelf next to Eric Carle's books, in case we wanted to read hers when we went to the reading center.

Finally, these students saw themselves as contributing authors to the text environment as viewed through what we consider to be ventriloquation. For example, when talking about the instructional aid labeled Circular Endings, Shanna pointed out that this text represents when she and her classmates learned about circular endings and then explained what circular endings are:

> Like when you're planting little seeds in the story [and that seed grows into a flower and] that flower it gets bigger and blooms . . . because like the people that read the book or see the movie, they don't really know what's going to happen at the end.

When we asked her if she uses circular endings in her writing, she answered with a resounding "yes" and, pointing to her poem, "I like to write poems!"

We Value Some Texts More than Others

While our findings thus far have indicated the importance of a variety of texts in the classrooms, some texts were valued by the students we interviewed more than other texts. For example, students told us that the most important texts in the classroom were those that they (and their peers) used often, such as the word walls. According to Shanna, the word walls in her classroom are helpful and she "would use it because I need a little help on my words and [pointing to a word on the wall] so, I barely know this word so I would need a little help on it." When asked what other texts their friends find helpful, Timothy said the games on the computer "tell you how to read." Students also valued texts that "help them become better writers," such as the "Where are you in your writing?" management chart, a circle hanging on the wall that lists the various stages of the writing process. Students move their clip based on where they are at the end of each writing period. Shanna said this chart can be very helpful to her (or her friends) if she "forgets where she is in the writing process."

Likewise, the texts students were most excited to tell us about appeared to be those that were local, or written by them, their teacher, or a combination. In fact, when we looked around the room at the texts inside these environments, we were taken aback by the percentage that were local in nature. It did not surprise us then that students in these classrooms talked first and foremost about the local texts and had a lot to say about them. For example, on the tour of Shanna's classroom, she pointed out the "Yellow Board," a poster hanging close to the reading carpet where she and her classmates spent free reading time. The Yellow Board was, in fact, the classroom rules. Shanna explained to us that it contained "what our class agreed to do, like hard work, be kind to each other, to our classmates and ourselves, careful of others." She went on to tell us that this text is very important to her and others in her class because it reminds them of how they should "treat each other."

Action

Rhodes and Shanklin (1993) frame their consideration of the literacy assessments teachers use in the classroom in terms of purposes. Assessments can inform the teacher and the student regarding development and strengths that are emerging. Assessments can become the basis for communication with the student and with others in problem solving and goal setting. Assessments can help teachers discover the power in their own teaching. We are quite certain that the application of the TEX-IN3 is similarly useful in guiding teacher learning across the purposes described by Rhodes and Shanklin. The TEX-IN3 can provide a window into literacy practices that become the basis for action. In this section, we focus on actions school leaders (principals, department heads, and literacy coaches, for example) can take, within a professional development framework, to improve the print environment of schools and classrooms, with special emphasis on what students understand and value about the print environment of their classrooms. We organize these suggestions around four broad themes: (a) gathering perspectives; (b) self-examination and literacy practices; (c) collaborative professional development environments; and (d) employing innovative practices. Each is explored in the following sections.

Gathering Perspectives

We are not the first (nor the last) to write about the importance of a print-rich environment for the literacy development of students. Earlier research talked about this topic in terms of structuring for a classroom "flooded" with print (Cambourne, 2000) and organizing for classrooms as "print laboratories" (Searfoss & Readence, 1983). We see the next steps for teachers and school administrators to learn more about the importance of these types of environments and how to organize instruction around them. Delving into the literature, we have identified a set of materials in Table 8.3 that might be helpful in approaching this topic. We provide a brief synopsis of each.

TABLE 8.3 Additional readings related to text environments

Reading	Summary
Sailors, M., Kumar, T., Blady, S., & Wilson, A. (2013). Print Environments as "Tools" for Literacy Teaching and Literacy Learning. In B. Taylor & N. Duke (Eds.). *Handbook on Effective Literacy Instruction* (pp. 46–71). New York: Guilford Press.	In this chapter, the authors present two extended case examples of the careful selection and use of literacy tools. One case is of an elementary classroom teacher and one is of a school leader. Both show how the print environment is structured to support literacy learning in light of research. The chapter concludes with critical reflection questions for teachers, instructional leaders, and teacher educators to consider in improving the print environment that surrounds students in classrooms and schools.
Sailors, M. (2013). Making Literacy a "Pervasive Part" of a Second Grade Classroom. *Pennsylvania Reads, 12,* 7–15.	In this case study, the author presents the print environment of one effective second grade teacher and the way she uses the print to equalize the educational experiences of the students in her classroom. The study presents the texts offered by the teacher, the way in which the print represented meaningful and purposeful literacy events, and how those events were grounded in her intentions and purposes for literacy.
Sailors, M., & Hoffman, J.V. (2011). Establishing a Print-rich Classroom and School Environment. In R.M. Bean & A.S. Dagen (Eds.), *Best Practices of Literacy Leaders in Schools* (p. 184–205). New York: Guilford Press.	In this chapter, the authors describe the findings of a study that explored the characteristics and qualities of the text environment in elementary and middle school classrooms that were linked to student growth in literacy. The authors also offer thoughts on the ways literacy leaders can support the growth of print-rich classrooms and schools.
Sailors, M., & Hoffman, J.V. (2010). The Text Environment and Learning to Read: Windows and Mirrors Shaping Literate Lives. In D. Wyse, R. Andrews, & J. Hoffman (Eds.), *The International Handbook of English, Language and Literacy Teaching* (pp. 294–304). New York: Routledge.	This chapter represents a literature review of the print environment in classrooms through the role of the windows and mirrors metaphor.
Maloch, B., Hoffman, J.V., & Patterson, B. (2004). Local Texts: Reading and Writing "of the Classroom." In J.V. Hoffman & D. Schallert (Eds.). *The Texts in Elementary Classrooms*. Michigan: Center for the Improvement of Early Reading Achievement.	This chapter explores the construct of "local" texts (those texts that are "of the classroom," p. 130), considers critical issues related to the use of and the potential value of local texts, and makes recommendations for teachers related to the inclusion of local texts in classrooms.

Self-Examination and Literacy Practices

We believe the TEX-IN3 can be used for self-evaluation as teachers explore the ways in which their print environment supports (or could be more supportive of) literacy development. Because we have written about the instrument in other venues (Hoffman & Sailors, 2004; Hoffman et al., 2004; Sailors & Hoffman, 2010, 2011) and above, we will not belabor the point here. What we believe is important for this conversation is that teachers work together to document and describe their text environment, the ways in which it is being used, and what the community members (teacher and students) believe and understand about it. Additionally, what is important is that teachers focus on what is there, versus what is not there, as taking an appreciative stance for what is present in classrooms and valuable to learners reduces the sense of being "judged" and encourages genuine dialogue around practice. The use of video recordings, audio recordings, and transcripts will help center attention on the language of students which will assist in the analysis of that language and what it means for "engagement" and "use."

Collaborative Professional Development Environments

As teachers and school leaders learn to improve the print environment of classrooms and whole schools, it is important that they work together to do so. Teachers should work in conjunction with each other (in teams) to identify those types of texts found in their classrooms and throughout their school and they should support each other in improving their print environments. A collaborative stance can be seen in the "ongoing process in which educators work together collaboratively in recurring cycles of collective inquiry and action research to achieve better results for the students they serve" (DuFour, DuFour, Eaker, & Many, 2010, p. 11) and are often called professional learning communities (PLCs). PLCs are structured in ways that allow teachers to trust each other, operate from a shared purpose, and encourage risk-taking around practice. This structure allows for teachers to explore, not only the types of texts they have in their classrooms, but how their students talk about the texts, what they understand about the texts, and what they value about the texts. We believe the interview section of the TEX-IN3 can serve as a focal point during meetings of the PLC that are focused on understanding how texts in classrooms work for students. We also believe that same section can assist teachers in reframing their classroom environment so students become fully participatory in their literacy community.

Employing Innovative Practices

In the cycle of teacher inquiry, evaluation is not the end but part of an ongoing process of "trying out" and examining progress toward goals. In development research, we work to create something that is powerful through small, iterative steps of change that are examined carefully.

School leaders can work with teachers to set goals for enhancing the text environment of their classrooms. This work may involve the introduction of or emphasis on more local texts in the classroom (Maloch et al., 2004; Sailors, 2013). This work may also involve the examination of the discourse used by teachers around texts and then looking for the effects in the ways the students talk.

Take Back the Practice

In a world of teacher accountability, high-stakes as it is, standardized teacher instruments are not capable of capturing all that is important (and complex) in teaching and learning. We view the TEX-IN3 as a self-study instrument that can not only provide teachers with a systematic way to examine their own practices, a way to begin conversations in PLCs, but also a way to "reclaim" their classroom. In the most print-rich classrooms in which we have spent time, teachers and students know exactly what text is in their room, what purpose that text serves, and how it both supports instruction and positions readers in the classroom as literate beings. In some ways, that text may also provide teachers with the evidence they need to demonstrate that they (a) are teaching literacy in ways that are conducive to literacy development and (b) that their practices are grounded in research. In other ways, the text environment can also serve as a means for teachers to advocate for the type of teaching they value for literacy development.

Take Action

We conclude this chapter with one of our favorite quotes about the need to examine the print environment in classrooms. Ayers (2001) states,

> Questioning everything in the environment, from the bottom up, is an important task for teachers. . . . We can peel the cover back a bit, peek underground, disclose the undisclosed. . . . And in telling what is untold, we can become stronger in shaping our own environments, until they become places that more fully reflect what we know and value.
>
> *(p. 51)*

Examining not only the print environment is important and thinking about the types of texts we make available to our students in order to raise reading achievement is important. Additionally, critically listening to and examining the language students use around those texts is equally important. We have argued in this chapter that literacy is a social practice, one that is defined not by how well students score on achievement measures or how well teachers perform on observation measures but by the way in which students perceive and understand the literacy environment that surrounds them. In a perfect world, teachers and students would create that environment in co-constructed ways. However, in this high-stakes testing environment in which teachers and students in the U.S. find themselves, that may not be entirely possible. What we have argued for in this chapter is a critical examination by teachers of their own environment (through the use of collaborative processes with other teachers), specifically through listening to students. What they say, how they say it, and who they ventriloquize is of the utmost importance in understanding their development.

References

Ayers, W. (2001). *To teach: The journey of a teacher.* New York: Teachers College Press.

Barton, D., & Hamilton, M. (1998). *Local literacies: Reading and writing in one community.* New York: Routledge.

Barton, D., & Hamilton, M. (2000). Literacy practices. In D. Barton, M. Hamilton, & R. Ivanic (Eds.), *Situated literacies: Reading and writing in context.* London: Routledge.

Barton, D., Hamilton, M., & Ivanic, R. (Eds.). (2000). *Situated literacies: Reading and writing in context.* London: Routledge.

Brandt, D., & Clinton, K. (2002). Limits of the local: Expanding perspectives on literacy as a social practice. *Journal of Literacy Research, 34*(3), 337–356.

Brophy, J., & Good, T. (1986). Teacher behavior and student achievement. In M.C. Wittrock (Ed.), *Handbook of research on teaching* (3rd ed.). New York: Macmillan.

Cambourne, B. (2000). Observing literacy learning in elementary classrooms: Twenty-nine years of classroom anthropology. *The Reading Teacher, 53*, 512–515.

Doyle, W. (1983). Academic work. *Review of Educational Research, 53*, 159–199.

DuFour, R., DuFour, R., Eaker, R., & Many, T. (2010). *Learning by doing: A handbook for professional communities at work.* Bloomington, IN: Solution Tree.

Dunkin, M., & Biddle, B. (1974). *The study of teaching.* New York: Holt, Rinehart and Winston.

Engeström, Y. (1993). Developmental studies of work as a test bench of activity theory: The case of primary care medical practice. In S. Chaiklin & J. Lave (Eds.), *Understanding practice: Perspectives on activity and context* (pp. 64–103). New York: Cambridge.

Evertson, C.M., & Green, J.L. (1986). Observation as inquiry and method. In M.C. Wittrock (Ed.), *Handbook of research on teaching* (pp. 162–213). New York: Macmillan.

Heath, S.B. (1983). *Ways with words: Language, life, and work in communities and classrooms.* New York: Cambridge University Press.

Hoffman, J.V., Roller, C.M., Maloch, B., Sailors, M.W., Duffy, G.G., & Beretvas, S.N. (2005). Teachers' preparation to teach reading and their experiences and practices in the first three years of teaching. *The Elementary School Journal, 105*(3), 267–289.

Hoffman, J.V. & Sailors, M. (2002). *Texts Inventory, Texts In-Use and Text Interviews Observation System.* Unpublished document: The University of Texas at Austin.

Hoffman, J.V., & Sailors, M. (2004). Reflecting on the literacy environment and literacy practices: The TEX-IN3. In J.V. Hoffman & D. L. Schallert (Eds.), *Read this room: The role of texts in beginning reading instruction.* Ann Arbor, MI: Center for the Improvement of Early Reading Achievement.

Hoffman, J.V., Sailors, M., Duffy, G.G., & Beretvas, N. (2004). The effective elementary classroom literacy environment: Examining the validity of the TEX-IN3 observation system. *Journal of Literacy Research, 36*(3), 289–320.

Maloch, B., Hoffman, J.V., & Patterson, B. (2004). Local texts: Reading and writing "of the classroom." In J.V. Hoffman & D. Schallert (Eds.), *The texts in elementary classrooms*. Ann Arbor, MI: Center for the Improvement of Early Reading Achievement.

Miettinen, R. (2001). Artifact mediation in Dewey and in cultural-historical activity theory. *Mind, Culture, and Activity, 8*, 297–308.

Oliver, D.G., Serovich, J.M., & Mason, T.L. (2005). Constraints and opportunities with interview transcription: Towards reflection in qualitative research. *Social Forces, 84*(2), 1273–1289.

Ormerod, F., & Ivanic, R. (2000). Texts in practices: Interpreting the physical characteristics of children's project work. In D. Barton, M. Hamilton, & R. Ivanic (Eds.), *Situated literacies: Reading and writing in context*. London: Routledge.

Rhodes, L., & Shanklin, N.W. (1993). *Windows into literacy: Assessing learners K-8*. New York: Heinemann.

Sailors, M. (2013). Making literacy a "pervasive part" of a second grade classroom. *Pennsylvania Reads, 12*, 7–15.

Sailors, M., & Hoffman, J.V. (2010). The text environment and learning to read: Windows and mirrors shaping literate lives. In D. Wyse, R. Andrews, & J. Hoffman (Eds.), *The International Handbook of English Language and Literacy Teaching* (pp. 294–304). New York: Routledge.

Sailors, M., & Hoffman, J.V. (2011). Establishing a print-rich classroom and school environment. In R.M. Bean & A.S. Dagen (Eds.), *Best practices of literacy leaders in schools* (pp. 184–205). New York: Guilford Press.

Sailors, M., Kumar, T., Blady, S., & Willson, A. (2013). Literacy tools created and used within print-rich classroom environments. In B.M. Taylor & N.K. Duke (Eds.), *Handbook of effective literacy instruction: Research-based practice K-8* (pp. 46–71). New York: Guilford Press.

Searfoss, L.W. & Readence, J.E. (1983). Guiding readers to meaning. *Reading Psychology, 4*, 29–36.

Shulman, L. S. (1986). Paradigms and research programs in the study of teaching: A contemporary perspective. In M.C. Wittrock (Ed.), *Handbook of research in teaching* (3rd ed., pp. 3-36). New York: Macmillan.

Stallings, J. (1975). Implementation and child effects of teaching practices in Follow Through classrooms. *Monographs of the Society for Research in Child Development, 40*, 7–8.

Tusting, K. (2000). The new literacy studies and time. In D. Barton, M. Hamilton, & R. Ivanic (Eds.), *Situated literacies: Reading and writing in context*. London: Routledge.

Yamagata-Lynch, L.C. (2010). Understanding cultural historical activity theory. *Activity Systems Analysis Methods: Understanding Complex Learning Environments, 2*, 13–26.

9

THE USE OF FORMATIVE ASSESSMENT TO IMPROVE INSTRUCTION OF ENGLISH LEARNERS AND EVALUATION OF TEACHERS

Francesca López, Patrick Proctor, and Martin Scanlon

The history of schools in the United States underserving students who are English language learners (ELLs) is well documented (Ovando, 2003). Yet, as this population continues to grow, so too has the knowledge base for strengthening their educational opportunities (e.g., August, Francis, Han-Ya, & Snow, 2006; Brisk, 2006; Rolstad, Mahoney, & Glass, 2005; Scanlan & Lopez, 2012). Nevertheless, effective pedagogical strategies for ELLs are not used to the extent that they should be (Alemán, 2007; Gandara, Rumberger, Maxwell-Jolly, & Callahan, 2003; Reeves, 2004), due in part to inadequate preparation of preservice teachers and insufficient support and guidance for practitioners. This underutilization of effective pedagogical strategies has been further complicated by the emergence of evaluation tools that do not reflect best practices for ELLs (National Comprehensive Center for Teacher Quality, 2012).

Within this context, the goal of this chapter is to support administrators in their efforts to help teachers improve literacy instruction for ELLs. It begins by providing perspectives on two bodies of literature: evaluation of teachers and formative assessment. While these two bodies of literature are frequently viewed as unrelated, we make the case that viewing them in tandem can be helpful for school administrators seeking to improve the educational opportunities of ELLs. We first provide an overview of the role of classroom observations in research and the limitations of current accountability frameworks that incorporate classroom observations into teacher evaluation. We then present evidence on the often-overlooked utility of formative assessment[1] as a way to improve teacher instruction. Finally, we merge what is known about the limitations of teacher evaluations with the utility of formative assessment in a description of a network of schools that are incorporating formative assessments to improve literacy instruction for ELLs and non-ELLs in dual language settings.

Classroom Observations and Evaluations of Quality

Classroom observations have long been used as a means to gather information about what teachers do and how that in turn influences how students perform. For many decades, classroom observations have helped researchers identify specific teaching practices that promote achievement (e.g., Good, 1988; Good & Brophy, 1969; Good & Grouws, 1975; Simon & Boyer, 1967). Classroom observations in educational research have varied substantially in both the focus of analysis and in the methods of documenting what is observed (see Good & Brophy, 1969; Pianta & Hamre, 2009; Silverman, Proctor, Harring, Doyle, Mitchell, & Meyer, 2014), but have cumulatively contributed a great deal to what we know about the kind of teaching we would hope to find in classrooms (e.g., Good & Brophy, 2010).

Formerly used mainly for purposes of educational research, classroom observations are increasingly being used to provide information about teacher effectiveness, enhance accountability measures, and provide professional development (Pianta & Hamre, 2009). Two widely used classroom observation measures include the Classroom Assessment Scoring System (CLASS; Pianta, LaParo, & Hamre, 2008) and the Framework for Teaching (FFT; Danielson, 2013). Both observation measures have been used extensively nationwide from prekindergarten through grade 12, and were the only observation measures selected to assess *general* classroom quality (other measures were selected for specific subject areas) by the Bill and Melinda Gates funded study, the Measures of Effective Teaching Project (MET)—the largest study conducted to date on teaching in the United States. The utility of classroom observations in accountability is underscored by Pianta and Hamre (2009), where they point out that "Systematic classroom observation systems provide a standard way of measuring and noting teachers' strengths and weaknesses and evaluating whether professional development activities are actually helping improve classroom interactions" (p. 110). Indeed, there is utility in using observations for improving teaching and enhancing the learning environment. For example, when teachers are involved in iterative feedback processes about their teaching that include opportunities to discuss practice with others and make adjustments, their opportunities for professional growth are enhanced. Advantages such as this notwithstanding, there are salient issues with the use of classroom observation protocols as measures of teacher quality for accountability purposes. We now turn to discuss in detail the problems with such a misappropriation of these instruments.

Observation Instrumentation Generalizability

According to the *Standards for Educational and Psychological Testing* (American Educational Research Association, American Psychological Association, & the National Council on Measurement in Education, 1999), the norming sample is central to the standardization of any instrument. In the case of classroom observation measures, there are two norming samples to consider: (1) teachers, whose behaviors are considered the criteria to which observed teacher behaviors are compared; and (2) the demographics of the students on which teaching quality is assessed. Despite the importance of norms in the development of any instrument, a review of existing observation measures to identify those that "extract examples of good or promising evaluation practices" (Boller, Atkins-Burnett, Malone, Baxter, & West, 2010, p. xi) revealed that *none* provided information on norms. Considering the high-stakes nature of teacher evaluations, it is imperative to have this information when making decisions.

In an attempt to understand the potentially egregious consequences of interpreting scores resulting from observation instruments that do not provide norming information, one could consider national demographics of teachers as an estimate of a nationally representative sample. In this case, comparisons of quality teaching will be made against a sample of teachers who tend to be overwhelmingly White (85%; National Center for Education Information, 2005). Although this will not present an issue in most cases, the norming sample may be potentially inappropriate for 15% of classrooms on average, but likely a much higher percentage in low-income, urban settings where student achievement often dips relative to more affluent communities and schools. These differences become particularly salient when one considers that teachers of color tend to leave the profession at much higher rates (Irizarry & Donaldson, 2012). Thus, if classroom observations are being used as professional development tools, this is an issue that merits consideration.

The issue of a comparable norming sample for students is also problematic. Pianta and Hamre (2009) assert that the extant research supporting the theoretical framework underlying the CLASS makes the instrument a valid and reliable source of information about the degree to which interactions among students and teachers will promote students' academic and/or social development as a consequence of experience in the classroom (p. 12). The majority (close to 80%) of the children who participated in the earliest validation efforts of CLASS, however, were White (Pianta et al., 2007), despite a focus on examining teacher behaviors as moderators of at-risk factors which tend to be (although not always) stratified by race and/or ethnicity. Taken together, careful consideration of using an instrument that has excluded an examination of the applicability of the norming sample across teachers and students precludes its validity across populations until an appropriate norming sample has been established.

Researchers who examine the relationship between teacher behaviors and student achievement have devised various ways to deal with the variability across classrooms that results from student or teacher background variables that are not included in an observation protocol or student achievement measure (e.g., Good & Grouws, 1975). The attempt to control for variables (e.g., ethnicity, socioeconomic status, EL status) is also often used in value-added modeling

(VAM), which attemps to quantify the contribution made by teachers (or schools, depending on the unit of measurement) in terms of students' achievement growth (see Anderman, Anderman, Yough, & Gimbert, 2010). In addition to the pervasive issues with attempting to use gain scores (Good, Sikes, & Brophy, 1973; Cronbach & Furby, 1970) that are typically ignored in VAM (see Good, Wiley, & Sabers, 2010; Newton, Darling-Hammond, Haertel, & Thomas, 2010), another key issue for school leaders to consider is the transparancy of limitations. Whereas researchers tend to explicitly acknowledge limitations with attempting to generalize findings beyond the scope of a given analytic sample, VAM researchers often make no attempt to acknowledge issues with generalizability. Indeed, most teacher evaluation protocol studies omit the discussion of generalizability (for an exception, see Baker, Gersten, Haager, & Dingle, 2006). Despite this consideration, research addressing the paucity of knowledge on the generalizability of student-teacher dynamics across different student populations (see López, 2011) underscores a need to examine teacher behaviors and classroom dynamics that promote achievement for traditionally marginalized youth in general, and ELLs in particular. Measures that do not generalize to diverse student populations undermine the results such measures produce—particularly in accountability settings. Given the centrality of classroom observation measures in accountability, and the paucity of evidence on the appropriateness of the student and teacher samples, it is important for school administrators to carefully evaluate whether the use of a particular instrument is appropriate for student populations who were not accurately represented in the norming samples.

One example of such an evaluation involves a cross-validation of the CLASS (Pianta, La Paro, & Hamre, 2008) with different student populations (López, 2011). The study took place in a large, urban Midwestern school district across 46 classrooms comprising approximately 1,000 students (68% of whom were Latino) in grades 3 through 5. Using standardized reading assessments administered at the end of the school year and controlling for student-level factors (e.g., beginning of the school year assessment scores and eligibility for free lunch), López found that the results for the non-Latino sample were consistent with prior studies using the CLASS. Namely, teacher behaviors were positively, and in various cases quite strongly, related to student outcomes. For the Latino sample, however, the teacher behaviors did *not* predict achievement, despite similar variability to the non-Latino sample and a larger sample size than the non-Latino sample. These findings do not suggest that the kind of behaviors examined by the measure (e.g., respecting students' contributions, providing opportunities for higher level thinking, and maximizing learning opportunities) are not important for Latino students. Indeed, the contribution of classroom experiences to student achievement has been established by the extant literature on teaching effectiveness as a whole as well as the literature on effective teaching for Latino students (e.g., Howes, James, & Ritchie, 2003). Rather, by considering issues with measuring student achievement presented elsewhere (e.g., Brophy, 1973) along with the findings in the López (2011) study, evidence suggests that in its current version, the CLASS does not generalize across populations as a measure of teacher *quality*.

CLASS is not the only observation instrument used in accountability settings. Along with the CLASS, FFT (Danielson, 2013) was used in the MET Project as an observation instrument to assess overall classroom quality. MET researchers found a substantial overlap in the scores of FFT and the CLASS, as well as the language arts instrument, the Protocol for Language Arts Observations (PLATO; Kane & Staiger, 2012). Examining the dimensions of both the FFT and CLASS reveals much overlap in the teacher behaviors evaluated, many of which are heavily language-dependent due to their reliance on teacher/student verbal interactions in scoring of the various dimensions. In classrooms with ELLs, however, a language-reliant observation instrument may fail to capture best practices. Indeed, scholars have found the FFT limited because it has not been modified to ensure that teachers are using best practices with English learners, "which in some cases differ from or are additional to practices used with English proficient students" (August, Garcia-Arena, & Myrtle, 2013, p. 12).

School administrators seeking to utilize classroom observation instruments that have not considered ELLs must accordingly be mindful of their limited applicability to some classrooms. Do they, for example, consider that some ELLs are in the earlier stages of English acquisition when determining the extent to which students respond? Unless the school administrator has had training in the particular needs of ELLs that he or she can incorporate into an existing measure, usually the answer is "no." The only mention of considerations for ELLs in the FFT (Danielson, 2013), for example, is, "Students whose first language is not English, as well as students with other special needs, must be considered when a teacher is planning lessons and identifying resources to ensure that all students will be able to learn" (p. 13). *What* those specific behaviors should reflect, however, is absent from the FFT. Similarly, the CLASS documentation states that "the CLASS measure does not specifically assess . . . teaching strategies specific to dual language learners[2]" (p. 7).

In sum, standardized classroom observation instruments are designed to be *general*, and do not focus on the particular needs of ELLs. For non-ELLs, the language used by the teacher and students *is* the medium used to access the curriculum. For ELLs, however, both language and content are often being learned simultaneously, and will thus not serve the same role or function. Hence, in accountability settings, considering the specialized needs of English learners is a critical issue. To be able to address this need, school administrators need to focus on what is known about promoting effective teaching practices for English learners.

What Do Teachers Need to Know?

A panel of experts (National Comprehensive Center for Teacher Quality, 2012) "convened a forum of distinguished experts in December 2011 to discuss current efforts to develop evaluation systems designed to assess how well teachers of ELLs are educating these students" (p. 1). Among several recommendations, participants suggested that evaluation systems should reflect rigor, high quality, and be applied to *all teachers*; and evaluation systems should also reflect the kind of specialized knowledge that is necessary for effectively teaching English learners. Thus, the use of observation measures such as CLASS or FFT is not inherently misguided—particularly when used as tools to help teachers improve. To build teacher capacity to serve ELLs, however, those evaluating teachers (usually school leaders) need to understand what knowledge, skills, and dispositions contribute to this end. With this knowledge, school leaders can *augment* existing observations to consider the particular needs of their students.

Scanlan and López (2012) synthesize empirical research identifying three areas—cultivating language proficiency, ensuring access to high-quality teaching and learning, and promoting sociocultural integration—as central for school leaders. In a recent study, López, Scanlan, and Gundrum (2013) examined the relationship between discrete requirements in each state's teacher education programs with fourth grade Latino ELLs' reading outcomes on the National Assessment of Educational Progress. They found that training in ESL/ELD had a marked effect on ELLs' achievement (approximately a .40 *SD* gain for students in states with stringent requirements compared to peers in states with the least stringent requirements). They assert, "All teachers, not just specialist teachers, should understand the developmental trajectory of ELLs' English proficiency as well as how to nurture and support it" (p. 20). They further explain,

> This includes knowledge about explicit English instruction and creating opportunities for students to express themselves, as well as modifying the level of English used to make content comprehensible. Supplementing teaching with visual aids, vocabulary instruction, and graphic organizers, for example, are all ways teachers can help ELs be successful. Requiring teachers to have knowledge about ESL/ELD can ameliorate the lack of preparation often felt by teachers while promoting achievement for ELs.
>
> *(p. 20)*

They also found that requiring knowledge regarding native language/English content assessment was associated with ELLs' achievement, which has been supported by the extant literature (Black & Wiliam, 1998; Stiggins, 1988, 2002). This knowledge involves understanding the degree to which students' English proficiency is influencing the score that would otherwise reflect students' understanding of content. To gauge students' understanding, it is important to know how to use accommodations that mitigate the degree to which proficiency is reflected in scores, which includes linguistic modifications that are the most promising in reducing bias (Abedi, Hofstetter, Baker, & Lord, 2001; Abedi, 2002). Nevertheless, very few programs require teachers to have training in the assessment of content for ELLs, and the focus that does exist relies on summative rather than formative assessment (López, Scanlan, & Gundrum, 2013). This limits the extent to which teachers can identify students' knowledge, which can inform the instruction that needs to take place.

Formative Assessment

Although school leaders observe teachers' practice to gauge the extent to which they are supporting students' academic growth, teachers need tools to gauge students' needs in classroom contexts and make instructional decisions in response to these needs. Despite the importance of knowing where students' weaknesses are, there is a paucity of training provided to preservice teachers on formative assessments (Black & Wiliam, 1998), which can have a particularly negative impact for ELLs. Indeed, López et al. (2013) assert:

> All teachers should know how to assess their students formatively. With an accurate understanding of students' content knowledge, teachers can adjust instruction and attend to gaps in learning. Certainly, this recommendation is not limited to teachers who work with ELs (Stiggins, 1988) but for teachers of ELs, formative assessment is essential if they are implementing strategies resulting from their knowledge of ESL/ELD.
>
> *(p. 20)*

Formative assessment can be described as "activities undertaken by teachers, and/or by students, which provide information to be used as feedback to modify the teaching and learning activities in which they are engaged" (Black & Wiliam, 1998). We focus our attention on a set of assessments that are designed to be used formatively: curriculum-based measures (CBM). Broadly speaking, CBM instruments are used as formative assessments in special and general education settings to monitor progress and guide instructional modifications in reading, writing, spelling, and mathematics (Reschly, Busch, Betts, Deno, & Long, 2009; Shinn & Bamonto, 1998; Stecker et al., 2005). Focusing more narrowly on ELLs, the body of empirical research exploring the use of CBM is limited but growing (Sandberg & Reschly, 2011). In reading, CBM instruments have been used to assess oral fluency for ELLs in first grade (Graves, Plasencia-Peinado, Deno, & Johnson, 2005) and to determine if reading in English correlates with standardized measures of reading achievement (Wiley & Deno, 2005). In writing, CBM instruments have been shown to provide valid indicators of general proficiency for ELLs in high school (Campbell, Espin, & McMaster, 2013; Espin et al., 2008). A potential benefit of measuring ELLs' progress in general education via CBM is that it can "signal the need for intense preventative intervention that can assist teachers in avoiding the misplacement of some ELs in special education" (Graves et al., 2005, p. 24). This is significant, since ELLs are disproportionately and often inappropriately labeled as having disabilities (Artiles & Klinger, 2006; Artiles, Rueda, Salazar, & Higareda, 2005).

A fundamental tenet of CBM is that the data produced are *formative*: "student performance is assessed continuously *during* instruction and regular decisions are made about whether student progress is satisfactory or unsatisfactory" (Shinn & Bamonto, 1998, p. 8, emphasis in original). This information, in turn, informs teaching strategies that should be used.

Implementing Formative Assessment for Monitoring Biliterate Development

These two perspectives—on teacher evaluation and student formative assessment— form the foundation for unpacking a key way to improve literacy instruction of ELLs, to which we now turn. As noted above, perspectives on teacher evaluation and student formative assessment are not typically presented together. Yet we argue that in conjunction, these two perspectives can contribute to improving literacy instruction for ELLs. To illustrate this point, we will describe the Two-Way Immersion Network of Catholic Schools (TWIN-CS; see www.twin-cs.org): a network of schools engaged in a systematic effort to transform into schools that more effectively serve their ELL population.

TWIN-CS is a multiyear effort supporting Catholic schools transitioning from monolingual to bilingual instructional environments by implementing the two-way immersion model (TWI; Howard & Sugarman, 2007). TWIN-CS was launched in 2013, with 12 schools across the United States selected from a competitive pool to be the inaugural members. We draw upon TWIN-CS to illustrate an effort to shape the ways educational leaders enhance evaluation of teachers by infusing the use of formative assessment data to improve teachers' pedagogical strategies—and in particular their literacy instruction—to better serve ELLs.

TWI Model

The TWI model is used to serve both ELs who share a common home language and students for whom English is a first language. The vast majority of TWI programs are Spanish/English (Center for Applied Linguistics, n.d.). This model, which seeks to foster bilingualism and biliteracy, strong academic attainment, and cross-cultural appreciation, is a prime example on a pedagogical approach for

ELLs that is at once effective and underutilized. In terms of efficacy, empirical research has consistently found the model to provide strong educational outcomes for ELLs (Collier & Thomas, 2012; Howard, Sugarman, & Christian, 2003). Evidence from a long-term developmental study of ELLs' academic performance across a variety of program placements (including ESL, transitional bilingual education, and sheltered English immersion) reveals that ELL students who are placed in TWI schools consistently outperform their counterparts in other programs (Collier & Thomas, 2012).

In a TWI classroom, students who are native English speakers and students who are ELLs (but share the same native language) all strive to develop bilingualism and biliteracy (de Jong, 2002; Mora, Wink, & Wink, 2001; Senesac, 2002). While the benefits of bilingualism (e.g., Adesope, Lavin, Thompson, & Ungerleider, 2010; Diaz, 1983) are theorized to accrue to all participants, ELLs stand to gain in particularly important ways. First, instead of ignoring the home language, the curricular and instructional designs of TWI naturally build upon ELLs' home language. This strategy is known to support their English language proficiency and content knowledge development (Rolstad et al., 2005; Slavin & Cheung, 2005). Second, in contrast to other approaches that segregate ELLs, the TWI model creates natural incentives for ELLs and their native English classmates to interact around language, since all are pursuing bilingualism and biliteracy. Interaction amongst ELLs and native English-speaking students has been shown to promote ELLs' development of conversational and academic English (Bunch, 2006; Lucas, Villegas, & Freedson-Gonzalez, 2008; Saenz, Fuchs, & Fuchs, 2005). Finally, when compared with their counterparts in English-only settings, ELLs in bilingual settings—such as TWI—develop stronger levels of self-competence (Collier & Thomas, 2012), one of the strongest predictors of future performance (Lopez, 2010).

Literacy development in TWI. Since TWIN-CS member schools are transitioning from monolingual institutions into bilingual ones, school leaders need to be particularly attentive to the literacy development therein. One way to do this is by promoting linguistically responsive teaching practices. Teachers engaging in linguistically responsive teaching demonstrate an "understanding of how [ELLs] with diverse sets of experiences, packaged individually into cultures, make meaning, communicate that meaning, and extend that meaning" and transforming such understanding "into pedagogy and curriculum that result in high academic performance" for these students (Garcia, Arias, Murri, & Serna, 2010, p. 139). Key concepts of linguistically responsive teaching include (Lucas et al., 2008):

- ELLs develop conversational language proficiency before academic language proficiency. Social interaction amongst ELLs and native English speakers fosters the development of both conversational and academic language proficiencies.
- ELLs who develop academic language proficiency in their home language are advantaged over ELLs who do not.

- When developing their second language, ELLs require opportunities to receive comprehensible input that is just beyond their current level of competence as well as to produce meaningful output.
- When developing their second language, ELLs require explicit attention to linguistic form and function, as well as safe, welcoming classroom environments that reduce anxieties about performing in a second language.

To apply these key concepts, linguistically responsive teachers engage in specific practices when working with ELLs, including identifying the language demands of classroom discourse and tasks, scaffolding instruction to promote their learning of both content and language, and building upon their language backgrounds and experiences (Lucas & Villegas, 2010).

Given that TWI settings are explicitly organized to support linguistically responsive teaching, how do school leaders help teachers in TWIN-CS schools learn to engage in these practices? Instead of relying on classroom evaluation tools like CLASS and FFT—which we describe as limited for settings with ELLs—school administrators in TWIN-CS are empowering teachers to use formative assessments to critically reflect on student work and make instructional adjustments accordingly. Consistent with the recommendations made by the panel of experts (National Comprehensive Center for Teacher Quality, 2012) we described earlier, school leaders directly and indirectly facilitate informal observations to gauge teachers' practices and areas that potentially require more support to be effective with ELLs. At different times, various individuals conduct these observations, including school leaders themselves, a mentor working with each of the schools in the transition to TWI, and fellow teachers. This process of observation and feedback on specific practices occurs within *communities of practice* (COP), to which we now turn.

Communities of practice supporting literacy development. The theory of action of TWIN-CS can be summarized in three statements. First, TWI settings are organized to promote linguistically responsive teaching in general, and bilingualism and biliteracy in particular. Second, CBM data on early biliteracy provides teachers valuable *formative* information to monitor student progress in early biliteracy skills and then to adjust instructional practices that will lead to improvements in students' knowledge and skills in this domain. Third, teachers have learned how to use CBM in a formative manner within COP. School leaders use classroom observations focused on the practices that teachers are developing to meet the needs of ELLs, and use the information acquired formatively to determine the additional support teachers require. Thus, this theory of action guides school leaders who are interested in improving literacy for ELLs to focus their attention toward supporting these COPs.

The concept of COP is grounded in sociocultural learning theory, holding that we learn through interactions with others in enterprises that are of value, as well as through experiences in the world (Lave & Wenger, 1991;Vygotsky, 1978). COPs are groups of individuals who share a common purpose and learn how to pursue this purpose from one another. They have three constituent characteristics: mutual engagement, joint enterprise, and shared repertoire (Wenger, 1998). Being mutually engaged in relationships defines the community. Through this engagement, members pursue a common enterprise, employing a repertoire of artifacts, both tangible (e.g., vocabulary, tools, symbols) and intangible (e.g., stories, concepts).

Coburn & Turner's (2011) *framework for data use* grounds this theory of action. This framework is a multidimensional depiction of how data are used in schools. At the heart of this framework is the process of "what actually happens when individuals interact with assessments, test scores, and other forms of data in the course of their ongoing work" (p. 175). This *process of data use* dimension is embedded in an *organizational and political context*, which includes the organizational routines and norms as well as resources (e.g., time, access to data), leadership, and power relations. Interventions to promote data use feed into this context, and potential outcomes emerge from it.

Figure 9.1 illustrates Coburn & Turner's (2011) framework as it applies to the TWIN-CS initiative. TWIN-CS promotes the use of data by directing participating schools in the use of CBM instruments in early biliteracy. This engenders the process of data use by teachers: monitoring student scores and trends on CBM instruments, interpreting what these scores mean, and constructing implications of these data for instructional adaptations. This use of data occurs within COPs in an organizational and political context. The potential outcomes from this data use include improved bilingualism and biliteracy amongst students and improved linguistically responsive teaching practices by the educators.

COPs promoting literacy development in TWIN-CS. School leaders across TWIN-CS schools support teachers' use of data to promote literacy development. The promotion of data use is embedded in schools' new TWI service delivery model that supports culturally and linguistically diverse students (upper left corner, Figure 9.1). Teachers and school leaders participated in training during the spring and early summer of 2013, when schools engaged in several steps to become members of TWIN-CS, such as participating in book discussions on linguistically responsive teaching (Howard & Sugarman, 2007; Miramontes, Nadeau, & Commins, 2011), participating in webinars on these texts, and participating in two face-to-face professional development sessions: an initial half-day workshop in April and an extensive 3.5-day academy in June of 2013. The spring workshop provided a basic overview of TWI. The summer academy served as an intensive retreat during which teams from each school participated in workshops on curriculum and instruction, assessment (both formative and summative), and organizational development. The formative assessment component of the academy encompassed the use of CBM in particular. During the 2013–2014 academic year these professional development activities continued with a series of webinars on the use of CBM assessments in the area of early biliteracy.

TWIN-CS initiative: **Promoting Formative Data Use**

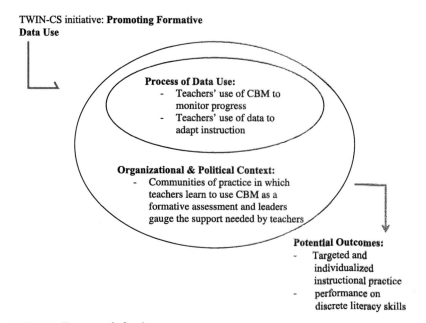

FIGURE 9.1 Framework for data use

Adapted from Coburn & Turner, 2011, p. 176.

These activities marked a shift into the *process of data use,* unfolding in a particular organizational and political context (center, Figure 9.1). Put another way, teachers and administrators in TWIN-CS learned to use CBM as a formative assessment with colleagues in several COPs. We draw on the key characteristics—mutual engagement, joint enterprise, and shared repertoire (refer back to Table 9.1)—to describe two COPs salient to the learning of CBM.

Implementation team. Within each school an "Implementation Team" COP formed. At a minimum, this team included several teachers, one to two administrators, and a mentor from outside. Schools were encouraged to also include parent representatives from the various cultural and linguistic backgrounds on the Implementation Team. These individuals are *mutually engaged* in relationships transforming the school to the TWI model. In other words, implementing the model is the *joint enterprise* that they share. Individuals have different roles in this transformation and rely on one another for support and guidance. For most of the teachers and administrators, the TWI model itself presents a new way to think about teaching and learning. For others, such as the mentor, the model is familiar, but the particular school context is novel. Thus, each of these communities of practice looks a little different.

These Implementation Teams developed a *shared repertoire* to accomplish the goal of transforming their school to the TWI model. This repertoire included the foundational books on TWI that they read, information from the summer academy, and information from the professional development webinars that were ongoing. Thus, information about using CBM as a formative assessment is part of this shared repertoire, and one that was monitored by school leaders to determine areas that needed support. For instance, directions for administering specific assessments, data tracking tools, charts of student progress, and meetings to analyze and respond to graphed data all are examples of tools, artifacts, and resources that formed the shared repertoire. Different members of the Implementation Team played specific roles as individuals to learn this repertoire. For instance, many mentors played a coaching role to teachers, who are learning to administer the assessments and make sense of them. Principals play a different role, identifying areas that need support, championing and resourcing the work to support teachers, while not usually bringing direct expertise.

Take Action

School administrators face many pressures to help teachers improve literacy instruction for ELLs. We began this chapter arguing that classroom evaluation tools such as CLASS and FFT will not necessarily help leaders effectively respond to these pressures. These tools are useful for gauging some general teaching practices, but problematic in that they have not necessarily considered the particular needs of ELL populations. Thus, they are limited in their ability to provide objective data about teacher performance in different settings. School administrators need more than just a healthy skepticism toward the utility of classroom observation tools. Rather, they need practical strategies to actually help teachers develop the requisite knowledge and skills to effectively serve ELLs. To that end, we hold that

- formative assessments can assist teachers in informing their practice, providing detailed information that classroom observations are generally not designed to provide; and
- teachers can learn to use data from formative assessments in communities of practice.

In conclusion, it is clear that helping teachers improve literacy instruction for ELLs is complex work. In tackling this task, administrators need to think carefully and strategically about where to invest their efforts. Formative assessments are one such place.

Notes

1 Although we discuss the literature on formative assessment broadly, we focus specifically on curriculum-based measurement (CBM). CBM emerged several decades ago in "an effort to decrease the separation between measurement and instruction—to make data

on student achievement more integral to daily teacher decision making" (Deno, 1985, p. 221). Thus, even though the focus is on the measures that fall under CBM, the discussion surrounding formative assessment can be generalized to other assessment tools used to inform instruction.

2 It is likely that the CLASS refers to dual language learners instead of English learners given its use in preschool settings, such as Head Start, which often use dual language approaches. Dual language learners, however, may not necessarily be "English learners."

References

Abedi, J. (2002). Standardized achievement tests and English language learners: Psychometrics issues. *Educational assessment, 8*(3), 231–257.

Abedi, J., Hofstetter, C., Baker, E., & Lord, C. (2001). NAEP math performance and test accommodations: Interactions with student language background (CSE Tech. Rep. No. 536). Los Angeles, CA: National Center for Research on Evaluation, Standards, and Student Testing. Retrieved October 1, 2008, from http://www.cse.ucla.edu/products/rsearch.asp

Abedi, J., Hofstetter, C., & Lord, C. (2004). Assessment accommodations for English language learners: Implications for policy-based empirical research. *Review of Educational Research, 74*, 1–28.

Adesope, O.O., Lavin, T., Thompson, T., & Ungerleider, C. (2010). A systematic review and meta-analysis of the cognitive correlates of bilingualism. *Review of Educational Research, 80*(2), 207–245.

Alemán, E. (2007). Situating Texas school finance policy in a CRT framework: How "substantially equal" yields racial inequity. *Educational Administration Quarterly, 43*(5), 525–558.

American Educational Research Association, American Psychological Association, & the National Council on Measurement in Education. (1999). *Standards for educational and psychological testing.* Washington, DC: American Educational Research Association.

Anderman, E.M., Anderman, L.H., Yough, M.S., & Gimbert, B.G. (2010). Value-added models of assessment: Implications for motivation and accountability. *Educational Psychologist, 45*(2), 123–137.

Artiles, A., & Klinger, J. (2006). Forging a knowledge base on English language learners with special needs: Theoretical, population, and technical issues. *Teachers College Record, 108*(11), 2187–2194.

Artiles, A., Rueda, R., Salazar, J.J., & Higareda, I. (2005). Within-group diversity in minority disproportionate representation: English language learners in urban school districts. *Exceptional Children, 71*(3), 283–300.

August, D., Garcia-Arena, P., & Myrtle, R. (2013). Draft final report Hartford Public Schools policies and practices for English language learners (ELLs). Retrieved from http://www.achievehartford.org/upload/files/AIR%20Final%20DRAFT%20Report%20Sept%20%2027%202013.pdf

August, D., Francis, D., Han-Ya, A.H., & Snow, C. (2006). Assessing reading comprehension in bilinguals. *The Elementary School Journal, 107*(2), 221–238.

Baker, S., Gersten R., Haager, D., & Dingle, M. (2006). Teaching practice and the reading growth of first-grade English learners: Validation of an observation instrument. *Elementary School Journal, 107*, 199–221.

Black, P. & Wiliam D. (1988) Inside the black box: Raising standards through classroom assessment. *Phi Delta Kappan, 80*(2) 139–148.

Black, P., & Wiliam, D. (1998) Assessment and classroom learning. Educational Assessment: Principles, Policies and Practices, 5, 7–74.

Boller, K., Atkins-Burnett, S., Malone, L.M., Baxter, G.P., & West, J. (2010). *Compendium of student, teacher, and classroom measures used in NCEE evaluations of educational interventions: Volume I. Measures selection approaches and compendium development methods.* NCEE 2010-4012. National Center for Education Evaluation and Regional Assistance.

Brisk, M.E. (2006). *Bilingual education: From compensatory to quality schooling.* Mahwah, NJ: Lawrence Erlbaum.

Bunch, G. (2006). "Academic English" in the 7th grade: Broadening the lens, expanding access. *Journal of English for Academic Purposes, 5*, 284–301.

Campbell, H., Espin, C., & McMaster, K. (2013). The technical adequacy of curriculum-based writing measures with English learners. *Reading and Writing, 26*(3), 431–452.

Center for Applied Linguistics. (n.d.). Center for Applied Linguistics directory of two-way immersion programs. Retrieved August 15, 2013 from: http://www.cal.org/twi/directory/

Coburn, C., & Turner, E. (2011). Research on data use: A framework and analysis. *Measurement, 9*(4), 173–206.

Collier, V., & Thomas, W. (2012). *Dual language education for a transformed world.* Albuquerque, NM: Fuente Press.

Cronbach, L. J., & Furby, L. (1970). How should we measure "change"?: Or should we? *Psychological Bulletin, 74*, 68–80.

Danielson, C. (2013). *The framework for teaching evaluation instrument.* Princeton, NJ: Danielson Group.

de Jong, E.J. (2002). Effective bilingual education: From theory to academic achievement in two-way bilingual program. *Bilingual Research Journal, 26*(1), 65–84.

Deno, S. (1985). Curriculum-based measurement: The emerging alternative. *Exceptional Children, 52*(3), 219–232.

Diaz, R.M. (1983). Thought and two languages: The impact of bilingualism on cognitive development. *Review of Research in Education, 10*(1), 23–54. doi: 10.3102/0091732x010001023

Espin, C., Wallace, T., Campbell, H., Lembke, E.S., Long, J.D., & Ticha, R. (2008). Curriculum-based measurement in writing: Predicting the success of high-school students on state standards tests. *Exceptional Children, 74*(2), 174–193.

Gandara, P., Rumberger, R., Maxwell-Jolly, J., & Callahan, R. (2003). English learners in California schools: Unequal resources, unequal outcomes. *Educational Policy Analysis Archives, 11*(36), 1–54.

Garcia, E., Arias, M.B., Murri, N.J.H., & Serna, C. (2010). Developing responsive teachers: A challenge for a demographic reality. *Journal of Teacher Education, 61*(1–2), 132–142.

Good, T.L. (1988). Observational research ... grounding theory in classrooms. *Educational Psychologist, 23*, 375–379.

Good, T.L., & Brophy, J. (1969). *Analyzing classroom interaction: A more powerful alternative.* ERIC Clearinghouse on Teaching and Teacher Education. Publication no. ED 041837.

Good, T., & Brophy, J. (2010). *Looking in classrooms* (10th ed.). Boston: Allyn and Bacon.

Good, T.L., Sikes, J. N., & Brophy, J. E. (1973). Effects of teacher sex and student sex on classroom interaction. *Journal of Educational Psychology, 65*(1), 74.

Good, T.L., & Grouws, D. (1975). *Process-product relationships in fourth grade mathematics classrooms.* Columbia: College of Education, University of Missouri. ERIC Clearinghouse on Teaching and Teacher Education. Publication no. ED 125907.

Good, T.L., Wiley, C.R.H., Sabers, D. (2010). Accountability and educational reform: A critical analysis of four perspectives and considerations for enhancing reform efforts. *Educational Psychologist, 45*, 138–148.

Graves, A., Plasencia-Peinado, J., Deno, S., & Johnson, J.R. (2005). Formatively evaluating the reading process of first-grade English learnings in multiple-language classrooms. *Remedial and Special Education, 26*(4), 215–225.

Howard, E., & Sugarman, J. (2007). Realizing the vision of two-way immersion: Fostering effective programs and classrooms. Washington, DC: Center for Applied Linguistics.

Howard, E., Sugarman, J., & Christian, D. (2003). Trends in two-way immersion education: A review of the research (p. 69). Baltimore: Center for Research on the Education of Students Placed At Risk (CRESPAR).

Howes, C., James, J., & Ritchie, S. (2003). Pathways to effective teaching. *Early Childhood Research Quarterly, 18*(1), 104–120.

Irizarry, J., & Donaldson, M.L. (2012). Teach for América: The Latinization of US schools and the critical shortage of Latina/o teachers. *American Educational Research Journal, 49*, 155–194.

Kane, T.J., & Staiger, D.O. (2012). Gathering feedback for teaching: Combining high-quality observations with student surveys and achievement gains. Research Paper, MET Project. Bill & Melinda Gates Foundation.

Lave, J., & Wenger, E. (1991). *Situated learning: Legitimate peripheral participation.* Cambridge: Cambridge University Press.

Lopez, F. (2010). Identity and motivation among Hispanic English language learners in disparate educational contexts. *Education Policy Analysis Archives, 18*(16), 1–33.

López, F. (2011). The nongeneralizability of classroom dynamics as predictors of achievement for Hispanic students in upper elementary grades. *Hispanic Journal of Behavioral Sciences, 33*, 350–376.

López, F., Scanlan, M., & Gundrum, B. (2013). Preparing teachers of English language learners: Empirical evidence and policy implications. *Education Policy Analysis Archives, 21*. Retrieved from: http://epaa.asu.edu/ojs/article/view/1132.

Lucas, T., & Villegas, A.M. (2010). The missing piece in teacher education: The preparation of linguistically responsive teachers. *National Society for the Study of Education, 109*(2), 297–318.

Lucas, T., Villegas, A.M., & Freedson-Gonzalez, M. (2008). Linguistically responsive teacher education: Preparing classroom teachers to teach English language learners. *Journal of Teacher Education, 59*(4), 361–373.

Miramontes, O., Nadeau, A., & Commins, N. (2011). *Restructuring schools for linguistic diversity: Linking decision making to effective programs* (2nd ed.). Boston: Teachers College Press.

Mora, J.K., Wink, J., & Wink, D. (2001). Dueling models of dual language instruction: A critical review of the literature and program implementation guide. *Bilingual Research Journal, 24*(4), 435–460.

National Center for Education Information. (2005). Profile of teachers in the U.S. Retrieved from: http://www.ncei.com/POT05PRESSREL3.htm

National Comprehensive Center for Teacher Quality. (2012). *Summary of "Expert Forum on the Evaluation of Teachers of English language Learners."* Center on Great Teachers and Leaders, American Institutes for Research. Retrieved at http://www.gtlcenter.org/sites/default/files/docs/ForumSummary_July2012.pdf

Newton, X.A., Darling-Hammond, L., Haertel, E., & Thomas, E. (2010). Value-added modeling of teacher effectiveness: An exploration of stability across models and contexts. *Education Policy Analysis Archives, 18*(23), n23.

Ovando, C. (2003). Bilingual education in the United States: Historical development and current issues. *Bilingual Research Journal, 27*(1), 1–25.

Pianta, R.C., Belsky, J., Houts, R., & Morrison, F., & the National Institute of Child Health and Human Development Early Child Care Research Network. (2007). Opportunities to learn in America's elementary classrooms. *Science, 315,* 1795–1796.

Pianta, R.C., & Hamre, B.K. (2009). Conceptualization, measurement, and improvement of classroom processes: Standardized observation can leverage capacity. *Educational Researcher, 38,* 109–119.

Pianta, R.C., La Paro, K.M., & Hamre, B.K. (2008). *Classroom Assessment Scoring System* (CLASS). Baltimore: Paul H. Brookes.

Reeves, J. (2004). "Like Everybody Else": Equalizing educational opportunity for English language learners. *TESOL Quarterly, 38*(1), 43–66.

Reschly, A., Busch, T., Betts, J., Deno, S., & Long, J.D. (2009). Curriculum-based measurement oral reading as an indicator of reading achievement: A meta-analysis of the correlational evidence. *Journal of School Psychology, 47*(6), 427–469.

Rolstad, K., Mahoney, K., & Glass, G.V. (2005). The big picture: A meta-analysis of program effectiveness research on English language learners. *Educational Policy, 19*(4), 572–594.

Saenz, L., Fuchs, D., & Fuchs, L.S. (2005). Peer-assisted learning strategies for English language learners with learning disabilities. *Exceptional Children, 71*(3), 231–247.

Sandberg, K., & Reschly, A. (2011). English learners: Challenges in assessment and the promise of curriculum-based measurement. *Remedial and Special Education, 32*(2), 144–154.

Scanlan, M., & Lopez, F. (2012). ¡Vamos! How school leaders promote equity and excellence for bilingual students. *Educational Administration Quarterly, 48*(4), 283–625.

Senesac, B.V.K. (2002). Two-way bilingual immersion: A portrait of quality schooling. *Bilingual Research Journal, 26*(1), 1–17.

Shinn, M.R., & Bamonto, S. (1998). Advanced applications of curriculum-based measurement: "Big ideas" and avoiding confusion. In M.R. Shinn (Ed.), *Advanced applications of curriculum-based measurement* (pp. 1–31). New York: Guilford.

Silverman, R.D., Proctor, C.P., Harring, J.R., Doyle, B., Mitchell, M.A., & Meyer, A.G. (2014). Teachers' instruction and students' vocabulary and comprehension: An exploratory study with English monolingual and Spanish–English bilingual students in grades 3–5. *Reading Research Quarterly, 49,* 31–60.

Simon, A., & Boyer, E.G. (Eds.). (1967). Mirrors for behavior: An anthology of classroom observation instruments. Philadelphia, PA: Research for Better Schools.

Slavin, R.E., & Cheung, A. (2005). A synthesis of research on language of reading instruction for English language learners. *Review of Educational Research, 75*(2), 247–284.

Stecker, P., Fuchs, L.S., & Fuchs, D. (2005). Using curriculum-based measurement to improve student achievement: Review of research. *Psychology in the Schools, 42*(8), 795–819.

Stiggins, R. (1988). Make sure your teachers understand student assessment. *Executive Educator, 10,* 24–30.

Stiggins, R.J. (2002). Assessment crisis: The absence of assessment for learning. *Phi Delta Kappan, 83,* 758–76.

Vygotsky, L.S. (1978). Mind in society: The development of higher mental process. Cambridge, MA: Harvard University Press.

Wenger, E. (1998). Communities of practice: Learning as a social system. *Systems thinker, 9*(5), 2–3.

Wiley, H.I., & Deno, S. (2005). Oral reading and maze measures as predictors of success for English learners on a state standards assessment. *Remedial and Special Education, 26*(4), 207–214.

10

WHAT DOES EFFECTIVE TEACHING REALLY LOOK LIKE?

The Observation of Effective Teaching in Reading (OET-Reading) Systems

Carol MacDonald Connor, Sarah Ingebrand, and Nicole Sparapani

Introduction

There are many things in students' lives that affect how well they learn to read. Some include the support their parents can provide both economically and academically, events in their lives such as divorce or natural disasters, their genes, the aptitudes and interests that they bring to school, their temperament, their ability to pay attention and follow the classroom rules, and their willingness to participate in classroom activities. With so many factors playing a role, educators begin to wonder if, for some students, there is anything that will make a difference. In fact, effective teaching can make a true difference in how well students learn to read, especially from kindergarten through third grade. We recently conducted the Individualized Student Instruction (ISI) longitudinal study where we followed students from first through third grade, randomly assigning their teacher to individualize each student's reading instruction or to a mathematics intervention (Connor et al., 2013). We found that even though half of the students lived in poverty and all had to endure hurricanes and the Gulf oil spill disaster during the three years of the study, students did better when their teachers learned how to individualize their reading instruction.

Although many of the differences we see in students' reading scores and how fast and well they learn to read are genetically based (Olson, 2008), teaching still plays a very important role in learning to read (Taylor, Roehrig, Connor, & Schatschneider, 2010). Studies have shown that when students have an ineffective teacher, they may fail to reach their genetic potential. However, when they have an effective teacher they are much more likely to attain their potential. There are many other studies that show teaching matters and that ineffective teaching can actually hurt children and create instructionally induced reading disabilities (Vellutino et al., 1996).

So if we know that teaching matters, do we know what effective teaching actually looks like? Unfortunately, although we know teaching matters, it is difficult to walk into a classroom and know whether or not we are watching effective teaching. For example, when teachers and principals were asked to rate whether a teacher was teaching math effectively or not (yes or no), they were right only half the time—no better than if they had guessed (Strong, Gargani, & Hacifazlioğlu, 2011). In a large study supported by the Gates Foundation, four observation systems designed to identify effective reading and English language arts (ELA) instruction could not fully differentiate teachers whose students did well on the state ELA tests and those who did not. Although, the systems did explain some of the variability in students' scores on the SAT, a standardized assessment of reading (Kane, Staiger, & McCaffrey, 2012).

That said, being able to identify effective reading instruction is incredibly important because it helps us explain what teachers do that works and what does not seem to work to improve students' outcomes. Knowing what effective teaching looks like helps us move to effective standards of practice so that all students can learn to read well by the time they reach third grade (Connor et al., 2013). Right now, 32% of students nationwide are reading below basic levels by fourth grade (although this is down from 38% in 1992), and in high-poverty schools the percentage rises to almost 50% (National Assessment of Educational Progress, 2014). Students who are not reading well by fourth grade are more likely to be referred to special education, to drop out of school, or even commit crimes.

However, effective teaching can help children read proficiently by fourth grade. Returning to findings from the ISI longitudinal study, where we followed students from first through third grade (Connor et al., 2013), 94% of the students who received individualized instruction in first, second, and third grade were reading proficiently by the end of third grade, with no students falling below basic levels. In contrast, only 78% of the students participating in control classrooms during the three-year study were reading proficiently by the end of third grade, and some exhibited very limited reading skills. This provides more evidence that teaching matters. Thus, being able to observe and identify whether or not teachers are using effective reading practices can guide professional development efforts, help teachers improve their teaching, and, in turn, improve students' literacy outcomes. In this chapter, we will discuss why classroom observation is important, why we are not very good at recognizing effective teaching when we see it, and what we do know right now that educational leaders can use to help their teachers teach reading more effectively.

Perspectives

Supporting the development of observation tools expressly designed to improve effectiveness in teaching is an important policy decision (IES Technical Working

Group, 2013) and classroom observation systems are important tools for educational leaders as they strive to make sure that students receive effective instruction. Another tool for evaluating effective instruction, mandated in many states, are teacher value-added scores, which are based on students' test scores. However, these value-added scores, even appropriately used (Raudenbush, 2004), do not provide any information about how and why students are achieving poorly or well and treat the classroom like a black box. Although value-added scores do reveal tremendous variability in the effectiveness of teaching (Konstantopoulos & Chung, 2011), they do not help teachers or educational leaders actually improve what happens in the classroom.

Another important consideration when thinking about classroom observation are different theories of teaching (Raudenbush, 2009). Steve Raudenbush describes the first theory of teaching as "privatized idiosyncratic practice" (p. 172). Such practice happens when teachers close their classroom doors and teach in the ways they believe to be best. The ideal teacher develops her own curriculum. For the most expert teachers, who have a good grasp of the current research, have expert and specialized knowledge of their content area, and who understand how to use research evidence to inform their practice, this instruction is probably highly effective. However, for teachers with less experience or a limited grasp of the research base, such privatized idiosyncratic practice may be highly ineffective and disastrous, particularly for the most vulnerable children, especially those from families of low socioeconomic status whose home learning environment and access to resources can be limited. Well-designed observation tools that actually predict student outcomes can help open the black box of the classroom and begin to move toward what Raudenbush calls "shared instructional regimes" where the best and most rigorous research on effective teaching in a specific content area is brought to bear. "Such explicit notions of instruction define the work of teaching, the expertise required for classroom success, and the role of incentives and accountability in motivating expert instruction" (p. 172). Such systems can elucidate what effective expert practice in the classroom actually looks like so that it can be shared among a community of professionals—educational leaders and teachers.

But why do the observation systems currently available fail to truly distinguish between effective and ineffective teaching? Perhaps the most important reason is that many current observation systems look for global characteristics of the classroom learning environment, such as classroom management, and fail to recognize classrooms as the dynamic and complex systems that they really are (Connor et al., 2014). For this reason, many theories typically widely used in education are not particularly helpful when trying to understand the classroom learning environment. Instead, dynamic systems theory, along with bio-ecological theories, offer helpful ways to conceptualize the dynamic nature of the classroom learning environment. We provide our model in Figure 10.1. A dynamic systems framework (Yoshikawa & Hsueh, 2001) holds that there are multiple sources of influence on children's learning (Bronfenbrenner & Morris, 2006), including the instruction they receive, how this instruction is delivered (Connor, Piasta, et al., 2009), the general climate of the classroom (Rimm-Kaufman, Paro, Downer, & Pianta, 2005), teacher characteristics (Raver, Blair, & Li-Grining, 2011), and students' characteristics, which includes peer influences (Connor & Morrison, 2012; Justice, Petscher, Schatschneider, & Mashburn, 2011). Further, these sources of influence interact in different ways with some seemingly important factors (e.g., teacher education) having relatively small effects on students' learning (Goldhaber & Anthony, 2003) and other factors (e.g., content and minutes of instruction) having large effects (Connor, Morrison, Schatschneider, et al., 2011).

For example, a student starts the day feeling hungry and sad because her mom just lost her job because of the Gulf oil spill. Although she is usually a model student, she just cannot focus on the lesson. At the same time, the teacher is worried about whether her husband is going to catch fish to sell because of the oil spill and hasn't really had time to prepare the lessons for the day, so she

FIGURE 10.1

relies on whole-class instruction and allows the students to spend extra time at recess. She is less patient with the students and is not sure why, but it may be due to minor stress-related depression (McLean & Connor, in press). The other students in the classroom have a wide range of interests and skills, and each of them contributes to the classroom learning environment as well. Finally, the school has implemented a new literacy curriculum and the teacher is still learning to use it effectively. Thus we see that the classroom learning environment is influenced by each individual student and what they are experiencing at home and in the community, the teacher who brings her attitudes and teaching skills, and school educational leaders who have provided a new literacy curriculum. Finally, the Gulf oil spill is affecting the teacher and many of her students. On any given day, these multiple sources of influence are impacting the classroom learning environment. Thus, to understand how and why a classroom learning environment is effective or not requires the observer to look at the teaching at the level of the individual student as well as considering the general classroom learning environment.

Evidence

This chapter focuses on evaluating *literacy* instruction from kindergarten through third grade. We do this because accumulating research shows that observation systems that focus on content-specific instruction are more likely to predict student outcomes in that content area than are more general systems (Connor, 2013). First we start with two aspects of the classroom learning environment, classroom organization and observation of student engagement, which are important but do not consistently distinguish between effective and ineffective instruction that lead to stronger student outcomes (Connor, Morrison, et al., 2009). These classroom characteristics are easy to observe and are sometimes, but not always, related to effective teaching and positive student outcomes. Thus, we consider these foundational aspects of the classroom learning environment that are necessary but not sufficient for student learning.

Just because a classroom is well managed doesn't mean it's effective. There are teachers whose classrooms appear highly disorganized, but their class discussions during the language arts instruction provide multiple rich learning opportunities that support students' comprehension of the text and overall learning (Carlisle, Kelcey, Berebitsky, & Phelps, 2011). At the same time, there are teachers who run a tight ship and keep their classroom tightly managed but who do not teach reading in ways that the students can comprehend and learn (Connor et al., 2014). Then there are truly chaotic classrooms, which are not good for teachers or students (Wachs, Gurkas, & Kontos, 2004). That is why focusing on how well managed a classroom appears seems to be necessary but not sufficient for identifying effective teaching.

Are students engaged or are they just "doing school"? Many observation systems suggest that the observer globally rate how engaged all the students are in classroom activities. Some tools differentiate passive (attending, silent reading) from active engagement (writing, raising hand, answering/asking questions; BOSS; Shapiro, 2003). Although student engagement should be a good predictor of academic outcomes, findings are mixed. Some studies show that engagement is integral for classroom learning (National Research Council, 2001, Ponitz et al., 2009), yet others show that engagement does not distinguish between effective and ineffective instruction, especially as students reach second and third grade and when observing the entire classroom. In fact, in one study, by third grade, global student engagement, based on observers' ratings, was associated with weaker literacy skill gains (Connor, Jakobsons, Crowe, & Meadows, 2009).

So What Does Predict Literacy Skills?

In our research, the best predictor of a student's literacy skill gains has always been the amount of time a student spends in meaningful instruction that aligns with his or her learning needs. This is particularly true when the instruction is provided by a knowledgeable teacher who is warm, responsive, organized, and supportive of her students' learning. In this next section we provide evidence about what we can observe in the classroom that can actually distinguish between effective and ineffective teaching. This section is divided in two parts: (1) evidence from observation research that focuses on the teacher; and (2) evidence from observation research that focuses on the individual student experience.

The extent to which the teacher is warm and responsive to her students and handles discipline in a supportive and caring way is associated with student reading outcomes. Accumulating research clearly shows that how teachers interact with their students, the extent to which they encourage and listen to their comments, and the extent to which they avoid harsh or punitive punishment predicts students language and literacy outcomes (Connor, Son, Hindman, & Morrison, 2005; Pianta, La Paro, Payne, Cox, & Bradley, 2002; Rimm-Kaufman et al., 2005). This also includes the kinds of discussions and types of questions used, for example, coaching versus telling (Taylor & Pearson, 2002). Research has shown that students whose teachers are more warm and responsive achieve greater gains in reading skills and vocabulary by the end of first grade.

There are certain ways that effective teachers encourage students to participate in lessons. Joanne Carlisle and colleagues (Carlisle et al., 2011) moved beyond judging the quality of instruction and examined third grade teachers' "actual instructional actions" (p. 430). They found that more effective teachers **modeled** the action or information they expected from students. For example, the teacher might use a think aloud to show how to figure out what an author means. More effective teachers also provided **support for student**

learning. PLATO (http://platorubric.stanford.edu), the Protocol for Language Arts Teaching Observation, assesses these characteristics as well, particularly for middle-school students (Grossman et al., 2010). This includes fostering discussion, using *why* and *how* questions, and giving students opportunities to ask questions, as well as assessing students' understanding and providing appropriate feedback. Not surprisingly, teachers were more likely to use these instructional actions when they had more specialized knowledge, which was assessed using a survey about how to teach reading.

Teachers' specialized knowledge about reading matters but so does what is taught and how much time students spend in meaningful instruction. A large part of effective teaching taps specialized knowledge about the content area—reading, math, science, social studies, etc.—and how to employ this knowledge in the classroom (e.g., Piasta, Connor, Fishman, & Morrison, 2009). Shayne Piasta and colleagues discovered that neither teachers' specialized knowledge about reading nor time spent in explicit reading instruction alone predicted first graders' reading gains. Highly knowledgeable teachers who did not provide any explicit instruction were no more effective than low-knowledge teachers. However, when high-knowledge teachers provided greater amounts of explicit instruction (teachers provided between 0 and 18 minutes/day of explicit reading instruction in this study), their students made significant gains in reading. Unfortunately, the more time low-knowledge teachers spent in explicit instruction, the worse their students' gains were. This is because they were spending time teaching concepts incorrectly. For example, one teacher said that the short "a" sound was in the word "above." Unfortunately, the short "a," sound as in "cat," is not in the word above—the "a" sound in above makes the schwa sound.

Students bring a wide array of skills, interests, and aptitudes to the classroom, so the amount and type of literacy instruction that is optimal for them will differ based on their reading and language skills. Most of our work in classroom observation has focused on individual differences among students and figuring out how to provide the amount and type of literacy instruction for each and every student in the classroom that is optimal for his or her learning. We have discovered that even students who share a classroom can have very different learning experiences—both good and bad. Instruction that might be considered high quality for one student might be ineffective for another because each student has a different profile of language and reading skills (Connor, Morrison, Fishman, et al., 2011; Connor, Morrison, Schatschneider, et al., 2011). For example, students who are struggling to learn to read make greater gains when they spend more time in explicit and systematic code-focused instruction. For example, a first grader who is having difficulty mastering the alphabetic principle—that letters and sounds go together to make words that have meaning—will make greater literacy skill gains when he spends more time with the teacher in a small group participating in code-focused learning activities (see

TABLE 10.1 Types of evidence-based literacy instruction in first grade

	Teacher/Student Managed	*Student/Peer Managed*
Code-focused	The teacher is working with a small group of students to improve their encoding. Each student has a small chalk board with the word "pin" on it. The teacher says, "change the /i/ in 'pin' to make the word 'pan.'"	In pairs, students are practicing fluent sight word reading using flash cards. One student holds the cards and the other reads the word on the card. Then they change places.
Meaning-focused	The teacher is reading a book, *Stone Soup*, to the students. After she reads a page, she stops and asks the students how the character planned to make soup from a stone. Several students respond with their ideas. She summarizes what the students said and then says, "Let's read some more and see what happens." She continues to read the book.	Students are reading a book of their choice independently.

Table 10.1). In contrast, for a first grader who is reading well, the same amount of time in teacher/child-managed code-focused instruction is a waste of instructional time since these skills have already been mastered. For this student, more time reading independently or being involved in other meaning-focused literacy activities, with only a limited amount of time in code-focused activities, will be more effective. We have been figuring out, based on students' decoding, comprehension, and vocabulary (or word knowledge) skills exactly how much time in certain types of literacy instruction is optimal. We discuss this more in the Take Action section.

Teachers' instructional actions and the time each student spends in particular types of literacy instruction operate synergistically so you have to consider both. We can do a better job of evaluating effective teaching when the observation system focuses on teachers' instructional actions *and* appropriate amounts of time in meaningful instruction, understanding that the latter varies by individual student (Connor et al., 2014). We take this finding to heart in the next section where we present an observation system designed for educational leaders that should reveal effective literacy instruction.

Take Action

In this section, we adapt our work to provide a system designed for educational leaders who are working to help their teachers improve their delivery of effective first grade literacy instruction. We call this the Observation of Effective Teaching in Reading (OET-Reading1). The most effective observation systems are designed for a specific purpose (Crawford et al., 2013; Reddy et al., 2013a, 2013b). Therefore, we have selected *first grade reading instruction* for this observation system because research shows clearly that kindergarten through second grade is the time when most students establish reading proficiency, that prevention is more effective than remediation (Torgesen, 2002), and that first grade is a critical year (Connor et al., 2013).

There is an important caveat with regard to the OET-Reading1 system. Although the findings presented in this chapter report evidence from rigorously tested systems, the OET-Reading1 system is an adaptation. This means that it should work. **However, it should not be used in any kind of high-stakes teacher evaluation. It has not been designed or tested for that purpose.**

The OET-Reading1 System for Educational Leaders

Start with Students. We have provided basic observation forms that can be adapted to meet the needs of the observer as well as examples from actual classrooms (see Appendix A). We recommend that observations be conducted during the dedicated literacy block for at least 30 minutes, but longer is better. Literacy blocks last anywhere from one to two hours and are associated with stronger student outcomes (Wharton-McDonald, Pressley, & Hampston, 1998). For our example, we have selected two different classrooms: the first is of highly effective teaching; the other is of less effective teaching. We judged effectiveness based on students gains on the Woodcock Johnson III Passage Comprehension assessment (Woodcock, McGrew, & Mather, 2001) from the beginning to the end of the school year. On average, students in the effective classroom made fall to spring gains in reading comprehension scores that were larger than the other classrooms we observed and when compared to the less effective classroom (an effect size $d = 1.0$). Note: all names in our examples are pseudonyms.

First, select two to four students with the following characteristics based on the most recent reading assessment results that you have. If there is a grade equivalent (GE) score, the charts in Appendix A will be easier to use:

1. Struggling and not progressing (reading skills half a GE behind; below 30th percentile or more; and no real progress). These should be the students you are most worried about).
2. Struggling (reading skills about half a GE behind; at or below 30th percentile).
3. Typical or Gifted but not progressing.
4. Typical or Gifted (use this student as a comparison for the others).

The scores for the students we observed are provided in Figure 10.2. As you can see, in both classrooms, students started with approximately the same reading levels with struggling readers about two months behind their typically reading peers. For the observation example, we used the winter scores.

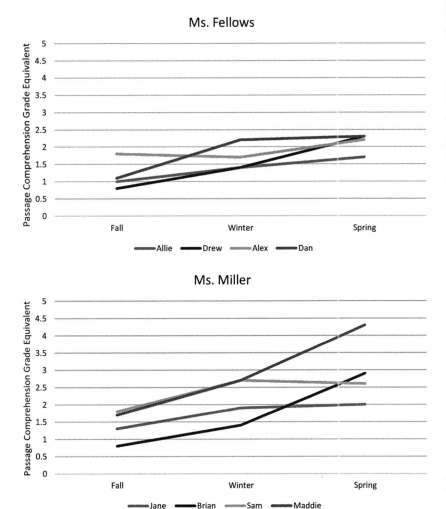

FIGURE 10.2 Student Passage Comprehension Grade Equivalent (GE) scores for fall, winter, and spring by classroom

Next, record the amount of time students are spending in small groups or whole class with the teacher, working with peers, or working independently at their desk and on a computer. Also record whether the activity is code-focused or meaning-focused, using Table 10.1 and our example as a guide. For example, in Ms. Miller's classroom, from 1:30 to 1:39, students were participating in different child-managed (CM) activities. Jane was working with a small group of students in a code-focused activity (CMCFSG) whereas Brian and Maddie were reading silently to themselves, which is a child-managed, meaning-focused activity (CMMF). We suggest that you briefly describe the activity in the first column.

Then watch the teacher lead a lesson—it can be either code- or meaning-focused. Watch how your target students are responding. Are they:

1. Raising their hands (when expected)? If so, make a hash mark. For example, in Ms. Fellows's class, Drew raised his hand six times.
2. Are they answering questions using more than one word? Again, make a hash mark for each answer that is more than one word. For example, in Ms. Miller's class, Sam answered questions twice using more than one word.
3. Do they participate in the classroom conversation? For example, when they raise their hands, does the teacher call on them? In Ms. Fellows's classroom, Drew is only called on once to make a contribution to the conversation.

Next, record whenever a target student is off task or is not receiving instruction using the space below the recorded activity. For example, in Ms. Fellows's class, at 11:19, Drew gets a drink of water and Alex goes to the bathroom. These are lost opportunities to learn.

Then look again at the teacher. Look for instructional actions that predict students' reading gains. What is the teacher doing during discussion when students are answering questions and participating in classroom conversations? In the column for the teacher, make a hash mark each time you observe one of the following instructional moves:

1. Models/Coaches (M/C)
2. Fosters discussion (FD)
3. Assesses students' learning and provides feedback (FB)
4. Asks *how* and *why* questions (H/W)
5. Encourages students to ask questions (S/Q)

As you can see in the completed observation form (Appendix A), when the target students in Ms. Miller's classroom were participating in TMCFWC instruction (2:05–2:37), she provided feedback (FB) four times, fostered discussion (FD) four times, and encouraged students to ask questions (S/Q) four times.

Also record when the teacher provides inaccurate or confusing instruction (ICI). For example, Ms. Fellows wanted to provide a water break for her students (11:16–11:39). But the directions she provided were confusing, so her students were confused and instruction time was wasted.

Record what the teacher is doing when the target students are off task or not responding. Note the following:

1. Is the teacher's feedback supportive or harsh?
2. Is there a system in place that helps students understand the classroom rules and routines and is the system used?

Making Sense of the Results

When the observation is finished, it is time to complete the summary sheet (see Appendix A). First, record the length of the observation. For example, we observed Ms. Miller's class twice—once for 28 minutes and again for 39 minutes. We observed Ms. Fellows's class for 35 minutes. We spent more time observing Ms. Miller's class because she taught a whole class lesson, met with students in a small group during learning stations or center time, as well as encouraged some students to work independently. Ms. Fellows provided instruction solely during a whole class lesson and did not organize her literacy block into learning stations. We encourage you to observe all types of instruction when possible. We provide graphs in Figures 10.3 and 10.4 (and a blank chart in Appendix A) that show recommended amounts of each type of instruction for students based on reading grade equivalent scores. For our example, we used students' winter scores because the observations were conducted in January and February.

Starting with Ms. Fellows, we see that, although Allie, Drew, Alex, and Dan had very different reading skills, they all got the same amount of TM instruction—5 minutes of code-focused and 14 minutes of meaning-focused instruction (see Figure 10.3). That is, except for Alex, who was on the computer during TMMFWC instruction. The students spent no time in CMCF instruction and

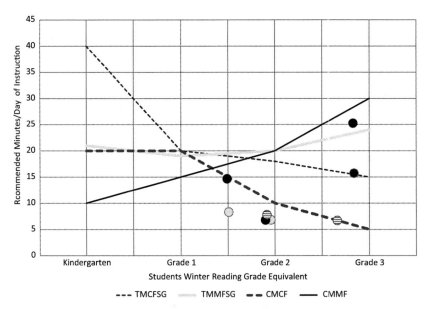

FIGURE 10.3 Recommended minutes of first grade reading instruction for Ms. Fellows's students. Dots represent students' recommended amount of each type of instruction by shade.

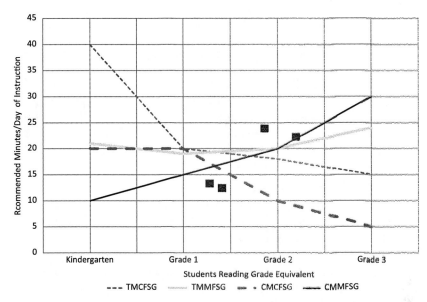

FIGURE 10.4 Recommended minutes of first grade reading instruction for Ms. Miller's students.

Squares represent student's recommended amount of each type of instruction by shade.

varying amounts of time in CMMF, with Alex receiving more time in CMMF because he was on the computer.

In Ms. Miller's class, most of the whole class time was spent in TMCFWC (about 32 minutes) with a small amount of TMMFWC instruction (see Figure 10.4). Jane spent part of that time in the bathroom, which is too bad because she is struggling with reading. During stations, we saw a good example of differentiated instruction. Jane who is struggling with reading, spent 7 minutes with the teacher in TMMFSG, 9 minutes in CMCF, and 8 minutes in CMMF. In contrast, Maddie, the typical student, spent the entire time in CMMF. Based on research, these are close to optimum for students with these different skill profiles. In general:

1. Struggling readers make greater gains when they spend more time in explicit and systematic code- and meaning-focused instruction conducted in small groups with their teacher—TMCFSG and TMMFSG.
2. Gifted students make greater gains when they are challenged and allowed to work independently and with peers—CMMF.
3. Typical readers may not be getting the right balance of systematic and explicit instruction versus challenging work.
4. When students are working independently or with peers:

a. The work should be meaningful and appropriately challenging.
b. Students should generally be on task.
c. Students who are good readers make greater gains when these student-managed times are meaning-focused (CMMF, reading, writing); they make weaker gains when the activities are code-focused (CMCF).
d. Students who are struggling with reading make greatest gains when they have time to practice the code-focused skills they are learning (CMCF) but still need opportunities to read and write independently (CMMF). The ideal amount of CMMF increases as the year progresses and students' reading skills improve.

If you examine Figures 10.3 and 10.4, you can see where we've plotted the small group (SG) and child-managed (CM) instruction for each student based on his or her reading scores in the winter. The closer the student is to the recommended amounts of each type of instruction, the stronger their reading gains will be. Ms. Miller's students are plotted as circles and Ms. Fellows as squares with shade matching the type of instruction (e.g., black for CMMF). Examination of the chart shows that Ms. Miller provided more of the recommended types of instruction and was fairly close to providing more optimal amounts of each type based on her students' winter scores. Ms. Fellows provided only CMMF opportunities and was also fairly close to providing optimal opportunities with less time for students who were struggling and more for students who had typical skills.

Based on the observations so far, we would encourage Ms. Fellows to provide more time with her students in small group TMCF and TMMF instruction, especially with students who are not making expected reading gains. We would commend Ms. Miller for individualizing her instruction to meet the needs of all of her students and encourage her to provide more time in small group time code-focused instruction.

Next, we examine the teachers' instructional actions during the lessons that are associated with greater student reading gains. Because we observed Ms. Miller longer than Ms. Fellows, we make the scores comparable by dividing the number of actions by the length of the observation (i.e., actions/minute). Ms. Miller modeled/coached 2 times, fostered discussion 4 times, provided feedback 7 times, used *how* and *why* questions 4 times, and encouraged students to ask questions 4 times for a total of 21 actions in 67 minutes or .31 actions/minute. Ms. Fellows modeled/coached 4 times, fostered discussion 2 times, and provided feedback 7 times. She did not use how/why questions or encourage students to ask questions. This gives a total of 13 actions over 35 minutes or .37 actions/minute.

Thus, based on observing both teachers' instructional actions, their teaching ratings were about the same but were qualitatively different. Ms. Fellows did not use *how* and *why* questions. Nor did she encourage her students to ask questions. In contrast Ms. Miller did use *how* and *why* questions and encouraged her students to ask questions. These are actions that generally foster student thinking and learning. Notice also that Ms. Miller used how and why questions during small group time. One reason teaching with smaller groups of students is frequently more effective than whole class is that it offers opportunities to use these kinds of instructional actions, particularly with students who might not participate actively during whole class instruction.

We also point out that Ms. Miller's lesson was code-focused for 32 minutes and meaning-focused for 4 minutes whereas Ms. Fellows's lesson was meaning-focused for 29 minutes and code-focused for 5 minutes. This means that Ms. Fellows was providing virtually no time in explicit systematic code-focused instruction with her first graders. Keep in mind that recommended daily amounts of TMCF are about 20 minutes/day for Allie and Drew.

Finally, we examined how the students were participating in instruction. This is another area where we see clear differences between classrooms. Although we did note some similarities in the instructional actions that both classroom teachers used, we observed dramatic differences in the students' responses to these actions. All four of the target students in Ms. Miller's class were actively participating in the whole class code-focused lesson, raising their hands and answering questions. In addition, Maddie, who had stronger reading skills, was also observed following along and writing. In contrast, during Ms. Fellows's whole class meaning-focused lesson, Drew was the only student actively participating in the lesson—he raised his hand and responded when called on. Allie was frequently observed to be off task and inattentive, and Ms. Fellows had to redirect her behavior two times. Further, Dan raised his hand but did not respond when the teacher called on him, and Alex was on the computer for most of the lesson and did not actively participate during the 3 minutes he was involved in the lesson. Thus we see that the same instructional actions associated with stronger student learning do not necessarily elicit similar levels of student participation. Both are important. Therefore, we suggest providing support to help Ms. Fellows encourage her students to actively participate in her classroom lessons as well as helping her ensure that her students are getting the appropriate amount of code- and meaning-focused instruction to maximize student learning.

Based on these observations, which teacher's students achieved stronger passage comprehension score gains? Based on the scores of all students, not just the target students, Ms. Miller's students were making reading skill gains that were greater than the students of the other 30 teachers in the study, whereas Ms. Fellows's students were making smaller gains than the other teachers' students. Based on the OET-Reading1 results, Ms. Miller was providing appropriate amounts of both code- and meaning-focused instruction and she individualized this instruction using stations. Although there was room for improvement with regard to her instructional actions and providing TCMCFSG instruction, still, her students were all active participants in the lesson, keeping in mind that two of the target students were not reading as well as the other students. In contrast, Ms. Fellows provided virtually no opportunities for her students to participate in code-focused instruction, she did not individualize instruction using stations or centers, and three of her students were not actively participating in the lessons she provided. Indeed, Allie, who, based on her test scores, was struggling with reading and not progressing from the fall to winter season, was observed to be off task. At the same time, Drew, who was struggling with reading at the beginning of the school year, did raise his hand and participate. Finally, Dan, who had above grade level reading skills, did not respond even when the teacher called on him. If we return to Figure 10.2, we see that Dan's reading skills stagnated from winter to spring as did Alex's and Allie's. The only student in Ms. Fellows's class who made real progress from winter to spring was Drew.

This observation system is designed to help educational leaders and literacy coaches target their professional development by elucidating aspects of instruction that are associated with first grade students' reading skill gains. We see that looking solely at what the teacher is doing, his or her instructional actions, does not differentiate effective from ineffective teaching—both of the teachers we observed made about the same number of moves. Rather, we identified three aspects of instruction that do predict students' literacy gains in first grade: (1) the extent to which each student receives amounts of instruction known to be important for first graders as they learn to read—teacher and child/peer managed code- and meaning-focused instruction are all important; (2) the reading instruction provided is evidence based and taught correctly—remember the "short a" example? (3) the use of practices that allow for individualized or differentiated reading instruction; and (4) the depth of students' active participation in the lessons. It is still worthwhile to observe teachers' instructional actions because teacher actions can promote student participation.

We encourage teachers, literacy coaches, and educational leaders to try the OET-Reading1 system and make adjustments so that it works in their school setting. Better understanding what effective expert practice in the classroom actually looks like will allow this knowledge to be shared among communities of professionals—educational leaders and teachers. Enacting these practices will provide stronger literacy outcomes for all students.

Appendix A   Sample Observation
OET-Reading First Grade Observation Form   Observer: Sarah M._____   Date: 2/26/2009

Activity	Time activity starts	Time activity ends	Student A – struggling and not progressing Name: Allie	Student B – Struggling Name: Drew	Student C – Typical/Gifted & not progression Name: Alex	Student D – Typical/Gifted Name: Dan	Comments & Teacher instructional actions Ms. Fellow
Editing – Individual work @ desk	11:13 AM	11:28 AM (15m)	CMMF	CMMF • raise hand & reads • OT	CMMF OT on computer during portion of lesson	CMMF OT	"Hurry up!" Little direction to students while they work. Some students to computer during Editing three
Off-Task Behavior or Student Not Present	11:16 11:19 11:27	11:17 11:21 11:39	Puts jacket away – OFF ———→	Gets Water	Bathroom CMMF COMPUTER		releases students if 8+ water are but they are confused (ICI)
Editing as a class	11:28	11:42 (14)	TMMFWC called on-1 off-task (minimal)	TMMFWC Called on -1 (wrong answer) Hand up - MF! Shouts - 1 But	ON COMPUTER TMMFWC 11:39-11:42	TMMFWC Hand up - III called on, but doesn't respond	FB: IIII - corrects Allie M/C: IIII FD: II
Off-Task Behavior or Student Not Present							
Write words (encode)	11:43	11:48	TMCFWC OT - mostly	OT ——→	OT ——→	↑ OT	FB: II
Off-Task Behavior or Student Not Present			OFF - III → not very long				Teacher disciplines Allie twice

OT = on task

OET-Reading Summary

Total Minutes Observed = ___35___   Teacher: ___Ms Fellows___

Student	TMCFSG (min)	TMMFSG	TMCFWC	TMMFWC	CMCF	CMMF	Total Min for Student	Student Active Participation	Comments on teacher/student interactions
Student A – struggling and not progressing Allie			5	14		14	33	Frequently off task caledon - 1	Teacher discipline twice
Student B – struggling Drew			5	15		13	32	Rashand 7 reads - 1 calledon - 1	
Student C – Typical/Gifted not progressing Alex			5	3		25	33	bathroom on computer	
Student D – Typical/Gifted Dan			5	14		15	34	hands up - 1 calledon - 1 (clicker rapport)	

Teacher	Model/Coaches	Fosters Discussion	Provides Feedback	How/Why Question	Students Ask Questions	**Total Observed**
(Number of times observed)	4	2	7			13

.37 actions/minute

Inaccurate or Confusing Information
1

Appendix A   Sample Observation
OET-Reading First Grade Observation Form   Observer: _Sarah M._   Date: _1/29/2009_

Activity	Time activity starts	Time activity ends	Student A – struggling and not progressing Name: Jane	Student B – Struggling Name: Brian	Student C – Typical/Gifted & not progression Name: Sam	Student D – Typical/Gifted Name: Maddie	Comments & Teacher instructional actions Mrs. Miller
Stations - rotation 1	1:30	1:39 (9 min)	CM CF SG working w/ words station OnTask	CM MF Individual Silent reading OnTask	CM MF SG read to partner OnTask	CM MF Individual Silent reading OnTask	Teacher organized stations then students then teacher called group
Off-Task Behavior or Student Not Present	1:38	1:39		→	OFF – Not Reading		
New Stations	1:42	1:50 (8 min)	CM MF SG read to partner OnTask	TM MF SG reading back called on / answer !! reads !!	CM MF silent reading OnTask	CM MF computer OnTask	FB	H/W	
Off-Task Behavior or Student Not Present							
New Station	1:51	1:58 (7 min)	TM MF SG Hand up- ## answer - || reads – |15 struggling	CM MF writing (individual) OnTask	CM CF SG working w/ words OnTask	CM MF writing (individual) OnTask	H/W - ||| FB -	FD -	
Off-Task Behavior or Student Not Present							

Appendix A   Sample Observation
OET-Reading First Grade Observation Form   Observer: __Sarah M.__   Date: 1/29/2009

Activity	Time activity starts	Time activity ends	Student A – struggling and not progressing Name: Jane	Student B – Struggling Name: Brian	Student C – Typical/Gifted & not progression Name: Sam	Student D – Typical/Gifted Name: Maddie	Comments & Teacher instructional actions Mrs. Miller
Letter-Sound Correspondence + phonemes	2:05 pm	2:37	T M C F WC raise hand ## answer – II good job from teacher	T M C F WC raise hand – 1 answer – 1 listening 4 on task Called on – 1	T M C F WC Hand up – III answer – II	T M C F WC Hand up – III answer – II following along + writing on let	FB-IIII "nice sight (iced Job) Encouraged students FD-III SQ-IIII MIL-II
Off-Task Behavior or Student Not Present	2:20	2:27	Bathroom			Flipping (twice) pencil	Discipline – II (reminder to raise hands)
Reviewing Story	2:40	2:44	T M M F WC →	Hand up – 1 →	Called on – 1	→	FB-1 asking about plot + setting after Students move to carpet
Off-Task Behavior or Student Not Present							
Off-Task Behavior or Student Not Present							

OET-Reading Summary

Total Minutes Observed = 39+ 26 = 67   Teacher: Ms. Miller

Student	TMCFSG (min)	TMMFSG	TMCFWC	TMMFWC	CMCF	CMMF	Total Min for Student	Student Active Participation	Comments on teacher/student interactions
Student A – struggling and not progressing		7	25	4	9	8	53	reads to partner, hand up -15, answer -3, reads - #2	Highly interactive
Student B – struggling		8	32	4		16	60	silent reading, read aloud, called on - 2, groups - 2, hand up - 1	
Student C – Typical/Gifted not progressing			32	4	7	16	59	read to partner, silent read alt, hand up >3, answer = 2, called on = 1	
Student D – Typical/Gifted			32	4		24	60	silent reading, writing = 2, hand up - 3, answer = 2	✓

Teacher	Model/Coaches	Fosters Discussion	Provides Feedback	How/Why Question	Students Ask Questions	**Total Observed**
(Number of times observed)	2	4	7	4	4	**21**

.31 actions / minute

Inaccurate or Confusing Information
0

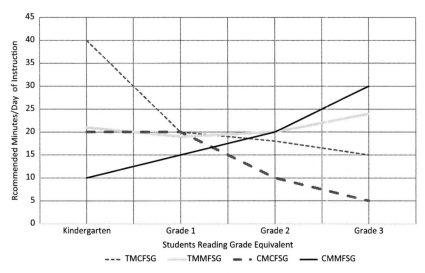

FIGURE 10.5 Recommendation minutes of first grade reading instruction based on students reading grade equivalent scores

References

Bronfenbrenner, U., & Morris, P.A. (2006). The bioecological model of human development. In R.M. Lerner & W. Damon (Eds.), *Handbook of child psychology: Theoretical models of human development* (6th ed., Vol. 1, pp. 793–828). Hoboken, NJ: John Wiley & Sons.

Carlisle, J.F., Kelcey, B., Berebitsky, D., & Phelps, G. (2011). Embracing the complexity of instruction: A study of the effects of teachers' instruction on students' reading comprehension. *Scientific Studies of Reading, 15*(5), 409–439.

Connor, C.M. (2013). Commentary on two classroom observation systems: Moving toward a shared understanding of effective teaching. *School Psychology Quarterly, 28*(4), 342–346. doi: 10.1037/spq0000045

Connor, C.M., Jakobsons, L.J., Crowe, E., Meadows, J. (2009). Instruction, differentiation, and student engagement in Reading First classrooms. *Elementary School Journal, 109*(3), 221–250.

Connor, C.M., & Morrison, F.J. (2012). Knowledge acquisition in the classroom: Literacy and content area knowledge In A.M. Pinkham, T. Kaefer, & S.B. Neuman (Eds.), *Knowledge development in early childhood: Sources of learning and classroom implications* (pp. 220–241). New York: Guilford Press.

Connor, C.M., Morrison, F.J., Fishman, B., Crowe, E.C., Al Otaiba, S., & Schatschneider, C. (2013). A longitudinal cluster-randomized controlled study on the accumulating effects of individualized literacy instruction on students' reading from first through third grade. *Psychological Science, 24*(8), 1408–1419. doi: 10.1177/0956797612472204

Connor, C.M., Morrison, F.J., Fishman, B., Giuliani, S., Luck, M., Underwood, P., . . . Schatschneider, C. (2011). Classroom instruction, child X instruction interactions and the impact of differentiating student instruction on third graders' reading comprehension. *Reading Research Quarterly, 46*(3), 189–221.

Connor, C.M., Morrison, F.J., Fishman, B., Ponitz, C.C., Glasney, S., Underwood, P., . . . Schatschneider, C. (2009). The ISI classroom observation system: Examining the literacy instruction provided to individual students. *Educational Researcher, 38*(2), 85–99.

Connor, C.M., Morrison, F.J., Schatschneider, C., Toste, J., Lundblom, E.G., Crowe, E., & Fishman, B. (2011). Effective classroom instruction: Implications of child characteristic by instruction interactions on first graders' word reading achievement. *Journal for Research on Educational Effectiveness, 4*(3), 173–207.

Connor, C.M., Piasta, S.B., Fishman, B., Glasney, S., Schatschneider, C., Crowe, E., . . . Morrison, F.J. (2009). Individualizing student instruction precisely: Effects of child by instruction interactions on first graders' literacy development. *Child Development, 80*(1), 77–100.

Connor, C.M., Son, S.-H., Hindman, A.H., & Morrison, F.J. (2005). Teacher qualifications, classroom practices, family characteristics, and preschool experience: Complex effects on first graders' vocabulary and early reading outcomes. *Journal of School Psychology, 43*, 343–375.

Connor, C.M., Spencer, M., Day, S.L., Giuliani, S., Ingebrand, S.W., McLean, L., & Morrison, F.J. (2014). Capturing the complexity: Content, type, and amount of instruction and quality of the classroom learning environment synergistically predict third graders' vocabulary and reading comprehension outcomes. *Journal of Educational Psychology, 106*(3), 762–778. doi: 10.1037/a0035921

Crawford, A.D., Zucker, T.A., Williams, J.M., Bhavsar, V., & Landry, S.H. (2013). Initial validation of the prekindergarten Classroom Observation Tool and goal setting system for data-based coaching. *School Psychology Quarterly, 28,* 277– 300. doi: 10.1037/spq0000033

Goldhaber, D., & Anthony, E. (2003). *Teacher quality and student achievement.* Urban Diversity Series (Report: UDS-115; 153). New York: Department of Education, Washington, DC.

Grossman, P., Loeb, S., Cohen, J., Hammerness, K., Wyckoff, J., Boyd, D., & Lankford, H. (2010). *Measure for measure: The relationship between measures of instructional practice in middle school English language arts and teachers' value-added scores* (No. 45). Washington, DC: National Center for Analysis of Longitudinal Data in Education Research.

IES Technical Working Group. (2013). *Researching college-and-career-ready standards to improve student outcomes.* Retrieved from: es.ed.gov/ncer/whatsnew/techworkinggroup/pdf/CCRSTWG.pdf

Justice, L.M., Petscher, Y., Schatschneider, C., & Mashburn, A. (2011). Peer effects in preschool classrooms: Is children's language growth associated with their classmates' skills? *Child Development, 82*(6), 1768–1777.

Kane, T., Staiger, D.O., & McCaffrey, D. (2012). Gathering feedback for teaching: Combining high-quality observations with student surveys and achievement gains. Bill and Melinda Gates Foundation. Retrieved from: http://eric.ed.gov/?id=ED540962

Konstantopoulos, S., & Chung, N. (2011). The persistence of teacher effects in elementary grades. *American Educational Research Journal, 48*(2), 361–386.

McLean, L., & Connor, C.M. (in press). Depressive symptoms in 3rd grade teachers: Relations to classroom quality and student achievement. *Child Development.*

National Assessment of Educational Progress. (2014). *Our nation's report card.* Retrieved March 2015, from: US Department of Education, National Center for Educational Statistics http://nationsreportcard.gov/reading_math_2013/—/what-knowledge

National Research Council. (2001). *Educating children with autism*. Committee on Educational Interventions for Children with Autism. Retrieved from: http://www.nap.edu/openbook.php?isbn=0309072697

Olson, R.K. (2008). Genetic and environmental influences on word-reading skills. In E.L. Grigorenko & A.J. Naples (Eds.), *Single-word reading: Behavioral and biological perspectives.* New directions in communication disorders research: Integrative approaches (pp. 233–253). Mahwah, NJ: Lawrence Erlbaum.

Pianta, R.C., La Paro, K.M., Payne, K., Cox, C., & Bradley, R.H. (2002). The relation of kindergarten classroom environment to teacher, family and school characteristics and child outcomes. *Elementary School Journal, 102*(3), 225–238.

Piasta, S.B., Connor, C.M., Fishman, B., & Morrison, F.J. (2009). Teachers' knowledge of literacy, classroom practices, and student reading growth. *Scientific Studies of Reading, 13*(3), 224–248.

Ponitz, C.C., McClelland, M.M., Matthews, J.S., & Morrison, F.J. (2009). A structured observation of behavioral self-regulation and its contribution to kindergarten outcomes. *Developmental Psychology, 45*, 605–619.

Raudenbush, S.W. (2004). What are value-added models estimating and what does this imply for statistical practice? *Journal of Educational and Behavioral Statistics, 29*(1), 121–129.

Raudenbush, S.W. (2009). The Brown Legacy and the O'Connor Challenge: Transforming schools in the images of children's potential. *Educational Researcher, 38*(3), 169–180. doi: 10.3102/0013189x09334840

Raver, C.C., Blair, C., & Li-Grining, C.P. (2012). *Extending models of emotion self-regulation to classroom settings: Implications for professional development.* Baltimore: Brookes.

Reddy, L., Fabiano, G., Dudek, C., & Hsu, L. (2013a). Development and construct validity of the Classroom Strategy Scale-Observer Form. *School Psychology Quarterly 28*, 317–34.

Reddy, L., Fabiano, G., Dudek, C., & Hsu, L. (2013b). Predictive validity of the Classroom Strategies Scale-Observer Form on statewide testing. *School Psychology Quarterly 28*, 301–316.

Rimm-Kaufman, S.E., Paro, K.M.L., Downer, J.T., & Pianta, R.C. (2005). The contribution of classroom setting and quality of instruction to children's behavior in kindergarten classrooms. *Elementary School Journal, 105*(4), 337–345.

Shapiro, E.S. (2003). Behavioral Observation of Students in Schools (BOSS). Computer Software. San Antonio, TX: Psychological Corporation.

Strong, M., Gargani, J., & Hacifazlioğlu, Ö. (2011). Do we know a successful teacher when we see one? Experiments in the identification of effective teachers. *Journal of Teacher Education, 64*(2), 367–382. doi: 10.1177/0022487110390221.

Taylor, B.M., & Pearson, D.P. (Eds.). (2002). *Teaching reading: Effective schools, accomplished teachers.* Mahwah, NJ: Lawrence Erlbaum.

Taylor, J.E., Roehrig, A.D., Connor, C.M., & Schatschneider, C. (2010). Teacher quality moderates the genetic effects on early reading. *Science, 328*, 512–514.

Torgesen, J.K. (2002). The prevention of reading difficulties. *Journal of School Psychology, 40*(1), 7–26.

Vellutino, F.R., Scanlon, D.M., Sipay, E.R., Small, S.G., Pratt, A., Chen, R., & Denckla, M.B. (1996). Cognitive profiles of difficult to remediate and readily remediated poor readers: Early intervention as a vehicle for distinguishing between cognitive and experiential deficits as basic causes of specific reading disability. *Journal of Educational Psychology, 88*(4), 601–638.

Wachs, T.D., Gurkas, P., & Kontos, S. (2004). Predictors of preschool children's compliance behavior in early childhood classroom settings. *Journal of Applied Developmental Psychology, 25*(4), 439–457.

Wharton-McDonald, R., Pressley, M., & Hampston, J.M. (1998). Literacy instruction in nine first-grade classrooms: Teacher characteristics and student achievement. *Elementary School Journal, 99*(2), 101–128.

Woodcock, R.W., McGrew, K.S., & Mather, N. (2001). *Woodcock-Johnson-III Tests of Achievement.* Itasca, IL: Riverside.

Yoshikawa, H., & Hsueh, J. (2001). Child development and public policy: Toward a dynamic systems perspective. *Child Development, 72*(6), 1887–1903.

11

WHEN LEADERSHIP SKILLS ARE NOT ENOUGH

The Role of Principals in High-Stakes Observations

Steven T. McAbee

Principals have an enormous responsibility when it comes to moving a school forward or moving a school from good to great. In a typical elementary school, some teachers introduce the world of education to five-year-olds while other teachers have students writing memoirs and using abstract mathematics operations by the end of fifth grade. Principals need the expertise to walk into every classroom and evaluate the quality of instruction being offered to all students. This was a bit overwhelming as I entered my position as elementary principal after spending my entire career as a middle school and high school teacher and administrator. I soon realized that I did not have the level of expertise needed to offer suggestions to all my teachers. I also realized that the observation instrument being used offered little value in spotting good and bad reading instruction. I had an amazing faculty, but I noticed things around the school that puzzled me; students were being given short speed-reading tests, teachers were making thousands of copies of worksheets that were part of a basal program, and there were no discussions about reading instruction other than the basal.

I was attending a new principal workshop in Knoxville. One of the presenters was Dr. Robert Lynn Canady; he was discussing creative scheduling for all grades. Scheduling is one of his areas of expertise but Dr. Canady is well versed in all areas of K-12 public schooling. During his presentation he veered off the discussion of scheduling to briefly mention research on early literacy. He stated, "If kindergarten students cannot read, cut up, and correctly reassemble the sentence 'The fat cat sat on the mat' by Halloween, then they are already behind." That one statement took my breath away because I knew from walking my halls that our kindergarten was doing a letter per week. Students in our kindergarten were on the letter "M" at Halloween, a far cry from reading simple sentences. I had also just recently met with my first grade teachers and asked them what every child needed to be able to do on day one of first grade to be successful. They replied that all students should know their letters and sounds. I had wonderful, hard-working teachers but I had a problem—a big problem: we had a reading instruction problem. Students were starting out behind expectations from the outset of their schooling. It was my duty to get us on the right track, but how? I am not a reading expert; I've never even taught a class younger than sixth grade.

Our elementary school was designated as a focus school because our students in poverty were not performing at the same levels as our more affluent students. Because of this status, I was able to apply for a grant to help improve our instruction. I wrote and received a $200,000 grant to improve reading instruction at the elementary level. I wanted the grant proposal to focus on high-quality professional development for our teachers and to purchase leveled texts for our students. The texts may need to be replaced from normal wear and tear, but it is hoped that the investment in professional development will give high returns for years to come. The proposal had three central components to help improve instruction; purchase hundreds of books at different reading levels for our students, bring in reading experts to provide bimonthly professional development for teachers, and build expertise in the faculty by partnering with the University of Tennessee at Knoxville. Through this partnership, eight of the teachers and I took courses and obtained our reading specialists degrees. The two years spent working toward this degree has allowed me to become much more expert in the field of child and adolescent literacy and thus become a much more effective teacher evaluator. Before this experience, I was an uninformed evaluator using a global observation instrument that is not designed to measure effective reading instruction. Combining a principal who is not expert in instruction with that instrument would lead to slow or no growth in teacher development.

There are two avenues I want to illuminate in the discussion of evaluating reading teachers from my perspective as an elementary school principal. First, many administrators know very little about highly effective reading instruction. We neither have a full grasp of the many components of a balanced literacy program nor know much about the research surrounding how to teach every child to read and write on grade level by third grade. Teacher performance is not so much a teacher issue as it is an administration issue. Teachers by and large want to be on a winning team. They want to be good at what they do—they want to be great teachers. Yet, administrators often do not have the expertise in reading instruction to give quality feedback after observing the teacher and, as is often the case, the administrator does not have a strong enough background to identify high-quality professional development needed for his or her school. All administrators and central offices provide professional development; it is just that few provide high-quality professional development relevant to the needs of teachers and students. There is a difference.

The other issue with teacher evaluation is the observation instruments that are not designed to paint a full picture of effective reading instruction. The observation methods used by most districts are global in nature. They help to measure if the teacher completes professional responsibilities, if the classroom is orderly and conducive to learning, if students know and understand daily routines, and so on. There is value in noticing these in each classroom, but the issue is that the observation instruments provide limited insight into the classroom experiences. As we will see later in this chapter, they give the evaluator a general impression of the classroom dynamics and instruction, but miss many of the nuances that distinguish effective reading instruction from ineffective reading instruction. Furthermore, the current observation models fail to measure aspects of reading growth that exist outside the school.

For example, we know that students in middle class and affluent families tend to improve in reading throughout the summer months. In contrast, students from poor families tend to "slide" backwards in reading achievement during the summer months. Consider a third grade student like Jennifer. Jennifer made a score of 768 on the reading/language arts portion of the end-of-the-year test. This score ranks Jennifer as proficient in reading. Her reading level as measured on running records is a Fountas and Pinnell (F&P) level P. Jennifer has few books at home and does very little reading over the summer months. She has little exposure to new vocabulary and forgets some of her reading strategies. When Jennifer returns to school to begin fourth grade she is given a running record and she is at an F&P level of O. She is a victim of "summer slide" (Allington & McGill-Franzen, 2013).

Jennifer has a wonderful fourth grade reading teacher who knows how to incorporate interactive read-alouds, guided reading groups, differentiated word study, and scaffolded independent reading time during class. At the end of the year Jennifer scores a 755 on the reading/language arts portion of the year-end test. This score is ranked as basic, the ranking just below proficient. Her F&P running record shows that she is reading at an R level. She has grown three F&P levels, which is considered a full year's growth. Her fourth grade teacher will suffer the consequences of the student having limited experiences with reading and writing during the summer months. Early on I would have been confused when examining the high stakes test scores at the end of Jennifer's fourth grade year because there is not much "growth." I would likely have had a conversation with the fourth grade teacher about this issue and tell the teacher to work harder next year when in actuality the teacher brought the child much farther than the value-added models (VAM) will ever show. I have included questions throughout the remainder of the chapter that will guide our thinking about an administrator's expertise in evaluating reading teachers and the value of current observation models.

Times Have Changed

There was a time when the qualifications for being an administrator were that you were a coach with two losing seasons and a master's degree. You were required to show up a little early to get the lights turned on and then head to your office to have a quick read of the newspaper and deal with unruly students and their parents. In today's schools the most knowledgeable person about instruction should be the principal. This is not the time to justify the importance of our leadership degrees; it is rather the time to decide if principals can consistently walk into classrooms and recognize high-quality reading instruction. Do we know as much about early literacy as we do adolescent literacy? Do we know how writing and reading go hand in glove to increase student achievement? Do we know what the research says about teaching every child to read and write on grade level? If we cannot answer the questions affirmatively, how can we effectively evaluate our reading teachers?

A Shift from Leadership Training to Instructional Training

In my experience, many administrators in public schools receive quality training in leadership theory and methods. This training is needed because of the many dynamics that come into play in our public schools. School safety policy, bullying issues, parental involvement, high-stakes testing, etc. are all components that administrators must be able to deal with quickly and effectively. And while most administrators are sufficient in these areas and some of the issues lead to school improvement and increased student achievement, there is an area lacking in administrator training: teacher observation. There are many models of teacher observation and they all tend to focus on aspects such as classroom management, professional responsibilities, communication with parents, and student engagement. At first blush one might think that a component like student engagement will allow the administrator to gauge the type of instruction being delivered to students.

An administrator will likely give a favorable evaluation if he enters the classroom and notices a quiet class which seems to be participating in the lesson and a teacher who is circulating throughout the room, and just think of the high reviews the teacher will receive if the principal notices that students are in learning centers! The administrator is too often oblivious to the important nuances that are happening in a classroom, such as whether students are reading authentic texts that are appropriate for them, whether students are engaged in effective word study and vocabulary lessons, and whether students know the strategies needed to be successful readers. One might argue that the administrator could simply ask the teacher these questions in a debriefing session after the observation and the teacher could explain the finer details of the lesson. This can be problematic if the teacher is weak in instruction and the administrator is not conversant in effective reading instruction. In this situation, the teacher gives a rational explanation of the lesson and since the administrator is rather limited in his/her knowledge of reading instruction, an effective observation score is given to the teacher.

One could also argue that the instrument is creating a situation where the teacher has to sacrifice quality instruction. Aspects like free reading time and books in the classroom are not listed on the rubric. Thus, the teacher could get a low observation score if the teacher has an unannounced observation during sustained silent reading time simply because engaged self-selected reading is not an indicator of effective instruction according to the characteristics listed on the generic rubric.

Professional Development

In their chapter within this volume (Chapter 10), Connor, Ingebrand, and Sparapani mention that principals are no better than chance at judging quality instruction. This may be because the observation models are not designed to measure reading instruction or because principals are simply not trained to recognize effective reading instruction. With the latter in mind, the importance of high quality professional development (PD) for administrators cannot be taken for granted. Principals need to understand balanced literacy as well as anyone in the building. Once the principal has adequate schema for literacy, he/she can begin to find professional development opportunities for faculty members at their school.

Measuring Effective Instruction

Administrators need to understand the types of instruments being used to measure student reading progress. Many times the instruments used to measure reading progress do not actually measure reading achievement. For example, teachers are told to progress monitor students' fluency using DIBELS. When speed of reading for one minute is emphasized over everything else, students learn to speed read words quickly but comprehend very little of what was read. I recall having a student read a page from her book for me the first year I was principal. She read the page as quickly as she could, with little intonation. Once she had completed the page she said to me, "How long did that take me?" I told her that I did not time her on the page. A look of disappointment came across her face. I asked her to describe what had taken place in the story. She stared at the page and didn't say a word. I then asked her if she could predict what might happen next in the story. She looked at me and then back to the page and finally responded "I don't know." It didn't take long for my gut to tell me something was wrong with this situation—a situation that existed throughout my entire school.

My teachers were not checking for fluency, they were measuring reading rate and whether a kid could sound out nonsense words. I had failed to fully realize the impact that our progress monitoring tool was having on our students' reading abilities. I had forgotten the truism that students are much more likely to learn what is taught than what is not taught! To complicate the matter, my district had adopted this instrument and mandated that every teacher use it with every student with fidelity. Our district was systematically creating speed readers in every school! Speed readers who had few strategies for understanding texts. As administrators we do not look forward to asking the central office to change district-wide policy, but at the end of the day a principal is responsible for his/her school. The principal must know not only what good reading instruction looks like, but also how to measure all components of reading. That said, we no longer use that instrument in my school.

Most of the current observation models lead administrators to notice things like: students are on task, classroom is conducive to learning, teacher is interacting with students, routines are established and understood by all students, teacher completes professional responsibilities, teacher consistently uses academic vocabulary with students, etc. Imagine that you enter a classroom and evaluate a teacher who receives high marks on all the components listed. You still know very little about her reading instruction. We know from the research that the most effective observation systems are designed for a specific purpose. The issue is that most schools do not have an observation system designed for evaluating reading instruction. This is compounded by the use of value-added models (VAM). VAMs may be beneficial at showing some growth added to the students' achievement by the teacher but they do very little to help teachers and principals know what to improve in the classrooms. The VAMs do little to show *how* and *why* certain students are progressing slowly or quickly. I will argue that the *how* and *why* are the most important facets for the principal to be able to recognize upon entering a classroom. It is the *how* and *why* that allows the teacher to reflect on her teaching and make meaningful connections to improve instruction and help students grow. It is also important to note that educators are teaching unobserved over 90% of the time. If we want this time to become more engaging and meaningful for the students, either the observation instrument must be more focused on effective reading instruction or evaluators need to be more expert in noticing effective reading instruction.

Noticing Instruction

Administrators must be able to systematically and regularly spot strong and weak instruction throughout the building. I want to briefly look inside a teacher's classroom as she goes through her reading block.

I enter Ms. Smith's first grade classroom at 8:10. The room is arranged with small desks and a few circle tables with a beautiful rug on the floor. There are lots of colorful posters and rules on the wall that have been purchased at the local teacher supply store. The students are sitting on the rug around her as she reads a book to them. Sitting in the back of the room is Mrs. Jones, a paraprofessional assigned to help Ms. Smith during the reading block. The students are very attentive and enjoy the story. After about 10 minutes Ms. Smith shuts the book and tells students it is time to go to centers. There are four center stations set up around the room.

Ms. Smith takes four students to a kidney-shaped table for small-group reading. The students have the "above" level decodable reader from the basal series. Another group goes to Mrs. Jones at another kidney-shaped table where they read with her from an old Lippincott book. A third group goes to a table with four computers and complete literacy activities online, and the rest of the students complete a skills worksheet using "ee" or "ea." I listen in as Ms. Smith conducts the reading group. They choral-read a page. She then has one student read a page. The student struggles to pronounce a word and she tells him to sound it out. After a couple of unsuccessful tries, she tells him the word and they move on. After 20 minutes has elapsed, Ms. Smith announces it is time to switch and each group goes to a different center. This continues until all groups have been to each center. The students have a wonderful grasp of the routine and there is little lost time during transitions. A few students go to the bathroom, which is located in the classroom, but there are no disruptions to the class.

Once the 90-minute reading block has ended, Mrs. Jones leaves the room and Ms. Smith begins a scripted phonics lesson. It is a whole group activity and Ms. Smith hands out a worksheet. She then tells the students to write the letter to the sound they hear. She says /a/. The students write down the letter *a*. Next she says /er/. Some students write *er*, some write down *ir*, and some write down *ir*, *er*, and *ur*. She stops and makes sure all students have all the correct responses. The students then begin to code words in a paragraph on the worksheet and those who finish early are allowed to read quietly.

Good Instruction or Effective Instruction?

This teacher most likely would have been given a satisfactory score on most observation models. The principal would have made note of the learning centers, the additional person in room for learning center instruction, classroom management was fine, differentiated opportunities were presented to the students. However, many reading experts would have given a poor score if they were looking at the instruction received by the students. Here are some things that would have been noticed:

- Some of the most ineffective classrooms have paraprofessionals delivering instruction to students. This is especially true if the paraprofessional works with struggling students. We must begin to utilize our paraprofessionals in many ways other than delivering instruction. (The only exception I see to this is if the paraprofessionals happen to be highly trained.)

- Student-created posters and anchor charts are more meaningful than store-bought materials that are placed on the wall.
- Simply reading a story to students is not sufficient. We know that it is much more effective to have a teaching point from the whole-group read-aloud and give students instructions on how to practice the point during their independent reading time.
- Students need many texts that are at their instructional and independent reading level. The above-, on-, and below-level supplementary books provided by basal series are not sufficient. In fact, we know that many of the supplemental below-level readers offered by the basal series are written at a more difficult level than the basal itself.
- Worksheets that deal with skills in isolation are not effective instructionally and are not necessarily at the level each student needs. Some students will struggle and become frustrated with the work while others will find it boring and unchallenging.
- The computer station may or may not be beneficial to the students. There are a few programs that seem to foster interest in reading for many students but we find that the struggling students need explicit instruction from a highly qualified teacher if accelerated growth is going to be accomplished.
- Ms. Smith has few questioning skills as she interacts with the students at her table. The only help she provides the student struggling to pronounce a word is "sound it out."
- Ms. Smith spends little time asking students to predict what will happen next, summarize what you just read, or make inferences about the text.
- Finally, Ms. Smith conducts a separate whole group phonics lesson that lasts 40 minutes. The lesson is in no way differentiated based on where students are in their word recognition development. Students spend a great amount of time making different marks on the words in the paragraph in an effort to "code" the words.

The administrator must know the nuances of good reading instruction in order to help Ms. Smith become a more effective reading teacher. Without this specific knowledge, Ms. Smith would be graded satisfactory as a reading teacher and would miss out on valuable feedback from her evaluator. It is also important to note that Ms. Smith is not a "lazy" teacher. She has spent a lot of time preparing for this lesson. She is trying to apply the things she knows about reading instruction. She is working really hard; she is simply working hard at the wrong things. And unfortunately for Ms. Smith, the principal who has given her high marks all year will look at the end of the year scores which will be much lower than was hoped for and will sit down with Ms. Smith and encourage her to work harder next year at increasing the reading achievement of her students. Just as Ms. Smith's only advice to her struggling reader was "sound it out," her principal's only piece of advice for becoming a more expert teacher is "work harder." It is an administrator problem when teachers fail to become more expert—it is not a teacher problem. As Peterson stated in her chapter, "[E]valuating teachers without providing the professional learning and collaborative support they need to change only leads to defeated and demoralized educators."

Take Action

There are still many aspects of K–12 education that I do not fully understand. With the help and guidance of many others, I have learned several things about developing a thoughtful and balanced literacy program in the elementary school. I now know that having students complete worksheets during a reading block is basically useless, struggling students need the most expert teacher to give them additional small group instruction (not the paraprofessionals), classrooms need hundreds of books written at different reading levels for students, and students need time during each day to read for the pleasure of reading. Below I have listed a few ideas that I hope will help you as the instructional leader of your school.

1. Reflect on the chapters of this book. List the ideas presented that you do not fully understand or do not know what it would look like in a classroom. For example, do you fully comprehend what Dr. Connor is describing with "teacher meaning" and "code-focused lessons"? Do you understand that each child in a class will need different amounts of instruction to achieve at the highest levels? I had to learn that some students didn't need the teacher right beside them and others needed more explicit instruction from the teacher. I learned that this is one of the best ways to accelerate the growth of both struggling and advanced students.
2. Decide if your belief system allows you to consider the thoughts in this book. For example, is it "fair" for the teacher to meet with a group of struggling students twice each day, four days per week, but to meet with a high-level group only twice the entire week? The evidence is compelling that this is very effective at increasing reading achievement for all students. However, if you are one who believes that every child deserves the same amount of time with the teacher, you will reject this research.
3. Decide who you will contact to help become more expert in reading instruction. Is there a reading specialist in the district? (I am talking about a legitimate reading specialist, someone with an advanced degree from a credible university, not just a teacher who has been given the title "reading specialist.") Is there a university nearby with a well-respected reading specialist degree program? If so, contact someone in charge at the university to see if they might be interested in partnering with your school.

4. Join literacy organizations and pay to receive their publications. I would begin with the International Literacy Association (formerly the International Reading Association). Their publications will provide you with valuable articles on important aspects of reading instruction. These publications provide great opportunities for discussions with and among your teachers.

5. Let your professional learning communities revolve around reading instruction until a common language is used throughout the entire school. We started with Jan Richardson's book *The Next Step in Guided Reading*. We knew we wanted to move in the direction of small group, leveled text reading instruction, and this book was recommended by our reading consultants.

   Once we began our course work with the University of Tennessee, the reading specialist cohort introduced Anne McGill-Franzen's book *Kindergarten Literacy* to our pre-K and kindergarten teachers. Next, we did a school-wide book study on Peter Johnston's book *Choice Words*. I want to make note here that the suggestion is not to just go out and buy a bunch of books and have your teachers read more. I am suggesting that you and your teachers decide on the professional books that will be relevant to their growth and helping all students in the school. Meet with them regularly to discuss what they are reading. Once you understand what they are researching, let different groups of teachers present the information to others during a faculty meeting. Most of the information presented to the faculty by the principal could be sent out as an email. Instead of discussing the mundane events of the school calendar, have a group of teachers present the research on effective reading instruction, another group present strategies for increasing comprehension, and another group of teachers discuss the importance of choice during free reading time. Each meeting can focus on a different topic of a balanced literacy program.

6. Investigate the instruments used by your school to measure reading growth. Consider things such as, what does it actually measure, how does it measure growth, and what does the research say about the effectiveness? For example, do you use DIBELS? If so, why do you use DIBELS? What are the strengths and weaknesses of DIBELS? What feedback do you receive from teachers about the instrument? There is an issue if the administrator is not the most knowledgeable person about the measurements used in the school.

7. Attend trainings and PD with your teachers and especially reading coaches/ specialists. This has the potential to accelerate the growth of the entire faculty. When the principal is learning with his teachers, dynamic conversations and learning take place. Both the instructor and evaluator are developing common knowledge and a common language about instruction. One drawback about administrators participating in teacher PD is that some teachers will be reluctant to ask questions and expose themselves as being uninformed. Plan ahead with the trainers to step out of the training at certain times so teachers can have a time of question and answers without you being present. I remember one such meeting when the reading consultant shared with

me that the teachers wanted to have PD on differentiated word study. I was excited about the opportunity and wanted to learn along with my teachers so I would know what it should look and sound like in the classrooms. I would sit in the training and participate with others and ask the questions I needed to know. I would excuse myself for 20 or 30 minutes so the teachers and trainers could have a Q and A session and return again for the next part of the training.

Conclusions

One of the hardest things for me as a principal who realized he needed help was knowing how and where to get help. I learned that all the information available is not always good information. Once I found out whom the leading experts were, my life became much easier because I could now begin to educate myself about reading instruction. There are many reputable reading experts around the country. My intentions are not to offend any of them by excluding their names, but I can only write of the one's who have helped me through their books or their conversations with me. So, the following is a list of people I highly recommend. I add this part because I wish someone had handed me this list years ago.

- Early literacy instruction: As an elementary school administrator I needed guidance in how to teach every five-year-old to read and write. More importantly, I wanted each five-year-old to love reading and writing. Books by Anne McGill-Franzen, Marie Clay, and Carol MacDonald Connor are great places to start. You already have a chapter by MacDonald Connor in this book and I think you can tell that my teachers and I love McGill-Franzen's book *Kindergarten Literacy*. It has been my experience that no one is more respected, cited, and appreciated than Marie Clay and her work with early literacy.
- Adolescent literacy: An elementary school spans the ages from four years old in pre-K to 11 years old in fifth grade. Kylene Beers has books that are chock-full of strategies and ideas for upper elementary and middle school reading teachers.
- Word study: Gone are the days where every student has the same spelling words to study Monday–Thursday and test on Friday. Students need instruction that meets them where they are in terms of spelling and orthographic development. We have found that *Words Their Way* is a series that meets the needs of students. The authors, Donald Bear, Marcia Invernizzi, Francine Johnston, and Shane Templeton, have years of research and experience in the field of word study.
- Guided reading: Guided reading is a cornerstone of small-group reading instruction. We have found Jan Richardson's work with guided reading to be an excellent source for this type of reading instruction.

- Research on effective reading instruction: Principals *must* know what the research says about effective reading instruction. You will not beat Richard Allington's knowledge of the research on effective reading instruction. You can read the research for accelerating struggling readers, developing an effective Response to Intervention program, and learn how to reduce 80% of the achievement gap that exists between poverty and non-poverty students.

This is a list of authors that I would start with in my search for understanding balanced literacy. Of course there are many others, some credible and some who are quacks. They make mention of many other reading experts in their writings, so the possibilities for growth are endless. I will leave it to them and their publications to guide you to other experts in the field.

Reference

Allington, R. L., & McGill-Franzen, A. (2013). *Summer reading: Closing the rich/poor reading achievement gap*. New York: Teachers College Press.

CONTRIBUTORS

Peter Afflerbach is a Professor of Reading in the Department of Curriculum and Instruction at the University of Maryland. His most recent work focuses on aspects of individual differences in reading development that are sometimes neglected in reading theory and practice, including motivation and engagement, metacognition, student self-efficacy and self-concept, and epistemic beliefs. Peter has published in numerous research and practitioner journals, including *The Reading Teacher, Journal of Reading, Journal of Adolescent and Adult Literacy, Journal of Educational Psychology, Language Arts, Elementary School Journal, Journal of Literacy Research, Reading Research Quarterly,* and *Cognition and Instruction.* He has also published several books, dozens of book chapters, policy briefs, technical reports, and position papers.

Richard L. Allington is a Professor of Education at the University of Tennessee. Previously he served as the Irving and Rose Fien Distinguished Professor of Education at the University of Florida, and as chair of the Department of Reading at the University at Albany–SUNY. Dick has served as the President of the International Reading Association, as President of the National Reading Conference, and as a member of the International Reading Association Board of Directors. He is the co-recipient of the Albert J. Harris Award from IRA in recognition of his work contributing to the understanding of reading and learning disabilities and the William S. Gray Citation of Merit for his contributions to the profession. In addition Dick has been named to the IRA Reading Hall of Fame.

David Coker is an Associate Professor in the School of Education at the University of Delaware and teaches courses on writing and reading instruction. Dr. Coker's research focuses on writing development, early writing assessment, and effective approaches to writing instruction. Currently he is the principal investigator of a project on the relationship between writing instruction and first-grade literacy outcomes. He has published a number of peer-reviewed articles and is co-author of two books published by Guilford Press in 2015: *Teaching Beginning Writers* and *Developing Strategic Writers through Genre Instruction: Resources for Grades 3–5*.

Carol MacDonald Connor is a Professor at Arizona State University. For the past decade, she has been in Developmental Psychology at Florida State University and the Florida Center for Reading Research. Her research has focused on examining the links between young children's language and literacy development with the goal of illuminating reasons for the perplexing difficulties children who are atypical and diverse learners have developing basic and advanced literacy skills. Most recently, her research interests have focused on children's learning in the classroom from preschool through third grade. Awarded the Presidential Early Career Award for Scientists and Engineers (PECASE, 2008), the Society for Research in Child Development (SRCD, 2009) Early Career Award, and the Richard Snow Award (APA, 2008), she is the principal investigator for studies funded by the U.S. Department of Education, Institute for Education Sciences, and the National Institute for Child Health and Human Development.

Elizabeth N. Farley-Ripple is an Assistant Professor in the School of Education at the University of Delaware. She has expertise in quantitative and mixed methods and applies a variety of methodological tools to research projects. Her research expertise is in policy analysis and evidence-based decision-making, and recent work includes studies of administrator mobility, school and teachers' use of data, teacher quality and effects, and equity in student outcomes. Dr. Farley-Ripple has been awarded grants from the Spencer Foundation and the Institute for Education Sciences and has published her research in a number of respected journals.

Rachael E. Gabriel is Assistant Professor of Reading Education, Neag School of Education, University of Connecticut, USA. She is author of *Reading's Non-Negotiables: Elements of Effective Reading Instruction* (Rowman & Littlefield, 2013) and co-editor of *Performances of Research: Critical Issues in K-12 Education* (Peter Lang, 2013). Rachael's career in education began as a middle school reading teacher in Washington, DC. Rachael is a former fellow of the Baker Center for Public Policy at the University of Tennessee and current associate of the Center for Education Policy Analysis (CEPA), and the Center on Postsecondary Education and Disability (CPED) at the University of Connecticut. Rachael's research interests include teacher preparation, development and evaluation, as well as literacy instruction, interventions, and related policies.

Robert Garry is currently the Principal at South Side School in Bristol, Connecticut Bob has been an educator for 22 years and has classroom and leadership experience at the elementary and middle school level. He has been recognized locally and nationally for his work in the classroom, as the 2004 Bristol Teacher of the Year and as a 2004 DisneyHand Teacher Award winner. He is currently working to earn a doctoral degree from the University of Connecticut.

James Hoffman is a Professor of Language and Literacy Studies at The University of Texas at Austin. Dr. Hoffman is a former editor of *The Reading Research Quarterly* and *The Yearbook of the National Reading Conference*. He has served as President of the National Reading Conference and as a member of the Board of Directors of the International Reading Association. Dr. Hoffman was an affiliated scholar with both the National Reading Research Center (NRRC) and the Center for the Improvement of Early Reading Achievement (CIERA). He was elected to the Reading Hall of Fame in 2002 and served as President of this organization from 2008 to 2010. The primary focus for his research has been on teaching and teacher preparation. Dr. Hoffman has published over 150 articles, books, and chapters on literacy-related topics. He has been active in international literacy projects in Central America, Africa, and Asia.

Sarah Ingebrand is a doctoral candidate in Developmental Psychology at Arizona State University. She earned her undergraduate degree at Northwestern in 2009 in Communication Science and Disorders, and her master's at Florida State University as part of the IES Predoctoral Fellowship program in 2013. Her research focuses on reading and writing instruction and learning in the classroom, classroom observation, and writing assessment development.

Allison Jackson is a doctoral candidate in the School of Education at the University of Delaware. Her area of specialization is Special Education. Her research interests are early literacy including early reading and writing development, assessment, and effective approaches to instruction. Currently, she is investigating executive function and beginning writing in first grade.

Alyson Lavigne (previously known as Alyson Lavigne Dolan), is an Assistant Professor in the College of Education at Roosevelt University. She received her Ph.D. in Educational Psychology from the University of Arizona. Her work in the area of teacher evaluation and supervision includes a co-edited *Teachers College Record* special issue on high-stakes teacher evaluation and two co-authored books. The most recent book, *Improving Teaching through Observation and Feedback: Going Beyond State and Federal Mandates*, will be released in 2015.

Francesca López is an Associate Professor of Educational Psychology at the University of Arizona. She began her career in education as a bilingual (Spanish/English) elementary teacher, and later as an at-risk high school counselor, in El Paso,

Texas. After completing her Ph.D. in Educational Psychology at the University of Arizona (2008), she served on the faculty of the Educational Policy and Leadership department at Marquette University (2008–2013). Her research is focused on the ways educational settings promote achievement for Latino youth and has been funded by the American Educational Research Association Grants Program and the Division 15 American Psychological Association Early Career Award. She is a 2013 National Academy of Education/Spencer Postdoctoral Fellow. She has served on the editorial board of the *Journal of Psychoeducational Assessment* and is currently an associate editor for *Reading and Writing Quarterly*.

Steven T. McAbee, EdD, is Principal at Benton Elementary School in Polk County, Tennessee. He is also an adjunct faculty member at the University of the Cumberlands where he teaches courses in Instructional Design and Curriculum, Classroom Management, and the Modern Secondary School. He recently received an Education Specialist degree as a reading specialist from University of Tennessee, Knoxville. His particular interests are developing teacher expertise through ongoing, job-embedded professional development as well as accelerating the reading growth of struggling readers living in rural poverty. He is a former middle and high school science teacher and administrator.

Tammy Oberg De La Garza is an Assistant Professor in the College of Education at Roosevelt University. She is dedicated to preparing skilled language and literacy teachers who have multicultural competence and are catalysts for social change. Her work and research with literacy and Latino communities were the catalysts for her book, *Salsa Dancing in Gym Shoes: Exploring Cross-Cultural Missteps with Latinos in the Classroom.* Tammy lives in Chicago with her remarkable husband and teenage children.

Patrick Proctor is an Associate Professor of Literacy & Bilingualism at Boston College. His principal area of interest and focus is with English language learners in U.S. public schools, and their language and literacy achievement. A former third- and fourth-grade bilingual teacher, Proctor is ultimately interested in how language and literacy development are affected by classroom instruction, and the various media through which that instruction is delivered. In his research on praxis, Dr. Proctor has co-developed an English vocabulary and comprehension intervention for fifth grade multilingual students, and actively works with principals and teachers in the Boston Public Schools on long-term literacy initiatives designed to promote reflective teaching.

Misty Sailors is a Professor of Literacy Education at The University of Texas at San Antonio in the department of Interdisciplinary Learning and Teaching. Dr. Sailors' scholarly pursuits center on the areas of (a) literacy tools found in elementary classrooms; (b) the professional development of reading teachers and literacy coaches; (c) local and international reading program development; and (d) reading research methodologies. Dr. Sailors' research accomplishments are demonstrated by her funding for research on the role of coaching in improving teachers' practices and the reading achievement of students in low-income schools in Texas and in Malawi, Africa. The Literacy Research Association (LRA), the American Association of University Women, and the University of Texas at San Antonio recognized her contributions to research on teaching and literacy learning. She currently serves as a member of the review board for *Reading Research Quarterly* and *The Reading Teacher* and is a member of the Board of Directors for the LRA. Dr. Sailors co-edited a special issue of *The Elementary School Journal* on coaching and has worked in classrooms and with teachers and literacy coaches in the U.S., Bangladesh, Cambodia, Malawi, Tanzania, South Africa, and Mozambique.

Martin Scanlon is an Associate Professor in Educational Policy and Leadership at Marquette University. He is currently a Visiting Associate Professor of Research in the Lynch School of Education at Boston College, with his work focusing on supporting the formation of TWIN-CS. His current research explores how to strengthen the communities of practice in schools to promote inclusion of students across multiple dimensions of diversity. His scholarship—which has focused primarily on reform in special education service delivery, bilingual education, and school-community collaboration—has been published in over two dozen articles in peer-reviewed journals, including *Educational Administration Quarterly* and *Teachers College Record*. Before joining higher education, Martin spent over a decade as a teacher and administrator in elementary and middle schools in Washington, D.C., Berkeley, California, and Madison, Wisconsin. He continues to work closely with building and district level administrators in an effort to apply research to practice.

Nicole Sparapani graduated with her Ph.D. in Communication Science and Disorders from Florida State University in 2013 and is currently a Postdoctoral Research Scholar in Developmental Psychology at Arizona State University in the Learning Sciences Institute. For over a decade, Nicole has worked as a Certified Speech-Language Pathologist serving children with Autism Spectrum Disorder (ASD) and their families within an interdisciplinary preschool program and through innovative, naturalistic home- and community-based interventions. Her clinical experiences have greatly influenced her research interests, which center on the student and environmental characteristics that relate to classroom performance and learning in students with diverse learning needs.

Debra S. Peterson, Ph.D., works as a teacher educator and consultant for the Minnesota Center for Reading Research and the Department of Curriculum and

Instruction in the College of Education and Human Development at the University of Minnesota. She has collaborated with teachers and schools to improve reading instruction and implement school-wide reform for the past 15 years. Current publications include articles in *Reading Research Quarterly, Elementary School Journal*, and *The Reading Teacher*. Awards include the International Reading Association Albert J. Harris Award for Reading Research. She has also written multiple book chapters and is the co-author of *No More Teaching to the Middle*.

Sultan Turkan is an Associate Research Scientist at the Center for Validity Research at ETS. Prior to joining ETS in 2010, Turkan was a doctoral candidate in the teaching and teacher education program at University of Arizona. Her research focuses on understanding and assessing the quality of teaching mathematics and science to English language learners, teacher education and professional development, and formative teacher assessments. Turkan's research interests expand across understanding how to develop fair and valid content assessments for ELLs as well as valid accommodations on large-scale content assessments.

Huijing Wen is a Ph.D. student in the School of Education at the University of Delaware. Her research interests focus on the role of writing-related knowledge in students' writing performance and the impact of instructional factors on students' writing development. She is also interested in developing valid and reliable affective reading and writing instruments in the Chinese language. She was a college English instructor in China and was awarded a Fulbright FLTA Fellowship in 2007–2008.

Sarah Woulfin is an Assistant Professor of Educational Leadership at the University of Connecticut's Neag School of Education. She studies the relationship between education policy, leadership, and instructional reform. Using lenses from organizational sociology, she investigates how leaders affect teachers' responses to school reform. She received a Ph.D. in Education from the University of California-Berkeley. Formerly, as an urban public school teacher and reading coach, she was dedicated to strengthening students' reading and writing skills to promote educational equity. As a scholar, her commitment to raising the quality of instruction motivates her research on how policy influences—and is influenced by—administrators and teachers.

INDEX